WILLIAM EDWARD BURGHARDT
DU BOIS was born in 1868 in
Great Barrington, Massachu-
setts. A brilliant student and natural leader, he experienced
little prejudice during his early years; it was while attend-
ing Fisk, a Southern university for Negroes, that the young
Du Bois first fully awoke to the realities of race in America.
His response was to make the cause of the black people
his own. After graduation from Fisk, he earned his Ph.D.
from Harvard, studied in Berlin, and became one of the
great pioneer sociologists. In 1903, *The Souls of Black
Folk* appeared. This prophetic masterpiece was but the
beginning of a long, often lonely crusade that saw Du Bois
forced into an increasingly radical position in his search
for a solution to the American racial dilemma. His final
years were marked by disillusionment with his native land,
renunciation of his citizenship, and final self-exile in Ghana,
where W. E. B. Du Bois died in 1963 at the age of ninety-
five.

W. E. BURGHARDT DU BOIS

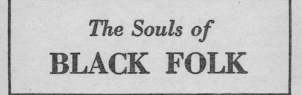

The Souls of
BLACK FOLK

With Introductions by

Dr. Nathan Hare
AND
Alvin F. Poussaint, M.D.

Revised and Updated Bibliography

A SIGNET CLASSIC

SIGNET CLASSIC
Published by the Penguin Group
Penguin Books USA Inc., 375 Hudson Street,
New York, New York 10014, U.S.A.
Penguin Books Ltd, 27 Wrights Lane,
London W8 5TZ, England
Penguin Books Australia Ltd, Ringwood,
Victoria, Australia
Penguin Books Canada Ltd, 2801 John Street,
Markham, Ontario, Canada L3R 1B4
Penguin Books (N.Z.) Ltd, 182–190 Wairau Road,
Auckland 10, New Zealand

Penguin Books Ltd, Registered Offices:
Harmondsworth, Middlesex, England

First Signet Classic Printing, June, 1969
21 20 19 18 17 16 15 14 13

Introduction Copyright © 1969 by
New American Library, a division of Penguin Books USA Inc.

Bibliography Copyright © 1982 by
New American Library, a division of Penguin Books USA Inc.
All rights reserved

Library of Congress Catalog Card Number: 71-82444

Printed in the United States of America

To Burghardt and Yolande
The Lost and the Found

PUBLISHERS' NOTE

In 1963, Dr. W. E. Burghardt Du Bois died at the age of 95 in Ghana, in self-imposed exile from his native land. Sixty years earlier, he had written *The Souls of Black Folk*, a book destined to become an influential American classic. Because of its significance, the publishers invited two eloquent black spokesmen, Drs. Nathan Hare and Alvin F. Poussaint, to supply interpretive essays for this extraordinary work.

HEREIN IS WRITTEN

The Forethought

HEREIN lie buried many things which if read with patience may show the strange meaning of being black here at the dawning of the Twentieth Century. This meaning is not without interest to you, Gentle Reader; for the problem of the Twentieth Century is the problem of the color line. I pray you, then, receive my little book in all charity, studying my words with me, forgiving mistake and foible for sake of the faith and passion that is in me, and seeking the grain of truth hidden there.

I have sought here to sketch, in vague, uncertain outline, the spiritual world in which ten thousand thousand Americans live and strive. First, in two chapters I have tried to show what Emancipation meant to them, and what was its aftermath. In a third chapter I have pointed out the slow rise of personal leadership, and criticised candidly the leader who bears the chief burden of his race to-day. Then, in two other chapters I have sketched in swift outline the two worlds within and without the Veil, and thus have come to the central problem of training men for life. Venturing now into deeper detail, I have in two chapters studied the struggles of the massed millions of the black peasantry, and in another have sought to make clear the present relations of the sons of master and man. Leaving, then, the white world, I have stepped within the Veil, raising it that you may view faintly its deeper recesses,—the meaning of its religion, the passion of its human sorrow, and the struggle of its greater souls. All this I have ended with a tale twice told but seldom written, and a chapter of song.

Some of these thoughts of mine have seen the light before in other guise. For kindly consenting to their republication here, in altered and extended form, I must thank the publishers of the *Atlantic Monthly, The World's Work,* the *Dial, The New World,* and the *Annals of the American Academy of Political and Social Science.* Before each chapter, as now printed, stands a bar of the Sorrow Songs,—some echo of haunting melody from the only American music which welled up from black souls in the dark past. And, finally, need I add that I who speak here am bone of the bone and flesh of the flesh of them that live within the Veil?

ATLANTA, GA., FEB. 1, 1903.　　　W.E.B. Du B.

W. E. Burghardt Du Bois: An Appreciation

A genius is sometimes said to be twenty-five years ahead of his time. W. E. Burghardt Du Bois, who was in many ways the father of serious black thought as we know it today, was about fifty years ahead of his. Indeed, both Du Bois and his times previewed the strife and conflicts of today, and they provide, on closer scrutiny, a model of black struggle and black innovation.

The prescience of Du Bois is apparent, for example, in his anticipation of many of the concepts currently in vogue among those black power advocates who assume these concepts are of their own creation. For instance: "conscious self-realization," "survival," "an all-black party," and the need for blacks to control their own organizations and work for the separate autonomy of the black community.

Du Bois was born in the puritanical New England community of Great Barrington, Massachusetts, in the dawn of the Reconstruction era. It was the beginning of a period of rapid industrial growth and social change, a period marked by a significant drive for recognition on the part of the black community. Du Bois regretted that sociology had not yet advanced as had the so-called "natural sciences" but instead had been reduced to "social work." He determined to "put science into sociology," but he had not reckoned with

the bitter opposition this objective was to engender—
though it was signaled by one of the essays, "Mr.
Booker T. Washington and Others," in *The Souls of
Black Folk.*

When *The Souls of Black Folk* appeared, ". . . the
great mass of Negro children were being trained in
Negro schools, the great mass of Negro churchgoers
were members of Negro churches," lived in Negro
neighborhoods, voted for the same political party and,
as Du Bois observed, "What was true in 1910 was still
true in 1940 and will be true in 1970."

What was true around 1910? During the high noon
of the Du Bois–Booker T. Washington conflict, the
crossroads of post-Reconstruction black direction, the
struggle between conservative assimilation and militant pluralism—now known as black power—came to
the fore. Equally important was the character of Du
Bois, which gave him a unique insight, timely to this
day, into the forces affecting the black man.

To consider these and other points, we must go
back to Great Barrington and sketch the young Du
Bois vis-à-vis the black struggle then in bloom. The
times in which he lived portended much of today's social situation.

For instance, relative family income of blacks and
whites was about the same as today, according to
U.S. Bureau of the Census economists. Although some
aspects of the blacks' position have changed for the
better, the difference is mainly a matter of small degree. Three times as much, for example, was spent
on white than on black education in those days.
Blacks were disfranchised in many of the Southern
states, and black voting today remains an act performed under the stress of intimidation while federal
officials frequently continue to look the other way.

The American society was generally characterized

by a high degree of geographic mobility and a corresponding social dislocation. In the area of social and occupational mobility, black aspirations had been spurred by the myth that every Negro was to receive forty acres and a mule, just as "poverty programs" would later promise to free them from want and squalor. Many ex-slaves felt they were due a share of the plantations in reparation for their past labor, and this cry is still echoed faintly by their descendants. Amid unrelenting frustrations, Africanization and other separatist programs inevitably appear, the only difference being that in Du Bois' early years they were advocated by whites (including Abraham Lincoln) as well as blacks. Today, however, cries for separatism are heard largely from black circles.

Blacks were leaving the South in droves in the 1890's just as they are today, mainly because of unfulfilled aspirations and a false notion of the opportunities existing for blacks in the North. This migration has shifted the focus of the black struggle northward. Du Bois and other Northern black intellectuals in those days generally traveled South for work and development. Du Bois, who assimilated the best that both Harvard and Heidelberg could offer only to be excluded from teaching in white American colleges, eventually was impelled to flit back and forth between North and South, though the impetus for *The Souls of Black Folk* came from the South.

Du Bois' introduction to the South occurred when, having taken pleasure all of his life in outdistancing his white New England schoolmates, he was refused admission to Harvard and instead had to enter Fisk in Nashville, Tennessee. Though disappointed at the death of his childhood ambition to study at Harvard, Du Bois looked forward to Fisk because of the chance —refreshing to him—to exchange the black isolation of

a small Massachusetts town for the fellowship of a
large number of black peers at Fisk.

In the South, he found easy access to public facilities in railroads and hotels. In churches and schools,
however, the situation was different. The central
theme of the Southern whites then as now was local
white rule, and in the years preceding *The Souls of
Black Folk*, the white establishment succeeded in ce-
menting Jim Crow regulations which were not to be
erased until the Civil Rights Act of 1964.

Social Darwinism had reached its apex as an alleged scientific justification for the cutthroat policies
of nineteenth-century capitalism, and the rise of industry had brought with it increasing technological
and social change. Black aspirations, on the other
hand, had been beaten down by the white South. In
the North, as is now the case in the South, constitutional and judicial decrees had legitimized black aspirations. But, contradictorily, more subtle forms of
oppression prevented the realization of black social
change in proportion to those lip-service ideals. There
were token appointments, then as now, but statisti-
cally speaking blacks either failed to move up as a
group or failed to move as fast as whites. Frustration
was rampant, of course, among both blacks and
whites; physical abuse was more blatant and apparent
than today. In addition, the violence was more frequently directed at persons rather than property, and
white citizens at large were more likely to take part in
the violence than in these times of notable police bru-
tality.

In the days of Du Bois and the making of *The
Souls of Black Folk*, racial overtones pervaded even
the professed beliefs of the white world. Backed by
Social Darwinism, prestige was bestowed on a book
such as Charles Carroll's *The Negro: a Beast*, an effort

to "prove in 1900 that blacks were lower animals." Many whites, moreover, were enraged and humiliated in response to Black Reconstruction. Andrew Johnson, for one, bemoaned the fact that blacks had taken Richmond, calling the incident "a citadel of racial treason . . . taken possession of by a lot of soldiers of African descent and led by a Dutchman. Now where is that bragging chivalry of the South, which flattered itself that one of them could whip five yankees in the beginning of the war, when now fifty thousand of them run from a thousand Negroes?"

Spurred by such sentiments after the war, whites wreaked violence on blacks both individually and collectively. Organized white mobs included the "Red Shirts," a militant arm of the Democratic Party. "Lynching," a phenomenon peculiar to the Southern United States frontier, came into the English language and soared to its peak in the late nineteenth century. Now and again the blacks fought back, as in the case of the Cane Hay Massacre, which occurred in South Carolina, October, 1876. A mob of whites was forced to retreat and several were killed by defending blacks. A rumor in 1882 alleged that Negroes had held a recent meeting and planned "an immense barbecue" of oppressive whites.

In this milieu, Du Bois, of mulatto, French Huguenot, Dutch, and African ancestry, acquired a sense of the "absolute division" of the black and white races. The white Southern community was largely closed to him by custom as a member of the black race, and the rest he rejected himself, seldom leaving the campus. He never rode a streetcar or visited a theater or concert hall. His public personality took on a brooding anguish. He rarely went off the campus except for necessary shopping, for he had his "island within" and "a desperate fear of intruding" where he was not wanted. This response was reinforced when he was finally admitted to Harvard, which brought him back to his home state of Massachusetts. Though he "had a good singing voice and loved music," he was rejected by the Harvard Glee Club—on the basis of his race, he felt. This aggravated his somewhat self-confessed "inferiority complex." In later life, he was to discover that he and white acquaintances could not "talk together." He disdained their company for the most part, rejecting invitations to spend weekends with H. G. Wells and declining an offer from the wife of Havelock Ellis to meet with Ellis and George Bernard Shaw. At times he could have met presidents of the United States and did not, attributing this to a fear, as he said, that "my color would interfere." To the world in general, Du Bois was nearly always "an outsider looking in," and he felt he knew far too few of his contemporaries. Even among his black fellows he felt somewhat set apart all his life, though highly regarded, "cocky and self-satisfied."

Some thought he was hard to know, not always realizing that he was "incomprehensibly shy." He was not a man who, like many of his rivals, "could slap people on the back and make friends of strangers." His exercise was walking instead of sports, but there again he "walked alone." He was a lone wolf, but he was not selfish—his disdain for material things was to leave him unemployed and virtually penniless at the age of seventy.

He was very close to his mother, who was lame. He credited this to the fact that, all his life, he had more friends among women than among men. During the early part of his life he had an "inexcusable ignorance of sex," though, and he was sexually uneducated until he attended Fisk. "Friendship and sex" was the one aspect of his life on which in later years he looked back with "mixed feelings." His New England upbringing, he confessed, had not taught him even the physical differences between men and women." This he readily learned as he began to talk with the fellows of girls and "looked at their legs."

Then came "rare kissing of the most unsatisfactory sort," and, finally, as a school teacher in the rural districts of Tennessee, he was "literally raped by the unhappy wife" who was his landlady. In Paris, as a graduate student, he had a brief fling with prostitutes and lived more or less in common law with a shopgirl in Berlin. These two experiences left him exhilarated but burdened with a sense of shame; and, at last, he was literally frightened into marrying before he was able to support a family because he was faced with being driven by certain fellow professors at Wilberforce into adultery with their wives. And yet he lived with his wife, Nina, for fifty-three years until her death, though the union was not absolutely ideal. For one thing, Nina had been brought up in a society with the mores of chastity and virginity which regarded sex as basically indecent, while Du Bois described himself as a "lusty young man."

Du Bois traveled a good deal, and his "work was out in the world and not at home," though he never neglected his home and family. He made his own bed mornings, prepared his own breakfast frequently, and left his bathtub cleaner than it was when he entered it. So far as Du Bois could tell, his marriage was a happy one. When his first-born died of a "careless sewage," his death, Du Bois recalled, "tore our lives in two." The child was eulogized in one of *The Souls of Black Folk* essays, and Du Bois threw himself completely into his work, while "most reason for living left the soul" of his wife.

Once a year during their life in the South, Du Bois took his family north on vacation for a "breath of fresh air and civilization." He abhorred the necessity of having to live, in the South, constantly on the verge of violence, though contrary to the opinions prevailing during the first half of the twentieth century, he was not loathe to fight back as a black man. Yet he never killed a bird nor shot a rabbit, and he claimed that he even let others kill the chickens he ate. Unlike his schoolmates at Fisk, he never carried a pistol. Once, however, when a professor at Atlanta University, he bought a shotgun and two thousand rounds of shells filled with buckshot and resolved that if a white mob were to cross the campus to his house he would, without hesitation, "spray their guts over the grass." The whites dutifully stayed away.

Du Bois advocated "effective guns in the hands of black people determined to sell their souls dearly" in order to stop the cowardly mobs, and eventually he came under criticism for "overtones of violence" in his writings. He told his critics that "no human group had ever achieved freedom without being compelled to murder thousands of its oppressors," and that though he hoped this would not be true for black Americans, he most emphatically was willing to stand behind the conviction that it might be necessary. No black American group took so firm a position until the Black Panthers more than half a century later, and it was not until the mid-1960's that blacks threw off the ridiculous taboo against the advocacy of simple self-defense on the part of blacks attacked by whites in the South. This was only one area of Du Bois's prescience, however.

As a matter of fact, the prescience portrayed in *The Souls of Black Folk*, particularly in the chapter "Of Mr. Booker T. Washington and Others," not only

created a school of thought running counter to conservative pluralism at a time when Washington and
his philosophy were regarded as messianic, but signaled, more than anything else prior to the "black
power" movement (whose concepts it largely anticipated), a crucial starting point in the black push for
recognition and self-determination. Though Du Bois
left out much of the more controversial portion of
what young blacks thought about the Booker T.
Washington school of acquiescence in those days, the
conflict became more personal and bitter than Du
Bois ever dreamed it would. Du Bois had refused to
be the leader of a counter-movement to Booker T.
Washington and was reluctant to criticize him publicly—partly because he did not disagree totally with
some of his "dangerous half-truths." Another reason
was that during the years surrounding the publication
of *The Souls of Black Folk* he regarded himself as a
"scientist, and neither a leader nor an agitator." Also,
the Tuskegee machine had been trying to attract him
there ever since 1900, at one point inviting him to
name his price. But after the publication of *The Souls
of Black Folk* and the subsequent outbreak of the
"Boston Riots"—a clash between Booker T. Washington and a faction of black "radicals" led by the jour-
nalist Monroe Trotter, at which Du Bois was not present, he was finally catapulted against his will into
leadership of the anti-Tuskegee forces.

After Booker T. Washington's Atlanta Exposition
Speech of 1895, in which he assured the nation that
the blacks could accept social separation and a sophisticated form of subordination, the whites had
rushed to translate Washington's ideas into Jim Crow
legislation which was underwritten by the Supreme
Court's "separate-but-equal" decree only one year
later. The molders of public opinion simultaneously

sought to shape Washington into the one recognized
Negro leader.

Most grants for black persons had to be approved
by Booker T. Washington even in the North, and Du
Bois would soon feel the pressures from forces behind
the Tuskegee concept—forces which he blamed for
undermining his study of the black race undertaken
at Atlanta. For ever so long, Du Bois had sought to
persuade Harvard and Columbia, as well as the
Negro colleges, to support his effort to put science
into sociology, particularly in the study of the race
problem. Unfortunately, there was no demand for the
"scientific work of the sort" he was doing. He had
pushed toward what was to become the field of sociology as a Harvard undergraduate, but sociology
was not a recognized major at Harvard until twenty
years later. Du Bois was probably the father of the
empirical approach to sociology in America, but, of
course, he was never given the credit—though his
study of the Philadelphia Negro, conducted late in
the nineteenth century, is still a highly regarded example of social research.

One day Du Bois himself was stunned when, on his
way to see Joel Chandler Harris, then editor of the
Atlanta Constitution, he noticed the knuckles of a
Negro who had recently been lynched and left on
mangled display in a grocery store. Du Bois was
shocked into the realization that he could no longer
remain a calm, cool, detached scientist while his black
brethren were being lynched and murdered and
starved.

He concluded that if people knew what was right
they would act. And so Du Bois—who had studied
with William James at Harvard, introduced mankind
to the scientific study of racial conflict, and constituted, during almost a century of life, a personal case

study of the social history of race relations in this country—decided to switch from science to "propaganda." His first major effort in that area, "Of Mr. Booker T. Washington and Others," the only essay in *The Souls of Black Folk* written expressly for that volume—a book called the "political life of the educated segment of the race"—ignited the controversy which put an end to his work at Atlanta University.

Du Bois had written *The Souls of Black Folk* just three years before an age of social change in which was born the modern push for such progressive reforms as freedom of speech, suffrage, and abolition of color caste—an age of lip service, at the least, to brotherhood and higher education for blacks. These demands were so in discord with the Booker T. Washington theory of achieving black self-uplift by condemning blacks as responsible for their own degradation that Du Bois was accused of being ashamed of his race. He sidestepped a later conflict with Marcus Garvey (who rallied six million blacks around a warning to the white man to clear out of Africa and make room for four million marching blacks) because he sympathized with him and embraced his goals—a "great and worthy dream"—though he regarded his methods as "bombastic and wasteful."

But this was only the beginning of Du Bois' remarkable prescience vis-à-vis the black struggle of today. His precocity had been apparent as early as the age of sixteen, when, as a high school student and a reporter for a local newspaper, he advised the people of Great Barrington to check with him before deciding which books to read. His life's endeavor was to share his education, and he regretted that blacks were rejecting the little education that was available to them. Later he came to understand the socio-psychological foundations of this condition and eventually

anticipated by more than forty years the present college cry for black studies! Going beyond the current
expressive stage of the black studies movement (and
its preoccupation with history and culture) to a more
pragmatic stage even now only nascent (with an emphasis on black politics, scientific and economic endeavor and inquiry), Du Bois criticized predominantly Negro colleges particularly for restricting their
vision and perpetuating a reign of terror to attract
white support. He believed that predominantly Negro
colleges, potentially black colleges, should reflect
black ideas, and despite his own deep preparation in
European and European-oriented scholarship of the
classical variety, Du Bois wanted to redirect the contemporary curricula toward greater relevancy to society's problems. But his particular focus, as the father
of the black intelligentsia, was the Negro college,
which he wanted to see achieve self-determination
and become more relevant to the black community
and its struggle. He advocated separate black schools
and indicted Negro colleges for having failed to make
available any of the chief studies of the black experience. His hope for black education was only a part of
his general program of black self-sufficiency toward a
black ethos and socio-cultural system. This brings us
to the core of his black power prescience.

Du Bois advocated black self-help and spoke of
"physical power"—and other varieties now made syn-
onymous with black power—at a time when Negroes
overwhelmingly resisted such ideas. These included
self-determination as a basis for the survival of the
black race and, more specifically, the establishment of
black cooperatives [1] and all-black parties built on a
base of black art and culture. All this he endeavored

1 Booker T. Washington was said to have adopted the idea in forming
the National Business League.

to put into actual operation, and he is credited with discovering such black cultural leaders as Langston Hughes and helping to usher in the so-called "New Negro renaissance." At the very least he wanted blacks to control their own protest organizations, as they now are striving to do, and came, consequently, into conflict with the NAACP, which he had joined as editor of its official organ, *The Crisis*. For example, in his effort to promote the idea that black is beautiful, he ran afoul of contemporary fashion when he used a dark Negro's picture for a *Crisis* cover. For this he was accused of accepting racism.

This accusation grew more acute when he urged blacks to take advantage of the disadvantage of segregation and demand black officers for black troops, just as blacks are now doing in the case of key civilian personnel. However, Du Bois' visions of black nationalism did not come to pass until after World War I and the great migration of blacks to the urban north. During the war, Du Bois, the major Negro leader after Booker T's death in 1915, had urged blacks to forget their grievances temporarily and "close ranks" with their white countrymen, who later would be grateful to blacks for helping to win the war for "democracy." Afterward, Du Bois admitted his error and returned to the antiwar policy he had advocated as a college student. He admitted that he had not always been right, but he had "always been sincere."

Du Bois, anticipating black sentiments now current, referred to whites as "shameless breeders of bastards," and said that "no Negro can afford to stoop to an Anglo-Saxon standard of morality." He once thanked God "that, though mixed with French and Dutch, I have no Anglo-Saxon blood." Du Bois was a natural critic, and in deriding black leaders such as Frederick Douglass (who, in his opinion, vacillated and were

"afraid to call a lie a lie"), he advocated a tough, uncompromising stand. Sometimes even the sponsors of
his lectures quivered before his barbed tongue. It was
his belief that black people "may and must criticize
America, describe how she has ruined her democracy,
sold out her jury system, and led her seats of justice
astray." He condemned America's attempts to "reduce
life to buying and selling," cheating and deceiving,
and he bewailed the "bankruptcy of white christianity." Having lost faith in the good intentions of his
white fellows, he complained that Negroes and West
Indians—and most of West Africa—were aping the ac-
quisitive white society, a tendency he fought all his
life, grounding his faith that these inclinations would
disappear on "an inner cultural ideal." Accordingly,
he pioneered the pan-African movement, was publicly
credited by Nkrumah and others with having inspired
the independence drive of many African nations, and
eventually worked toward the "unity of nonwhite nations the world over"—the rallying cry of the current
Third World movement.

Du Bois' prescience was both a positive virtue and
a flaw in that it kept him so far above the black masses—indeed above the black vanguard of the day—that
he could not swing adequate black support to offset
the opposition to his concepts—concepts which were
regarded as audacious even by scholars, many of
whom had been his academic inferiors at Harvard.
Except for a few Negro colleges "in understandable
self-defense," as Du Bois put it, no American college
even honored him for his high scholarship. White
journals for the most part closed their pages to him
after he complained of being "shaken by white sociologists' distortion of fact and warm license of fancy"
while "gleefully counting the black man's bastards

and his prostitutes" in an "all-pervading desire to inculcate disdain for everything black."

He regretted in later life that he did not concentrate more on writing and publishing than in getting caught up in other things which needed to be done. However, he was able to say—after losing faith in the black "Talented Tenth" as potential saviors of the race and turning his back at the age of ninety-five on both the white and black bourgeoisie to live and die at the end of "a twisted life" in Accra, Ghana—that the secret of whatever good he had ever done was the fact that he had been able to earn a living "by doing the work which I wanted to do and work that the world needed done." This included *The Souls of Black Folk,* his first "commercial" book, which had a greater effect on the black race, in the view of James Weldon Johnson, than any other since *Uncle Tom's Cabin.*

Du Bois had sworn while in his teens to work toward exterminating racism so long as he lived. And he still lives . . . in *The Souls of Black Folk.*

Dr. Nathan Hare
Chairman, Department of Black Studies
San Francisco State College
San Francisco, Calif.

The Souls of Black Folk: A Critique

There have been over twenty-odd editions of *The Souls of Black Folk* printed in the United States since its original publication in 1903. It is regarded by many as a minor classic, by some, as merely an accomplished gathering of fact. It has been hailed at one time or another for its historical significance, its sociological insight, and its literary sophistication. It has also been dismissed as a document no longer relevant to the post-1954 struggle of the black man in America. Although much of the book has been unavoidably dated by the passage of time, it still stands as a monument to the black man's struggle in this country.

The Souls of Black Folk is primarily a historical document which delves into the "Negro Problem" as it existed immediately following the Civil War. But it is also the mirror of a highly volatile, ceaselessly energetic, and amazingly prolific champion of the black man's cause, W. E. Burghardt Du Bois.

W. E. B. Du Bois was born a mulatto and an only child in 1868 in the small New England town of Great Barrington, Massachusetts, and he died in 1963, a black American in voluntary exile in the land of his heritage, Africa. His father left the family permanently when Du Bois was quite young, and his mother, a loving and ambitious woman, alone took over the charge of rearing and supporting her child. Du Bois grew up in a world that had little touch with the daily miseries endured by the mass of blacks in America at that time. The few black inhabitants of Great Barrington were hardly numerous enough to constitute a problem to the white community, and Du Bois received the gift of a splendid isolation from many of the more cruel realities of American racism. The community opened to him; he attended school, played, laughed, and explored the world, surrounded and apparently "accepted" by his white peers. In looking back on this period of his life, Du Bois could recall little experience of segregation or color discrimination. Not only did Du Bois share in the world of his white classmates, in many respects he led them in that world. His scholastic and extracurricular achievements were impressive. Not the least impressed by his record was Du Bois himself. At the age of fifteen he was putting together and annotating his collected papers. The town of Great Barrington reasoned that it was only fitting that such a talent be allowed to continue its development, and accordingly, money was found to allow Du Bois to continue his education beyond his high school years.

And here appears the first small crack in the idyllic upward surge of Du Bois' existence in Great Barrington. It was decided that Du Bois would be sent to Fisk, a southern center of learning for black students, as opposed to Harvard or Amherst, which were quite nearby and which Du Bois, in his state of youthful naïveté and self-importance, had fully expected to attend. There was no possible basis for this decision other than color, and the realization of this sent Du Bois down to Fisk with the first stirrings of doubt and with questions which he spent the rest of his life attempting to answer. *The Souls of Black Folk,* pub-

XXX   W. E. BURGHARDT DU BOIS

lished some fifteen years after Du Bois' graduation
from Fisk, constitutes his first valiant attempt at an
answer. To understand and interpret that answer adequately, it is necessary to follow Du Bois' intellectual
and academic progression a bit more closely.

As might be expected, Du Bois' sojourn at Fisk was
an academic success. The white teaching staff accepted him and he gloried in the instruction. More
importantly, however, Du Bois found himself in a
community of black men whose personalities and
background spoke of a life experience totally removed
from the easy tranquility of Great Barrington, Massachusetts. While at Fisk, two summers were spent
teaching in a nearby rural black community, where
Du Bois came face to face with demoralizing poverty
and hunger for the first time. The glaring injustices
endured by these black men struck Du Bois with tremendous force, and he began to see the glimmerings
of a direction for his talents and energies. At nine-
teen, he embraced the black man's misery with an almost jubilant cry, and the lifelong battle commenced.

Harvard was the next step in Du Bois' preparation.
He finally arrived at this venerable center of white
American learning, but without the capacity for
warmth and enthusiasm he would have brought to it
four years earlier. Du Bois' three-year detour to Fisk
had shattered his New England isolation and, consequently, turned Harvard into a mere way of learning
rather than of living, a means rather than an end. He
now knew firsthand of the existence of racial prejudice in this country. However, he still considered it to
be limited to certain areas and classes of people. His
four years at Harvard and the following two years
studying in Berlin cemented Du Bois' belief in several
general principles. Among them was the conviction
that the intellectual, of no matter what race, is above

unreasoning prejudice. His professors at both universities encouraged Du Bois' thirst for knowledge and opened themselves to him in intellectual camaraderie. The role of the scholar, the selfless Seeker of Truth, became increasingly attractive to Du Bois. The white man's world of Harvard and Berlin had given him the tools which he saw as necessary for his attack on the black man's plight in America, and Du Bois set to work with a passion that would quickly have exhausted lesser men.

His studies had convinced him of the infallibility of scientific research, not only as a source of truth, but as a conqueror of oppression. In speaking of color prejudice, he stated:

> They must be recognized as facts, but unpleasant facts, things that stand in the way of civilization and religion and common decency. They can be met in but one way—by the breadth and broadening of human reason, by catholicity of taste and culture.

Du Bois genuinely believed that if he could utilize his training in gathering and presenting the facts concerning the misery of the black man in America, those facts, indisputable in their logic and clarity, would move the white man to right the wrongs now made visible to him. This belief was based on an assumption which presupposed the existence of a willingness, a reservoir of goodwill and simple goodness, within the white man which would move him inevitably to correct the injustice of the black man's plight:

> . . . natural questions cannot be evaded, nor on the other hand must a Nation naturally skeptical as to Negro ability assume an unfavorable answer without careful inquiry and patient openness to conviction. We must not forget that most Americans answer all queries regarding the Negro a priori, and that the

least that human courtesy can do is to listen to the
evidence.

Du Bois was an extraordinary product of nineteenth-
century white America: a black man of unique background and innate talent, trained in the highest intellectual tradition of the white world. Consequently,
Du Bois sought to use that talent and training and
meet the white man on his own professed level of fact
and reason. It was not a simple task, and Du Bois
himself realized that:

. . . the would-be black *savant* was confronted by
the paradox that the knowledge his people needed
was a twice-told tale to his white neighbors, while
the knowledge which would teach the white world
was Greek to his own flesh and blood.

The Souls of Black Folk is the classic culmination
of Du Bois' thought at that time. All that had
preceded the publication of this volume in 1903
pointed inevitably to this effort to produce a clear,
scientific, objective and dispassionate presentation of
the Negro cause. This volume is written primarily for
a white audience, and though some of what is said is
outdated, it still powerfully exemplifies the fierce belief in man's willingness to reason with man. Perhaps,
even more importantly, *Souls* represents not only the
effort of one man, but of many men—many black men
in America who have, before and since Du Bois, been
exposed to the inner sanctums of white higher education in this country. *The Souls of Black Folk* symbol-
izes an ever-recurring stage which most black intellectuals reach at some point in their cultural development. Indeed, until the 1954 Supreme Court decision
and the sit-in movement of the '60's, this stage of rea-
soning, of continued unflagging belief in the white
man's good will, represented the thinking of the ma-

jority of educated blacks in this country. And even now, when the black masses have in many ways reached a point of sophisticated skepticism concerning the basic inner make-up of the white man, the young black academician often finds himself hard-pressed to dispose ipso facto of the promise of informed reason as a basis for dialogue between the races. There is constantly the temptation to indulge himself to some extent in the thought that perhaps the problem has never been presented to the white man in a way that he could truly understand, that perhaps *this* time *he* would find a way, a language, a medium for transmitting the urgency of black America to the white man—for surely the progress of civilization has proven that reason can sometimes prevail, illumine, create; and certainly, the alternatives of continuing anguish, hatred, and ultimate suicidal warfare are unbearable! This desperate need of young, educated American blacks to cling to the voice of reason in the face of violent alternatives often leads them into heartrending debates with their white peers. These confrontations leave them with an enormous sense of frustration at their own inability to break through the barriers created by three hundred years of history. W. E. B. Du Bois did more than debate; he immortalized his argument for black equality in a volume which rests today as a symbol of the black intellectuals' perpetually recurring fury and folly.

The Souls of Black Folk was a revolutionary document at the time of its publication in 1903, and in some respects, remains so today. In attempting to approach the subject of the "Negro Problem" fairly and objectively, Du Bois not only pointed out the failings of the black American population, but more crucially, placed the inadequacies of white America squarely before the white man's eyes. He maintained that it was not only unjust, but illogical for the white community to continue attempting to thrust the blame for the black man's condition solely on to the shoulders of the former slaves. The blame was shared by both races, but it was up to the whites as the economically and politically stronger of the two to initiate the necessary steps involved in correcting the situation. Du Bois counseled his white audience:

> . . . when you fasten crime upon this race as its peculiar trait, they answer that slavery was the arch-crime, and lynching and lawlessness its twin abortion; that color and race are not crimes, and yet it is they which in this land receive most unceasing condemnation, North, East, South and West.

With this unequivocating stand, Du Bois established that blacks had the right to expect white people to take up their share of the responsibility for the racial situation. The next step in the progression was to wait for the white man's first efforts to right the wrongs.

By the 1960's, the young black people of America had grown tired of waiting for those efforts, and took to street demonstrations and marches in order to bring the white man to an immediate confrontation with his guilt, assuming that his shame at that confrontation would be the catalyst for those long-awaited efforts. The black people of the early '60's had learned that one of Du Bois' basic assumptions espoused in *The Souls of Black Folk* was wrong. It was not simply a matter of presenting their misery in an objectively palatable fashion. The goodwill of the white man went only so far as to partly acknowledge his guilt. It was therefore left again to the black people to go a step further and force him to act upon that guilt.

In *The Souls of Black Folk*, Du Bois apparently did not envisage such a massive rise of his people to the streets. Obviously, this would be unnecessary, as he firmly believed that reason would prevail. Indeed, in the early 1900's Du Bois was not genuinely concerned with the masses of the black population, nor for that matter of the white. His vision and call for action was directed to the "Talented Tenth," that educated elite of the black and white worlds which had the cultural and academic talents to lead the masses.

Du Bois' background and training set him at a great distance from the average black American of his time. Even had he then wished to, it is extremely doubtful that he could have communicated with the largely unlettered mass of blacks. His language and the language of *Souls* was designed for the ears of the aristocrat. His style of writing is often riddled with flowery, overly abstruse imagery.

> I sit with Shakespeare and he winces not. Across the color line I move arm in arm with Balzac and Dumas, where smiling men and welcoming women glide in gilded halls. From the caves of evening that swing between the strong-limbed earth and the tracery of the stars, I summon Aristotle and Aurelius and what soul I will, and they come all graciously with no scorn nor condescension. So, wed with Truth, I dwell above the Veil.

When he speaks of his poorer black brothers and sisters, it is from a distance too great to presuppose true comprehension:

> They used to have a certain magnificent barbarism about them that I liked. They were never vulgar, never immoral, but rather rough and primitive, with an unconventionality that spent itself in loud guffaws, slaps on the back, and naps in the corner.

And at a later point, Du Bois goes on to remark:

They are not happy, these black men whom we meet throughout this region. There is little of the joyous abandon and playfulness which we are wont to associate with the plantation Negro.

Though Du Bois had a general philosophical love for the people of the black race, he could not base his program for advancement on this nebulous mass, as he had little emotional comprehension of the individual black man. Du Bois spoke directly to those who had risen out of the nebulous mass and who stood as products of a broad, higher education. The colleges and universities which provided this education held a place of tremendous importance in Du Bois' scheme. His rather romanticized view of their function is made clear when he states:

Here, amid a wide desert of caste and proscription, amid the heart-hurting slights and jars and vagaries of a deep race-dislike, lies this green oasis, where hot anger cools, and the bitterness of disappointment is sweetened by the springs and breezes of Parnassus; and here men may lie and listen, and learn of a future fuller than the past, and hear the voice of Time.

The products of these universities, both black and white, empowered with the knowledge of great civilizations and imbued with the tradition of learning and reason, could place themselves above the everyday strife of racial conflict and create a channel of communication. Du Bois maintained that their clear vision would provide the basis of a program for the general benefit of the masses, and the university was where it all was to begin.

In a very real sense, Du Bois was correct. It was from the colleges and universities of this country that came the thousands of young people who pushed for-

ward the sit-in movement of the 1960's. The goals also
of that movement have many of their roots in Du
Bois' integrationist vision of 1903:

> I insist that the question of the future is how best
> to keep these millions (of black men) from brooding
> over the wrongs of the past and the difficulties of
> the present, so that all their energies may be bent
> toward a cheerful striving and cooperation with their
> white neighbors toward a larger, juster, and fuller
> future.

Du Bois spoke of a program that would lift the black
man out of his position of subservience, and permit
him to share equally with the white man in the fruits
of the American dream:

> . . . there are today no truer exponents of the pure
> human plight of the Declaration of Independence
> than the American Negroes.

The black man had to embrace the accepted goals of
hard work, thrift, honesty, and education. He had to
play his part in the democratic framework by using
the strength of the ballot. He had to strive to reach
the models of citizenship set down by the founding
fathers. Du Bois knew it would be hard. The black
man had a long, upward struggle to go, and it was
possible, but only with the help of white America—
help which Du Bois asserted was owed to the black
man. He did not demand this help; instead, he reasoned and coaxed and explained patiently the right-
ness of his cause. Yet, he did warn his white audience
of the consequences should they fail to respond to his
words:

> They are not fools, they have tasted of the Tree of
> Life, and they will not cease to think, will not cease
> attempting to read the riddle of the world. By tak-

ing away their best equipped teachers and leaders,
by slamming the door of opportunity in the faces of
their bolder and brighter minds, will you make them
satisfied with their lot? Or will you not rather
transfer their leading from the hands of the men
taught to think to the hands of untrained demagogues?

That white America did not respond quickly
enough is amply illustrated by the black power movement of today. Du Bois, in *The Souls of Black Folk*,
had established the black man's right to expect his
equal place in America, and he had thought those expectations would be answered through the "courtesy"
and goodwill of the white man. The black students of
the 1960's had thought those expectations would be
filled through the guilt and shame of the white man.
They have both been proven wrong by the passage of
time, and now the black man no longer simply ex-
pects, he demands. The "reason" that Du Bois clung
to so steadfastly has been pushed to the background;
indeed, the educated black man today is often held in
skepticism and distrust by his black brothers; and the
hope of a shared democracy of blacks and whites is
fast being relegated to the realm of pessimistic speculation.

Du Bois, the Scholar of 1903 whose learned voice
rings out so clearly from the pages of this book, seems
far removed from the black man's position today.
However, in reading the beautifully moving "Of the
Passing of the First-Born" included in this volume,
one glimpses briefly the anguish and passion of Du
Bois, the man, the black father. The piece is a lament
at the death of his infant son, a lament at first deeply
and touchingly sorrowful, which turns suddenly into a
cry of joy, of anguished gratitude that this child

would not have to know the living death of a black man in America:

> Well sped, my boy, before the world had dubbed your ambition insolence, had held your ideals unattainable, and taught you to cringe and bow. Better far this nameless void that stops my life than a sea of sorrow for you.

Du Bois hints at the great reservoir of empassioned bitterness he, the Scholar, held in check to produce the patient clarity of the other essays which make up *Souls*. It is a glimpse of the furious, uncompromising fighter for black dignity and independence which Du Bois was to become in later years. The stages of Du Bois' development from *The Souls of Black Folk* pose a remarkable parallel to the development of the black movement in America. It is a sign of this man's greatness that in 1903 he was speaking the words which echoed again in the sit-in marches of the 1960's, that in the 1920's he was espousing many of the programs which have since become known as the basis for black power, "black is beautiful," negritudo, etc.

In 1913, Du Bois produced a pageant, "The Star of Ethiopia," and revived it again in 1925 with a cast of 350 actors. It was a tale of the "eldest and strongest race of mankind" in which he chronicled a long list of of the black man's gifts to the world: the gifts of freedom, laughter, hope, faith, and humility. The black man and the Semite had made Egypt the first nation of the world; and the black man alone had spread Mohammedism over half the world.

By 1924, Du Bois' view of the role of the university in the black man's struggle had undergone a radical change. It was no longer a haven from the battle, but a center where the battle should be initiated. When

three-fourths of the students at Fisk went on strike
against the school administration for catering to white
supporters and ignoring student wishes, Du Bois
praised their "radicalism." Du Bois moved increasingly toward the position that only black support and
control of their own universities could make them
effective tools for the black community. He spoke out
for black schools teaching black history, black sociology, and black art. Gone was the call for a special
class of black men educated in white institutions,
versed in the historical fragments of white culture.
Du Bois cried out for black men whose education
was thoroughly grounded in the problems of contemporary black America.

By 1930, Du Bois had already begun formulating a
program for black economic self-sufficiency. He favored the plan of black manufacturers and consumers
cooperatives. Raw materials drawn from black farmers, transported by black-owned trucks, and transformed into finished products in black-owned factories would be bought by black customers patronizing
black cooperative stores. He encouraged the use of
the economic boycott in forcing concessions from
white businessmen. Du Bois was no longer speaking
to the white man, for they had not listened; his heart,
soul, and voice were directed in an urgent call to his
black brothers, telling them they had to do it alone.
He felt that America in his day would not yield any
substantial ground in the racial struggle, and Negroes
were without enough power or alliances to force com-
pliance.

When Du Bois expressed the hopelessness of outside
help, he spoke not only of the white world, but of the
black world beyond America's shores. He believed
firmly in the spiritual unity of black men around the
world, and worked feverishly toward this goal

through a Pan-African movement primarily led by him. But Du Bois came to feel that the black American could not afford to indulge himself in dreams of immediately effective worldwide black unity. The Black American's battle was on American soil. He had earned his right to his place as an equal in this society, and he must fight to get it immediately, with the tools at hand. Du Bois saw that the black man in this country had to deal with the cruel realities of his situation. Escaping to Africa was not the answer. A separate "country" within the United States was not practicable. But a pooling of black economic resources was a beginning.

When Du Bois turned his attention to the arts, he called for a generation of black writers and painters who would use their talents for the uplift of the masses. He dismissed all efforts which showed the black man in anything other than a favorable light. He demanded that all black artists not only believe, but use their art to prove, that "black is beautiful."

By 1932, Du Bois had also reversed his position on the validity of the ballot as an effective power tool for the black man. The vote could get the black community only the smallest bits of political patronage: a new school here, street lights there, etc. It did not offer real solutions to the pressing problems. Du Bois came to feel that the answer lay in black America's turning its energies inward, to gain control of its own communities. Friends and enemies alike of Du Bois vigorously criticized his programs, calling them "voluntary segregation," just as today the black power movement is labeled "racist" and "separatist."

The years following the publication of *The Souls of Black Folk* brought W. E. B. Du Bois to a radical reversal of his views. In his thoughts and writings of this later period are evident not only the roots, but the very framework for the various programs of black leaders today. The nonviolent voter registration drives and the economic boycott which he spoke of were later used as the basis for the civil rights movement of the early 1960's, the programs of SNCC, SCLC, and Dr. Martin Luther King. The current programs for black economic independence, political control by blacks of their own communities, the sudden outgrowth of courses in Afro-American history, art, etc. taught by blacks for blacks in centers of learning across the country, the heavy emphasis on the psychological uplifting of the black masses by concentrating on the positive aspects of blackness—all were part of Du Bois' message, and all are part of the current movement in black America today. Indeed, the whole concept of what is today known as black consciousness found its beginnings in the mind of Du Bois.

Perhaps it was inevitable that it took some thirty years before the black man finally began listening to Du Bois. Perhaps it was also inevitable that the white man has not yet begun to truly listen. He may be awakened by the terrible silence which may come should all black Americans, like Du Bois, exhaust themselves in efforts to communicate, and finally stop talking to white America. But for all those who wish to know how we arrived at our present juncture in this heartrending struggle, read on. The beginnings are here in *The Souls of Black Folk*, in the heart of W. E. B. Du Bois.

Alvin F. Poussaint, M.D.
Assistant Professor of Psychiatry
Tufts University School of Medicine,
Boston, Mass.

I

Of Our Spiritual Strivings

O water, voice of my heart, crying in the sand,
　All night long crying with a mournful cry,
As I lie and listen, and cannot understand
　　The voice of my heart in my side or the voice of the sea,
　O water, crying for rest, is it I, is it I?
　All night long the water is crying to me.

Unresting water, there shall never be rest
　Till the last moon droop and the last tide fail,
And the fire of the end begin to burn in the west;
　　And the heart shall be weary and wonder and cry like the
　　　sea,
　All life long crying without avail,
　　As the water all night long is crying to me.

ARTHUR SYMONS.

BETWEEN me and the other world there is ever an unasked question: unasked by some through feelings of delicacy; by others through the difficulty of rightly framing it. All, nevertheless, flutter round it. They approach me in a half-hesitant sort of way, eye me curiously or compassionately, and then, instead of saying directly, How does it feel to be a problem? they say, I know an excellent colored man in my town; or, I fought at Mechanicsville; or, Do not these Southern

outrages make your blood boil? At these I smile, or
am interested, or reduce the boiling to a simmer, as
the occasion may require. To the real question, How
does it feel to be a problem? I answer seldom a word.

And yet, being a problem is a strange experience,—
peculiar even for one who has never been anything
else, save perhaps in babyhood and in Europe. It is in
the early days of rollicking boyhood that the revelation first bursts upon one, all in a day, as it were. I
remember well when the shadow swept across me. I
was a little thing, away up in the hills of New England, where the dark Housatonic winds between
Hoosac and Taghkanic to the sea. In a wee wooden
schoolhouse, something put it into the boys' and girls'
heads to buy gorgeous visiting-cards—ten cents a
package—and exchange. The exchange was merry, till
one girl, a tall newcomer, refused my card,—refused it
peremptorily, with a glance. Then it dawned upon me
with a certain suddenness that I was different from
the others; or like, mayhap, in heart and life and
longing, but shut out from their world by a vast veil.
I had thereafter no desire to tear down that veil, to
creep through; I held all beyond it in common contempt, and lived above it in a region of blue sky and
great wandering shadows. That sky was bluest when
I could beat my mates at examination-time, or beat
them at a foot-race, or even beat their stringy heads.
Alas, with the years all this fine contempt began to
fade; for the words I longed for, and all their daz-
zling opportunities, were theirs, not mine. But they
should not keep these prizes, I said; some, all, I
would wrest from them. Just how I would do it I
could never decide: by reading law, by healing the
sick, by telling the wonderful tales that swam in my
head,—some way. With other black boys the strife
was not so fiercely sunny: their youth shrunk into

tasteless sycophancy, or into silent hatred of the pale world about them and mocking distrust of everything white; or wasted itself in a bitter cry, Why did God make me an outcast and a stranger in mine own house? The shades of the prison-house closed round about us all: walls strait and stubborn to the whitest, but relentlessly narrow, tall, and unscalable to sons of night who must plod darkly on in resignation, or beat unavailing palms against the stone, or steadily, half hopelessly, watch the streak of blue above.

After the Egyptian and Indian, the Greek and Roman, the Teuton and Mongolian, the Negro is a sort of seventh son, born with a veil, and gifted with second-sight in this American world,—a world which yields him no true self-consciousness, but only lets him see himself through the revelation of the other world. It is a peculiar sensation, this double-consciousness, this sense of always looking at one's self through the eyes of others, of measuring one's soul by the tape of a world that looks on in amused contempt and pity. One ever feels his twoness,—an American, a Negro; two souls, two thoughts, two unreconciled strivings; two warring ideals in one dark body, whose dogged strength alone keeps it from being torn asunder.

The history of the American Negro is the history of this strife,—this longing to attain self-conscious manhood, to merge his double self into a better and truer self. In this merging he wishes neither of the older selves to be lost. He would not Africanize America, for America has too much to teach the world and Africa. He would not bleach his Negro soul in a flood of white Americanism, for he knows that Negro blood has a message for the world. He simply wishes to make it possible for a man to be both a Negro and an American, without being cursed and spit upon by his fellows, without having the doors of Opportunity closed roughly in his face.

This, then, is the end of his striving: to be a co-worker in the kingdom of culture, to escape both death and isolation, to husband and use his best powers and his latent genius. These powers of body and mind have in the past been strangely wasted, dispersed, or forgotten. The shadow of a mighty Negro past flits through the tale of Ethiopia the Shadowy and of Egypt the Sphinx. Through history, the powers of single black men flash here and there like falling stars, and die sometimes before the world has rightly gauged their brightness. Here in America, in the few days since Emancipation, the black man's turning hither and thither in hesitant and doubtful striving has often made his very strength to lose effectiveness, to seem like absence of power, like weakness. And yet it is not weakness,—it is the contradiction of double aims. The double-aimed struggle of the black artisan —on the one hand to escape white contempt for a nation of mere hewers of wood and drawers of water, and on the other hand to plough and nail and dig for a poverty-stricken horde—could only result in making him a poor craftsman, for he had but half a heart in either cause. By the poverty and ignorance of his people, the Negro minister or doctor was tempted toward quackery and demagogy; and by the criticism of the other world, toward ideals that made him ashamed of his lowly tasks. The would-be black *savant* was confronted by the paradox that the knowledge his people needed was a twice-told tale to his white neighbors, while the knowledge which would teach the white world was Greek to his own flesh and blood. The innate love of harmony and beauty that set the ruder souls of his people a-dancing and a-singing raised but confusion and doubt in the soul of the black artist; for the beauty revealed to him was the soul-beauty of a race which his larger audience despised, and he could not articulate the message of another people. This waste of double aims, this seeking to satisfy two unreconciled ideals, has wrought sad havoc with the courage and faith and deeds of ten thousand thousand people,—has sent them often wooing false gods and invoking false means of salvation, and at times has even seemed about to make them ashamed of themselves.

Away back in the days of bondage they thought to see in one divine event the end of all doubt and disappointment; few men ever worshipped Freedom with half such unquestioning faith as did the American Negro for two centuries. To him, so far as he thought and dreamed, slavery was indeed the sum of all villainies, the cause of all sorrow, the root of all prejudice; Emancipation was the key to a promised land of sweeter beauty than ever stretched before the eyes of wearied Israelites. In song and exhortation swelled one refrain—Liberty; in his tears and curses the God he implored had Freedom in his right hand. At last it came,—suddenly, fearfully, like a dream. With one wild carnival of blood and passion came the message in his own plaintive cadences:—

> "Shout, O children!
> Shout, you're free!
> For God has bought your liberty!"

Years have passed away since then,—ten, twenty, forty; forty years of national life, forty years of renewal and development, and yet the swarthy spectre sits in its accustomed seat at the Nation's feast. In vain do we cry to this our vastest social problem:—

> "Take any shape but that, and my firm nerves
> Shall never tremble!"

The Nation has not yet found peace from its sins; the
freedman has not yet found in freedom his promised
land. Whatever of good may have come in these years
of change, the shadow of a deep disappointment rests
upon the Negro people,—a disappointment all the
more bitter because the unattained ideal was un-
bounded save by the simple ignorance of a lowly people.

The first decade was merely a prolongation of the
vain search for freedom, the boon that seemed ever
barely to elude their grasp,—like a tantalizing will-o'-
the-wisp, maddening and misleading the headless
host. The holocaust of war, the terrors of the Ku-Klux
Klan, the lies of carpet-baggers, the disorganization of
industry, and the contradictory advice of friends and
foes, left the bewildered serf with no new watchword
beyond the old cry for freedom. As the time flew,
however, he began to grasp a new idea. The ideal of
liberty demanded for its attainment powerful means,
and these the Fifteenth Amendment gave him. The
ballot, which before he had looked upon as a visible
sign of freedom, he now regarded as the chief means
of gaining and perfecting the liberty with which war
had partially endowed him. And why not? Had not
votes made war and emancipated millions? Had not
votes enfranchised the freedmen? Was anything impossible to a power that had done all this? A million
black men started with renewed zeal to vote themselves into the kingdom. So the decade flew away, the
revolution of 1876 came, and left the half-free serf
weary, wondering, but still inspired. Slowly but steadily, in the following years, a new vision began gradually to replace the dream of political power,—a powerful movement, the rise of another ideal to guide the
unguided, another pillar of fire by night after a
clouded day. It was the ideal of "book-learning"; the

curiosity, born of compulsory ignorance, to know and test the power of the cabalistic letters of the white man, the longing to know. Here at last seemed to have been discovered the mountain path to Canaan; longer than the highway of Emancipation and law, steep and rugged, but straight, leading to heights high enough to overlook life.

Up the new path the advance guard toiled, slowly, heavily, doggedly; only those who have watched and guided the faltering feet, the misty minds, the dull understandings, of the dark pupils of these schools know how faithfully, how piteously, this people strove to learn. It was weary work. The cold statistician wrote down the inches of progress here and there, noted also where here and there a foot had slipped or some one had fallen. To the tired climbers, the horizon was ever dark, the mists were often cold, the Canaan was always dim and far away. If, however, the vistas disclosed as yet no goal, no resting-place, little but flattery and criticism, the journey at least gave leisure for reflection and self-examination; it changed the child of Emancipation to the youth with dawning self-consciousness, self-realization, self-respect. In those sombre forests of his striving his own soul rose before him, and he saw himself,—darkly as through a veil; and yet he saw in himself some faint revelation of his power, of his mission. He began to have a dim feeling that, to attain his place in the world, he must be himself, and not another. For the first time he sought to analyze the burden he bore upon his back, that dead-weight of social degradation partially masked behind a half-named Negro problem. He felt his poverty; without a cent, without a home, without land, tools, or savings, he had entered into competition with rich, landed, skilled neighbors. To be a poor man is hard, but to be a poor race in a land of dollars is the very bottom of hardships. He felt the weight of his ignorance,—not simply of letters, but of life, of business, of the humanities; the accumulated sloth and shirking and awkwardness of decades and centuries shackled his hands and feet. Nor was his burden all poverty and ignorance. The red stain of bastardy, which two centuries of systematic legal defilement of Negro women had stamped upon his race, meant not only the loss of ancient African chastity, but also the hereditary weight of a mass of corruption from white adulterers, threatening almost the obliteration of the Negro home.

A people thus handicapped ought not to be asked to race with the world, but rather allowed to give all its time and thought to its own social problems. But alas! while sociologists gleefully count his bastards and his prostitutes, the very soul of the toiling, sweating black man is darkened by the shadow of a vast despair. Men call the shadow prejudice, and learnedly explain it as the natural defence of culture against barbarism, learning against ignorance, purity against crime, the "higher" against the "lower" races. To which the Negro cries Amen! and swears that to so much of this strange prejudice as is founded on just homage to civilization, culture, righteousness, and progress, he humbly bows and meekly does obeisance. But before that nameless prejudice that leaps beyond all this he stands helpless, dismayed, and well-nigh speechless; before that personal disrespect and mockery, the ridicule and systematic humiliation, the distortion of fact and wanton license of fancy, the cynical ignoring of the better and the boisterous welcoming of the worse, the all-pervading desire to inculcate disdain for everything black, from Toussaint to the devil,—before this there rises a sickening despair that would disarm and discourage any nation save that black host to whom "discouragement" is an unwritten word.

But the facing of so vast a prejudice could not but bring the inevitable self-questioning, self-disparagement, and lowering of ideals which ever accompany repression and breed in an atmosphere of contempt and hate. Whisperings and portents came borne upon the four winds: Lo! we are diseased and dying, cried the dark hosts; we cannot write, our voting is vain; what need of education, since we must always cook and serve? And the Nation echoed and enforced this self-criticism, saying: Be content to be servants, and nothing more; what need of higher culture for half-men? Away with the black man's ballot, by force or fraud,—and behold the suicide of a race! Nevertheless, out of the evil came something of good,—the more careful adjustment of education to real life, the clearer perception of the Negroes' social responsibilities, and the sobering realization of the meaning of progress.

So dawned the time of *Sturm und Drang*: storm and stress to-day rocks our little boat on the mad waters of the world-sea; there is within and without the sound of conflict, the burning of body and rending of soul; inspiration strives with doubt, and faith with vain questionings. The bright ideals of the past,—physical freedom, political power, the training of brains and the training of hands,—all these in turn have waxed and waned, until even the last grows dim and overcast. Are they all wrong,—all false? No, not that, but each alone was over-simple and incomplete, —the dreams of a credulous race-childhood, or the fond imaginings of the other world which does not know and does not want to know our power. To be really true, all these ideals must be melted and welded into one. The training of the schools we need

to-day more than ever,—the training of deft hands,
quick eyes and ears, and above all the broader,
deeper, higher culture of gifted minds and pure
hearts. The power of the ballot we need in sheer self-
defence,—else what shall save us from a second slavery? Freedom, too, the long-sought, we still seek,—the
freedom of life and limb, the freedom to work and
think, the freedom to love and aspire. Work, culture,
liberty,—all these we need, not singly but together,
not successively but together, each growing and aiding each, and all striving toward that vaster ideal that
swims before the Negro people, the ideal of human
brotherhood, gained through the unifying ideal of
Race; the ideal of fostering and developing the traits
and talents of the Negro, not in opposition to or contempt for other races, but rather in large conformity
to the greater ideals of the American Republic, in
order that some day on American soil two world-races
may give each to each those characteristics both so
sadly lack. We the darker ones come even now not altogether empty-handed: there are to-day no truer ex-
ponents of the pure human spirit of the Declaration
of Independence than the American Negroes; there is
no true American music but the wild sweet melodies
of the Negro slave; the American fairy tales and folk-
lore are Indian and African; and, all in all, we black
men seem the sole oasis of simple faith and reverence
in a dusty desert of dollars and smartness. Will America be poorer if she replace her brutal dyspeptic blundering with light-hearted but determined Negro humility? or her coarse and cruel wit with loving jovial
good-humor? or her vulgar music with the soul of the
Sorrow Songs?

Merely a concrete test of the underlying principles
of the great republic is the Negro Problem, and the
spiritual striving of the freedmen's sons is the travail

of souls whose burden is almost beyond the measure of their strength, but who bear it in the name of an historic race, in the name of this the land of their fathers' fathers, and in the name of human opportunity.

And now what I have briefly sketched in large outline let me on coming pages tell again in many ways, with loving emphasis and deeper detail, that men may listen to the striving in the souls of black folk.

II

Of the Dawn of Freedom

Careless seems the great Avenger;
  History's lessons but record
One death-grapple in the darkness
  'Twixt old systems and the Word;
Truth forever on the scaffold,
  Wrong forever on the throne;
Yet that scaffold sways the future,
  And behind the dim unknown
Standeth God within the shadow
  Keeping watch above His own.

LOWELL.

THE problem of the twentieth century is the problem
of the color-line,—the relation of the darker to the
lighter races of men in Asia and Africa, in America
and the islands of the sea. It was a phase of this problem that caused the Civil War; and however much
they who marched South and North in 1861 may have
fixed on the technical points of union and local autonomy as a shibboleth, all nevertheless knew, as we

know, that the question of Negro slavery was the real cause of the conflict. Curious it was, too, how this deeper question ever forced itself to the surface despite effort and disclaimer. No sooner had Northern armies touched Southern soil than this old question, newly guised, sprang from the earth,—What shall be done with Negroes? Peremptory military commands this way and that, could not answer the query; the Emancipation Proclamation seemed but to broaden and intensify the difficulties; and the War Amendments made the Negro problems of to-day.

It is the aim of this essay to study the period of history from 1861 to 1872 so far as it relates to the American Negro. In effect, this tale of the dawn of Freedom is an account of that government of men called the Freedmen's Bureau,—one of the most singular and interesting of the attempts made by a great nation to grapple with vast problems of race and social condition.

The war has naught to do with slaves, cried Congress, the President, and the Nation; and yet no sooner had the armies, East and West, penetrated Virginia and Tennessee than fugitive slaves appeared within their lines. They came at night, when the flickering camp-fires shone like vast unsteady stars along the black horizon: old men and thin, with gray and tufted hair; women with frightened eyes, dragging whimpering hungry children; men and girls, stalwart and gaunt,—a horde of starving vagabonds, homeless, helpless, and pitiable, in their dark distress. Two methods of treating these newcomers seemed equally logical to opposite sorts of minds. Ben Butler, in Virginia, quickly declared slave property contraband of war, and put the fugitives to work; while Fremont, in Missouri, declared the slaves free under martial law. Butler's action was approved, but Fremont's was hast-

ily countermanded, and his successor, Halleck, saw
things differently. "Hereafter," he commanded, "no
slaves should be allowed to come into your lines at
all; if any come without your knowledge, when owners call for them deliver them." Such a policy was difficult to enforce; some of the black refugees declared
themselves freemen, others showed that their masters
had deserted them, and still others were captured
with forts and plantations. Evidently, too, slaves were
a source of strength to the Confederacy, and were
being used as laborers and producers. "They constitute a military resource," wrote Secretary Cameron,
late in 1861; "and being such, that they should not be
turned over to the enemy is too plain to discuss." So
gradually the tone of the army chiefs changed; Congress forbade the rendition of fugitives, and Butler's
"contrabands" were welcomed as military laborers.
This complicated rather than solved the problem, for
now the scattering fugitives became a steady stream,
which flowed faster as the armies marched.

Then the long-headed man with care-chiselled face
who sat in the White House saw the inevitable, and
emancipated the slaves of rebels on New Year's, 1863.
A month later Congress called earnestly for the Negro
soldiers whom the act of July, 1862, had half grudg-
ingly allowed to enlist. Thus the barriers were lev-
elled and the deed was done. The stream of fugitives
swelled to a flood, and anxious army officers kept in-
quiring: "What must be done with slaves, arriving almost daily? Are we to find food and shelter for
women and children?"

It was a Pierce of Boston who pointed out the way,
and thus became in a sense the founder of the Freedmen's Bureau. He was a firm friend of Secretary
Chase; and when, in 1861, the care of slaves and
abandoned lands developed upon the Treasury

THE SOULS OF BLACK FOLK

officials, Pierce was specially detailed from the ranks to study the conditions. First, he cared for the refugees at Fortress Monroe; and then, after Sherman had captured Hilton Head, Pierce was sent there to found his Port Royal experiment of making free working-men out of slaves. Before his experiment was barely started, however, the problem of the fugitives had assumed such proportions that it was taken from the hands of the over-burdened Treasury Department and given to the army officials. Already centres of massed freedmen were forming at Fortress Monroe, Washington, New Orleans, Vicksburg and Corinth, Columbus, Ky., and Cairo, Ill., as well as at Port Royal. Army chaplains found here new and fruitful fields; "superintendents of contrabands" multiplied, and some attempt at systematic work was made by enlisting the able-bodied men and giving work to the others.

Then came the Freedmen's Aid societies, born of the touching appeals from Pierce and from these other centres of distress. There was the American Missionary Association, sprung from the *Amistad,* and now full-grown for work; the various church organizations, the National Freedmen's Relief Association, the American Freedmen's Union, the Western Freedmen's Aid Commission,—in all fifty or more active organizations, which sent clothes, money, school-books, and teachers southward. All they did was needed, for the destitution of the freedmen was often reported as "too appalling for belief," and the situation was daily growing worse rather than better.

And daily, too, it seemed more plain that this was no ordinary matter of temporary relief, but a national crisis; for here loomed a labor problem of vast dimensions. Masses of Negroes stood idle, or, if they worked spasmodically, were never sure of pay; and if perchance they received pay, squandered the new thing thoughtlessly. In these and other ways were camp-life and the new liberty demoralizing the freedmen. The broader economic organization thus clearly demanded sprang up here and there as accident and local conditions determined. Here it was that Pierce's Port Royal plan of leased plantations and guided workmen pointed out the rough way. In Washington the military governor, at the urgent appeal of the superintendent, opened confiscated estates to the cultivation of the fugitives, and there in the shadow of the dome gathered black farm villages. General Dix gave over estates to the freedmen of Fortress Monroe, and so on, South and West. The government and benevolent societies furnished the means of cultivation, and the Negro turned again slowly to work. The systems of control, thus started, rapidly grew, here and there, into strange little governments, like that of General Banks in Louisiana, with its ninety thousand black subjects, its fifty thousand guided laborers, and its annual budget of one hundred thousand dollars and more. It made out four thousand pay-rolls a year, registered all freedmen, inquired into grievances and redressed them, laid and collected taxes, and established a system of public schools. So, too, Colonel Eaton, the superintendent of Tennessee and Arkansas, ruled over one hundred thousand freedmen, leased and cultivated seven thousand acres of cotton land, and fed ten thousand paupers a year. In South Carolina was General Saxton, with his deep interest in black folk. He succeeded Pierce and the Treasury officials, and sold forfeited estates, leased abandoned plantations, encouraged schools, and received from Sherman, after that terribly picturesque march to the sea, thousands of the wretched camp followers.

Three characteristic things one might have seen in

Sherman's raid through Georgia, which threw the new situation in shadowy relief: the Conqueror, the Conquered, and the Negro. Some see all significance in the grim front of the destroyer, and some in the bitter sufferers of the Lost Cause. But to me neither soldier nor fugitive speaks with so deep a meaning as that dark human cloud that clung like remorse on the rear of those swift columns, swelling at times to half their size, almost engulfing and choking them. In vain were they ordered back, in vain were bridges hewn from beneath their feet; on they trudged and writhed and surged, until they rolled into Savannah, a starved and naked horde of tens of thousands. There too came the characteristic military remedy: "The islands from Charleston south, the abandoned rice-fields along the rivers for thirty miles back from the sea, and the country bordering the St. John's River, Florida, are reserved and set apart for the settlement of Negroes now made free by act of war." So read the celebrated "Field-order Number Fifteen."

All these experiments, orders, and systems were bound to attract and perplex the government and the nation. Directly after the Emancipation Proclamation, Representative Eliot had introduced a bill creating a Bureau of Emancipation; but it was never reported. The following June a committee of inquiry, appointed by the Secretary of War, reported in favor of a temporary bureau for the "improvement, protection, and employment of refugee freedmen," on much the same lines as were afterwards followed. Petitions came in to President Lincoln from distinguished citizens and organizations, strongly urging a comprehensive and unified plan of dealing with the freedmen, under a bureau which should be "charged with the study of plans and execution of measures for easily guiding, and in every way judiciously and humanely aiding, the passage of our emancipated and yet to be emancipated blacks from the old condition of forced labor to their new state of voluntary industry."

Some half-hearted steps were taken to accomplish this, in part, by putting the whole matter again in charge of the special Treasury agents. Laws of 1863 and 1864 directed them to take charge of and lease abandoned lands for periods not exceeding twelve months, and to "provide in such leases, or otherwise, for the employment and general welfare" of the freedmen. Most of the army officers greeted this as a welcome relief from perplexing "Negro affairs," and Secretary Fessenden, July 29, 1864, issued an excellent system of regulations, which were afterward closely followed by General Howard. Under Treasury agents, large quantities of land were leased in the Mississippi Valley, and many Negroes were employed; but in August, 1864, the new regulations were suspended for reasons of "public policy," and the army was again in control.

Meanwhile Congress had turned its attention to the subject; and in March the House passed a bill by a majority of two establishing a Bureau for Freedmen in the War Department. Charles Sumner, who had charge of the bill in the Senate, argued that freedmen and abandoned lands ought to be under the same department, and reported a substitute for the House bill attaching the Bureau to the Treasury Department. This bill passed, but too late for action by the House. The debates wandered over the whole policy of the administration and the general question of slavery, without touching very closely the specific merits of the measure in hand. Then the national election took place; and the administration, with a vote of renewed confidence from the country, addressed itself to the matter more seriously. A conference between the two branches of Congress agreed upon a carefully drawn measure which contained the chief provisions of Sumner's bill, but made the proposed organization a department independent of both the War and the Treasury officials. The bill was conservative, giving the new department "general superintendence of all freedmen." Its purpose was to "establish regulations" for them, protect them, lease them lands, adjust their wages, and appear in civil and military courts as their "next friend." There were many limitations attached to the powers thus granted, and the organization was made permanent. Nevertheless, the Senate defeated the bill, and a new conference committee was appointed. This committee reported a new bill, February 28, which was whirled through just as the session closed, and became the act of 1865 establishing in the War Department a "Bureau of Refugees, Freedmen, and Abandoned Lands."

This last compromise was a hasty bit of legislation, vague and uncertain in outline. A Bureau was created, "to continue during the present War of Rebellion, and for one year thereafter," to which was given "the supervision and management of all abandoned lands and the control of all subjects relating to refugees and freedmen," under "such rules and regulations as may be presented by the head of the Bureau and approved by the President." A Commissioner, appointed by the President and Senate, was to control the Bureau, with an office force not exceeding ten clerks. The President might also appoint assistant commissioners in the seceded States, and to all these offices military officials might be detailed at regular pay. The Secretary of War could issue rations, clothing, and fuel to the destitute, and all abandoned property was placed in the hands of the Bureau for

eventual lease and sale to ex-slaves in forty-acre par-
cels.

Thus did the United States government definitely
assume charge of the emancipated Negro as the ward
of the nation. It was a tremendous undertaking. Here
at a stroke of the pen was erected a government of
millions of men,—and not ordinary men either, but
black men emasculated by a peculiarly complete system of slavery, centuries old; and now, suddenly, vio-
lently, they come into a new birthright, at a time of
war and passion, in the midst of the stricken and embittered population of their former masters. Any man
might well have hesitated to assume charge of such a
work, with vast responsibilities, indefinite powers, and
limited resources. Probably no one but a soldier
would have answered such a call promptly; and, indeed, no one but a soldier could be called, for Congress had appropriated no money for salaries and ex-
penses.

Less than a month after the weary Emancipator
passed to his rest, his successor assigned Major-Gen.
Oliver O. Howard to duty as Commissioner of the
new Bureau. He was a Maine man, then only thirty-
five years of age. He had marched with Sherman to
the sea, had fought well at Gettysburg, and but the
year before had been assigned to the command of the
Department of Tennessee. An honest man, with too
much faith in human nature, little aptitude for business and intricate detail, he had had large opportunity of becoming acquainted at first hand with much of
the work before him. And of that work it has been
truly said that "no approximately correct history of
civilization can ever be written which does not throw
out in bold relief, as one of the great landmarks of political and social progress, the organization and administration of the Freedmen's Bureau."

On May 12, 1865, Howard was appointed; and he assumed the duties of his office promptly on the 15th, and began examining the field of work. A curious mess he looked upon: little despotisms, communistic experiments, slavery, peonage, business speculations, organized charity, unorganized almsgiving,—all reeling on under the guise of helping the freedmen, and all enshrined in the smoke and blood of the war and the cursing and silence of angry men. On May 19 the new government—for a government it really was —issued its constitution; commissioners were to be appointed in each of the seceded states, who were to take charge of "all subjects relating to refugees and freedmen," and all relief and rations were to be given by their consent alone. The Bureau invited continued coöperation with benevolent societies, and declared: "It will be the object of all commissioners to introduce practicable systems of compensated labor," and to establish schools. Forthwith nine assistant commissioners were appointed. They were to hasten to their fields of work; seek gradually to close relief establishments, and make the destitute self-supporting; act as courts of law where there were no courts, or where Negroes were not recognized in them as free; establish the institution of marriage among ex-slaves, and keep records; see that freedmen were free to choose their employers, and help in making fair contracts for them; and finally, the circular said: "Simple good faith, for which we hope on all hands for those concerned in the passing away of slavery, will especially relieve the assistant commissioners in the discharge of their duties toward the freedmen, as well as promote the general welfare."

No sooner was the work thus started, and the general system and local organization in some measure begun, than two grave difficulties appeared which

changed largely the theory and outcome of Bureau
work. First, there were the abandoned lands of the
South. It had long been the more or less definitely expressed theory of the North that all the chief problems of Emancipation might be settled by establishing the slaves on the forfeited lands of their masters,
—a sort of poetic justice, said some. But this poetry
done into solemn prose meant either wholesale confis-
cation of private property in the South, or vast appro-
priations. Now Congress had not appropriated a cent,
and no sooner did the proclamations of general am-
nesty appear than the eight hundred thousand acres
of abandoned lands in the hands of the Freedmen's
Bureau melted quickly away. The second difficulty
lay in perfecting the local organization of the Bureau
throughout the wide field of work. Making a new machine and sending out officials of duly ascertained fit-
ness for a great work of social reform is no child's
task; but this task was even harder, for a new central
organization had to be fitted on a heterogeneous and
confused but already existing system of relief and
control of ex-slaves; and the agents available for this
work must be sought for in an army still busy with
war operations,—men in the very nature of the case ill
fitted for delicate social work,—or among the questionable camp followers of an invading host. Thus,
after a year's work, vigorously as it was pushed, the
problem looked even more difficult to grasp and solve
than at the beginning. Nevertheless, three things that
year's work did, well worth the doing: it relieved a
vast amount of physical suffering; it transported seven
thousand fugitives from congested centres back to the
farm; and, best of all, it inaugurated the crusade of
the New England schoolma'am.

The annals of this Ninth Crusade are yet to be
written,—the tale of a mission that seemed to our age

far more quixotic than the quest of St. Louis seemed to his. Behind the mists of ruin and rapine waved the calico dresses of women who dared, and after the hoarse mouthings of the field guns rang the rhythm of the alphabet. Rich and poor they were, serious and curious. Bereaved now of a father, now of a brother, now of more than these, they came seeking a life work in planting New England schoolhouses among the white and black of the South. They did their work well. In that first year they taught one hundred thousand souls, and more.

Evidently, Congress must soon legislate again on the hastily organized Bureau, which had so quickly grown into wide significance and vast possibilities. An institution such as that was well-nigh as difficult to end as to begin. Early in 1866 Congress took up the matter, when Senator Trumbull, of Illinois, introduced a bill to extend the Bureau and enlarge its powers. This measure received, at the hands of Congress, far more thorough discussion and attention than its predecessor. The war cloud had thinned enough to allow a clearer conception of the work of Emancipation. The champions of the bill argued that the strengthening of the Freedmen's Bureau was still a military necessity; that it was needed for the proper carrying out of the Thirteenth Amendment, and was a work of sheer justice to the ex-slave, at a trifling cost to the government. The opponents of the measure declared that the war was over, and the necessity for war measures past; that the Bureau, by reason of its extraordinary powers, was clearly unconstitutional in time of peace, and was destined to irritate the South and pauperize the freedmen, at a final cost of possibly hundreds of millions. These two arguments were unanswered, and indeed unanswerable: the one that the extraordinary powers of the Bureau threatened the civil rights of all citizens; and the other that the government must have power to do what manifestly must be done, and that present abandonment of the freedmen meant their practical re-enslavement. The bill which finally passed enlarged and made permanent the Freedmen's Bureau. It was promptly vetoed by President Johnson as "unconstitutional," "unnecessary," and "extrajudicial," and failed of passage over the veto. Meantime, however, the breach between Congress and the President began to broaden, and a modified form of the lost bill was finally passed over the President's second veto, July 16.

The act of 1866 gave the Freedmen's Bureau its final form,—the form by which it will be known to posterity and judged of men. It extended the existence of the Bureau to July, 1868; it authorized additional assistant commissioners, the retention of army officers mustered out of regular service, the sale of certain forfeited lands to freedmen on nominal terms, the sale of Confederate public property for Negro schools, and a wider field of judicial interpretation and cognizance. The government of the unreconstructed South was thus put very largely in the hands of the Freedmen's Bureau, especially as in many cases the departmental military commander was now made also assistant commissioner. It was thus that the Freedmen's Bureau became a full-fledged government of men. It made laws, executed them and interpreted them; it laid and collected taxes, defined and punished crime, maintained and used military force, and dictated such measures as it thought necessary and proper for the accomplishment of its varied ends. Naturally, all these powers were not exercised continuously nor to their fullest extent; and yet, as General Howard has said, "scarcely any subject that has to be legislated upon in civil society failed, at one time or another, to demand the action of this singular Bureau."

To understand and criticise intelligently so vast a work, one must not forget an instant the drift of things in the later sixties. Lee had surrendered, Lincoln was dead, and Johnson and Congress were at loggerheads; the Thirteenth Amendment was adopted, the Fourteenth pending, and the Fifteenth declared in force in 1870. Guerrilla raiding, the ever-present flickering after-flame of war, was spending its forces against the Negroes, and all the Southern land was awakening as from some wild dream to poverty and social revolution. In a time of perfect calm, amid willing neighbors and streaming wealth, the social uplifting of four million slaves to an assured and self-sustaining place in the body politic and economic would have been a herculean task; but when to the inherent difficulties of so delicate and nice a social operation were added the spite and hate of conflict, the hell of war; when suspicion and cruelty were rife, and gaunt Hunger wept beside Bereavement,—in such a case, the work of any instrument of social regeneration was in large part foredoomed to failure. The very name of the Bureau stood for a thing in the South which for two centuries and better men had refused even to argue,—that life amid free Negroes was simply unthinkable, the maddest of experiments.

The agents that the Bureau could command varied all the way from unselfish philanthropists to narrow-minded busybodies and thieves; and even though it be true that the average was far better than the worst, it was the occasional fly that helped spoil the ointment.

Then amid all crouched the freed slave, bewildered between friend and foe. He had emerged from slavery,—not the worst slavery in the world, not a slavery

that made all life unbearable, rather a slavery that
had here and there something of kindliness, fidelity,
and happiness,—but withal slavery, which, so far as
human aspiration and desert were concerned, classed
the black man and the ox together. And the Negro
knew full well that, whatever their deeper convictions
may have been, Southern men had fought with
desperate energy to perpetuate this slavery under
which the black masses, with half-articulate thought,
had writhed and shivered. They welcomed freedom
with a cry. They shrank from the master who still
strove for their chains; they fled to the friends that
had freed them, even though those friends stood
ready to use them as a club for driving the recalci-
trant South back into loyalty. So the cleft between the
white and black South grew. Idle to say it never
should have been; it was as inevitable as its results
were pitiable. Curiously incongruous elements were
left arrayed against each other,—the North, the government, the carpet-bagger, and the slave, here; and
there, all the South that was white, whether gentleman or vagabond, honest man or rascal, lawless murderer or martyr to duty.

Thus it is doubly difficult to write of this period
calmly, so intense was the feeling, so mighty the
human passions that swayed and blinded men. Amid
it all, two figures ever stand to typify that day to coming ages,—the one, a gray-haired gentleman, whose fathers had quit themselves like men, whose sons lay in
nameless graves; who bowed to the evil of slavery because its abolition threatened untold ill to all; who
stood at last, in the evening of life, a blighted, ruined
form, with hate in his eyes;—and the other, a form
hovering dark and mother-like, her awful face black
with the mists of centuries, had aforetime quailed at
that white master's command, had bent in love over

the cradles of his sons and daughters, and closed in death the sunken eyes of his wife,—aye, too, at his behest had laid herself low to his lust, and borne a tawny man-child to the world, only to see her dark boy's limbs scattered to the winds by midnight marauders riding after "damned Niggers." These were the saddest sights of that woful day; and no man clasped the hands of these two passing figures of the present-past; but, hating, they went to their long home, and, hating, their children's children live to-day.

Here, then, was the field of work for the Freedmen's Bureau; and since, with some hesitation, it was continued by the act of 1868 until 1869, let us look upon four years of its work as a whole. There were, in 1868, nine hundred Bureau officials scattered from Washington to Texas, ruling, directly and indirectly, many millions of men. The deeds of these rulers fall mainly under seven heads: the relief of physical suffering, the overseeing of the beginnings of free labor, the buying and selling of land, the establishment of schools, the paying of bounties, the administration of justice, and the financiering of all these activities.

Up to June, 1869, over half a million patients had been treated by Bureau physicians and surgeons, and sixty hospitals and asylums had been in operation. In fifty months twenty-one million free rations were distributed at a cost of over four million dollars. Next came the difficult question of labor. First, thirty thousand black men were transported from the refuges and relief stations back to the farms, back to the critical trial of a new way of working. Plain instructions went out from Washington: the laborers must be free to choose their employers, no fixed rate of wages was prescribed, and there was to be no peonage or forced labor. So far, so good; but where local agents differed *toto cœlo* in capacity and character, where the *personnel* was continually changing, the outcome was necessarily varied. The largest element of success lay in the fact that the majority of the freedmen were willing, even eager, to work. So labor contracts were written, —fifty thousand in a single State,—laborers advised, wages guaranteed, and employers supplied. In truth, the organization became a vast labor bureau,—not perfect, indeed, notably defective here and there, but on the whole successful beyond the dreams of thoughtful men. The two great obstacles which confronted the officials were the tyrant and the idler,—the slaveholder who was determined to perpetuate slavery under another name; and the freedman who regarded freedom as perpetual rest,—the Devil and the Deep Sea.

In the work of establishing the Negroes as peasant proprietors, the Bureau was from the first handicapped and at last absolutely checked. Something was done, and larger things were planned; abandoned lands were leased so long as they remained in the hands of the Bureau, and a total revenue of nearly half a million dollars derived from black tenants. Some other lands to which the nation had gained title were sold on easy terms, and public lands were opened for settlement to the very few freedmen who had tools and capital. But the vision of "forty acres and a mule"—the righteous and reasonable ambition to become a landholder, which the nation had all but categorically promised the freedmen—was destined in most cases to bitter disappointment. And those men of marvellous hindsight who are today seeking to preach the Negro back to the present peonage of the soil know well, or ought to know, that the opportunity of binding the Negro peasant willingly to the soil was lost on that day when the Commissioner of the Freed-men's Bureau had to go to South Carolina and tell the weeping freedmen, after their years of toil, that their land was not theirs, that there was a mistake—some-where. If by 1874 the Georgia Negro alone owned three hundred and fifty thousand acres of land, it was by grace of his thrift rather than by bounty of the government.

The greatest success of the Freedmen's Bureau lay in the planting of the free school among Negroes, and the idea of free elementary education among all classes in the South. It not only called the school-mis-tresses through the benevolent agencies and built them schoolhouses, but it helped discover and sup-port such apostles of human culture as Edmund Ware, Samuel Armstrong, and Erastus Cravath. The opposition to Negro education in the South was at first bitter, and showed itself in ashes, insult, and blood; for the South believed an educated Negro to be a dangerous Negro. And the South was not wholly wrong; for education among all kinds of men always has had, and always will have, an element of danger and revolution, of dissatisfaction and discontent. Nev-ertheless, men strive to know. Perhaps some inkling of this paradox, even in the unquiet days of the Bureau, helped the bayonets allay an opposition to human training which still to-day lies smouldering in the South, but not flaming. Fisk, Atlanta, Howard, and Hampton were founded in these days, and six million dollars were expended for educational work, seven hundred and fifty thousand dollars of which the freedmen themselves gave of their poverty.

Such contributions, together with the buying of land and various other enterprises, showed that the ex-slave was handling some free capital already. The chief initial source of this was labor in the army, and his pay and bounty as a soldier. Payments to Negro soldiers were at first complicated by the ignorance of the recipients, and the fact that the quotas of colored regiments from Northern States were largely filled by recruits from the South, unknown to their fellow soldiers. Consequently, payments were accompanied by such frauds that Congress, by joint resolution in 1867, put the whole matter in the hands of the Freedmen's Bureau. In two years six million dollars was thus distributed to five thousand claimants, and in the end the sum exceeded eight million dollars. Even in this system fraud was frequent; but still the work put needed capital in the hands of practical paupers, and some, at least, was well spent.

The most perplexing and least successful part of the Bureau's work lay in the exercise of its judicial functions. The regular Bureau court consisted of one representative of the employer, one of the Negro, and one of the Bureau. If the Bureau could have maintained a perfectly judicial attitude, this arrangement would have been ideal, and must in time have gained confidence; but the nature of its other activities and the character of its *personnel* prejudiced the Bureau in favor of the black litigants, and led without doubt to much injustice and annoyance. On the other hand, to leave the Negro in the hands of Southern courts was impossible. In a distracted land where slavery had hardly fallen, to keep the strong from wanton abuse of the weak, and the weak from gloating insolently over the half-shorn strength of the strong, was a thankless, hopeless task. The former masters of the land were peremptorily ordered about, seized, and imprisoned, and punished over and again, with scant courtesy from army officers. The former slaves were intimidated, beaten, raped, and butchered by angry and revengeful men. Bureau courts tended to become centres simply for punishing whites, while the regular civil courts tended to become solely institutions for perpetuating the slavery of blacks. Almost every law and method ingenuity could devise was employed by the legislatures to reduce the Negroes to serfdom,—to make them the slaves of the State, if not of individual owners; while the Bureau officials too often were found striving to put the "bottom rail on top," and gave the freedmen a power and independence which they could not yet use. It is all well enough for us of another generation to wax wise with advice to those who bore the burden in the heat of the day. It is full easy now to see that the man who lost home, fortune, and family at a stroke, and saw his land ruled by "mules and niggers," was really benefited by the passing of slavery. It is not difficult now to say to the young freedman, cheated and cuffed about who has seen his father's head beaten to a jelly and his own mother namelessly assaulted, that the meek shall inherit the earth. Above all, nothing is more convenient than to heap on the Freedmen's Bureau all the evils of that evil day, and damn it utterly for every mistake and blunder that was made.

All this is easy, but it is neither sensible nor just. Someone had blundered, but that was long before Oliver Howard was born; there was criminal aggression and heedless neglect, but without some system of control there would have been far more than there was. Had that control been from within, the Negro would have been re-enslaved, to all intents and purposes. Coming as the control did from without, perfect men and methods would have bettered all things; and even with imperfect agents and questionable methods, the work accomplished was not undeserving of commendation.

Such was the dawn of Freedom; such was the work

of the Freedmen's Bureau, which, summed up in brief, may be epitomized thus: for some fifteen million dollars, beside the sums spent before 1865, and the dole of benevolent societies, this Bureau set going a system of free labor, established a beginning of peasant proprietorship, secured the recognition of black freedmen before courts of law, and founded the free common school in the South. On the other hand, it failed to begin the establishment of good-will between ex-masters and freedmen, to guard its work wholly from paternalistic methods which discouraged self-reliance, and to carry out to any considerable extent its implied promises to furnish the freedmen with land. Its successes were the result of hard work, supplemented by the aid of philanthropists and the eager striving of black men. Its failures were the result of bad local agents, the inherent difficulties of the work, and national neglect.

Such an institution, from its wide powers, great responsibilities, large control of moneys, and generally conspicuous position, was naturally open to repeated and bitter attack. It sustained a searching Congressional investigation at the instance of Fernando Wood in 1870. Its archives and few remaining functions were with blunt discourtesy transferred from Howard's control, in his absence, to the supervision of Secretary of War Belknap in 1872, on the Secretary's recommendation. Finally, in consequence of grave intimations of wrong-doing made by the Secretary and his subordinates, General Howard was court-martialed in 1874. In both of these trials the Commissioner of the Freedmen's Bureau was officially exonerated from any wilful misdoing, and his work commended. Nevertheless, many unpleasant things were brought to light,—the methods of transacting the business of the Bureau were faulty; several cases of defal-

cation were proved, and other frauds strongly suspected; there were some business transactions which
savored of dangerous speculation, if not dishonesty;
and around it all lay the smirch of the Freedmen's
Bank.

Morally and practically, the Freedmen's Bank was
part of the Freedmen's Bureau, although it had no
legal connection with it. With the prestige of the government back of it, and a directing board of unusual
respectability and national reputation, this banking
institution had made a remarkable start in the development of that thrift among black folk which slavery
had kept them from knowing. Then in one sad day
came the crash,—all the hard-earned dollars of the
freedmen disappeared; but that was the least of the
loss,—all the faith in saving went too, and much of the
faith in men; and that was a loss that a Nation which
to-day sneers at Negro shiftlessness has never yet
made good. Not even ten additional years of slavery
could have done so much to throttle the thrift of the
freedmen as the mismanagement and bankruptcy of
the series of savings banks chartered by the Nation
for their especial aid. Where all the blame should
rest, it is hard to say; whether the Bureau and the
Bank died chiefly by reason of the blows of its selfish
friends or the dark machinations of its foes, perhaps
even time will never reveal, for here lies unwritten
history.

Of the foes without the Bureau, the bitterest were
those who attacked not so much its conduct or policy
under the law as the necessity for any such institution
at all. Such attacks came primarily from the Border
States and the South; and they were summed up by
Senator Davis, of Kentucky, when he moved to enti-
tle the act of 1866 a bill "to promote strife and conflict between the white and black races . . . by a

grant of unconstitutional power." The argument gathered tremendous strength South and North; but its very strength was its weakness. For, argued the plain common-sense of the nation, if it is unconstitutional, unpractical, and futile for the nation to stand guardian over its helpless wards, then there is left but one alternative,—to make those wards their own guardians by arming them with the ballot. Moreover, the path of the practical politician pointed the same way; for, argued this opportunist, if we cannot peacefully reconstruct the South with white votes, we certainly can with black votes. So justice and force joined hands.

The alternative thus offered the nation was not between full and restricted Negro suffrage; else every sensible man, black and white, would easily have chosen the latter. It was rather a choice between suffrage and slavery, after endless blood and gold had flowed to sweep human bondage away. Not a single Southern legislature stood ready to admit a Negro, under any conditions, to the polls; not a single Southern legislature believed free Negro labor was possible without a system of restrictions that took all its freedom away; there was scarcely a white man in the South who did not honestly regard Emancipation as a crime, and its practical nullification as a duty. In such a situation, the granting of the ballot to the black man was a necessity, the very least a guilty nation could grant a wronged race, and the only method of compelling the South to accept the results of the war. Thus Negro suffrage ended a civil war by beginning a race feud. And some felt gratitude toward the race thus sacrificed in its swaddling clothes on the altar of national integrity; and some felt and feel only indifference and contempt.

Had political exigencies been less pressing, the opposition to government guardianship of Negroes less bitter, and the attachment to the slave system less strong, the social seer can well imagine a far better policy,—a permanent Freedmen's Bureau, with a national system of Negro schools; a carefully supervised employment and labor office; a system of impartial protection before the regular courts; and such institutions for social betterment as savings-banks, land and building associations, and social settlements. All this vast expenditure of money and brains might have formed a great school of prospective citizenship, and solved in a way we have not yet solved the most perplexing and persistent of the Negro problems.

That such an institution was unthinkable in 1870 was due in part to certain acts of the Freedmen's Bureau itself. It came to regard its work as merely temporary, and Negro suffrage as a final answer to all present perplexities. The political ambition of many of its agents and *protégés* led it far afield into questionable activities, until the South, nursing its own deep prejudices, came easily to ignore all the good deeds of the Bureau and hate its very name with perfect hatred. So the Freedmen's Bureau died, and its child was the Fifteenth Amendment.

The passing of a great human institution before its work is done, like the untimely passing of a single soul, but leaves a legacy of striving for other men. The legacy of the Freedmen's Bureau is the heavy heritage of this generation. To-day, when new and vaster problems are destined to strain every fibre of the national mind and soul, would it not be well to count this legacy honestly and carefully? For this much all men know: despite compromise, war, and struggle, the Negro is not free. In the backwoods of the Gulf States, for miles and miles, he may not leave the plantation of his birth; in well-nigh the whole rural South the black farmers are peons, bound by law and custom to an economic slavery, from which the only escape is death or the penitentiary. In the most cultured sections and cities of the South the Negroes are a segregated servile caste, with restricted rights and privileges. Before the courts, both in law and custom, they stand on a different and peculiar basis. Taxation without representation is the rule of their political life. And the result of all this is, and in nature must have been, lawlessness and crime. That is the large legacy of the Freedmen's Bureau, the work it did not do because it could not.

I have seen a land right merry with the sun, where children sing, and rolling hills lie like passioned women wanton with harvest. And there in the King's Highways sat and sits a figure veiled and bowed, by which the traveller's footsteps hasten as they go. On the tainted air broods fear. Three centuries' thought has been the raising and unveiling of that bowed human heart, and now behold a century new for the duty and the deed. The problem of the Twentieth Century is the problem of the color-line.

III

Of Mr. Booker T. Washington and Others

From birth till death enslaved; in word, in deed, unmanned!

. . . .

Hereditary bondsmen!   Know ye not
Who would be free themselves must strike the blow?

BYRON.

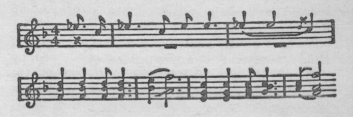

EASILY the most striking thing in the history of the American Negro since 1876 is the ascendancy of Mr. Booker T. Washington. It began at the time when war memories and ideals were rapidly passing; a day of astonishing commercial development was dawning; a sense of doubt and hesitation overtook the freedmen's sons,—then it was that his leading began. Mr. Washington came, with a single definite programme, at the psychological moment when the nation was a little ashamed of having bestowed so much sentiment on Negroes, and was concentrating its energies on Dollars. His programme of industrial education, conciliation of the South, and submission and silence as to civil and political rights, was not wholly original;

79

the Free Negroes from 1830 up to war-time had
striven to build industrial schools, and the American
Missionary Association had from the first taught various trades; and Price and others had sought a way of
honorable alliance with the best of the Southerners.
But Mr. Washington first indissolubly linked these
things; he put enthusiasm, unlimited energy, and perfect faith into his programme, and changed it from a
by-path into a veritable Way of Life. And the tale of
the methods by which he did this is a fascinating
study of human life.

It startled the nation to hear a Negro advocating
such a programme after many decades of bitter complaint; it startled and won the applause of the South,
it interested and won the admiration of the North;
and after a confused murmur of protest, it silenced if
it did not convert the Negroes themselves.

To gain the sympathy and coöperation of the various elements comprising the white South was Mr.
Washington's first task; and this, at the time Tuskegee
was founded, seemed, for a black man, well-nigh impossible. And yet ten years later it was done in the
word spoken at Atlanta: "In all things purely social
we can be as separate as the five fingers, and yet one
as the hand in all things essential to mutual progress."
This "Atlanta Compromise" is by all odds the most
notable thing in Mr. Washington's career. The South
interpreted it in different ways: the radicals received
it as a complete surrender of the demand for civil and
political equality; the conservatives, as a generously
conceived working basis for mutual understanding. So
both approved it, and to-day its author is certainly
the most distinguished Southerner since Jefferson
Davis, and the one with the largest personal following.

Next to this achievement comes Mr. Washington's

work in gaining place and consideration in the North. Others less shrewd and tactful had formerly essayed to sit on these two stools and had fallen between them; but as Mr. Washington knew the heart of the South from birth and training, so by singular insight he intuitively grasped the spirit of the age which was dominating the North. And so thoroughly did he learn the speech and thought of triumphant commercialism, and the ideals of material prosperity, that the picture of a lone black boy poring over a French grammar amid the weeds and dirt of a neglected home soon seemed to him the acme of absurdities. One wonders what Socrates and St. Francis of Assisi would say to this.

And yet this very singleness of vision and thorough oneness with his age is a mark of the successful man. It is as though Nature must needs make men narrow in order to give them force. So Mr. Washington's cult has gained unquestioning followers, his work has wonderfully prospered, his friends are legion, and his enemies are confounded. To-day he stands as the one recognized spokesman of his ten million fellows, and one of the most notable figures in a nation of seventy millions. One hesitates, therefore, to criticise a life which, beginning with so little, has done so much. And yet the time is come when one may speak in all sincerity and utter courtesy of the mistakes and shortcomings of Mr. Washington's career, as well as of his triumphs, without being thought captious or envious, and without forgetting that it is easier to do ill than well in the world.

The criticism that has hitherto met Mr. Washington has not always been of this broad character. In the South especially has he had to walk warily to avoid the harshest judgments,—and naturally so, for he is dealing with the one subject of deepest sensitiveness

to that section. Twice—once when at the Chicago celebration of the Spanish-American War he alluded to
the color-prejudice that is "eating away the vitals of
the South," and once when he dined with President
Roosevelt—has the resulting Southern criticism been
violent enough to threaten seriously his popularity. In
the North the feeling has several times forced itself
into words, that Mr. Washington's counsels of submission overlooked certain elements of true manhood,
and that his educational programme was unnecessar-
ily narrow. Usually, however, such criticism has not
found open expression, although, too, the spiritual
sons of the Abolitionists have not been prepared to
acknowledge that the schools founded before Tuskegee, by men of broad ideals and self-sacrificing spirit,
were wholly failures or worthy of ridicule. While,
then, criticism has not failed to follow Mr. Washington, yet the prevailing public opinion of the land has
been but too willing to deliver the solution of a weari-
some problem into his hands, and say, "If that is all
you and your race ask, take it."

Among his own people, however, Mr. Washington
has encountered the strongest and most lasting opposition, amounting at times to bitterness, and even to-
day continuing strong and insistent even though
largely silenced in outward expression by the public
opinion of the nation. Some of this opposition is, of
course, mere envy; the disappointment of displaced
demagogues and the spite of narrow minds. But aside
from this, there is among educated and thoughtful
colored men in all parts of the land a feeling of deep
regret, sorrow, and apprehension at the wide currency and ascendancy which some of Mr. Washington's theories have gained. These same men admire
his sincerity of purpose, and are willing to forgive
much to honest endeavor which is doing something

worth the doing. They coöperate with Mr. Washington as far as they conscientiously can; and, indeed, it is no ordinary tribute to this man's tact and power that, steering as he must between so many diverse interests and opinions, he so largely retains the respect of all.

But the hushing of the criticism of honest opponents is a dangerous thing. It leads some of the best of the critics to unfortunate silence and paralysis of effort, and others to burst into speech so passionately and intemperately as to lose listeners. Honest and earnest criticism from those whose interests are most nearly touched,—criticism of writers by readers, of government by those governed, of leaders by those led,—this is the soul of democracy and the safeguard of modern society. If the best of the American Negroes receive by outer pressure a leader whom they had not recognized before, manifestly there is here a certain palpable gain. Yet there is also irreparable loss,—a loss of that peculiarly valuable education which a group receives when by search and criticism it finds and commissions its own leaders. The way in which this is done is at once the most elementary and the nicest problem of social growth. History is but the record of such group-leadership; and yet how infinitely changeful is its type and character! And of all types and kinds, what can be more instructive than the leadership of a group within a group?— that curious double movement where real progress may be negative and actual advance be relative retrogression. All this is the social student's inspiration and despair.

Now in the past the American Negro has had instructive experience in the choosing of group leaders, founding thus a peculiar dynasty which in the light of present conditions is worth while studying. When

sticks and stones and beasts form the sole environment of a people, their attitude is largely one of determined opposition to and conquest of natural forces.
But when to earth and brute is added an environment
of men and ideas, then the attitude of the imprisoned
group may take three main forms,—a feeling of revolt
and revenge; an attempt to adjust all thought and action to the will of the greater group; or, finally, a determined effort at self-realization and self-development despite environing opinion. The influence of all
of these attitudes at various times can be traced in the
history of the American Negro, and in the evolution
of his successive leaders.

Before 1750, while the fire of African freedom still
burned in the veins of the slaves, there was in all
leadership or attempted leadership but the one motive of revolt and revenge,—typified in the terrible
Maroons, the Danish blacks, and Cato of Stono, and
veiling all the Americas in fear of insurrection. The
liberalizing tendencies of the latter half of the eighteenth century brought, along with kindlier relations
between black and white, thoughts of ultimate adjustment and assimilation. Such aspiration was especially
voiced in the earnest songs of Phyllis, in the martyr-
dom of Attucks, the fighting of Salem and Poor, the
intellectual accomplishments of Banneker and Der-
ham, and the political demands of the Cuffes.

Stern financial and social stress after the war cooled
much of the previous humanitarian ardor. The disappointment and impatience of the Negroes at the persistence of slavery and serfdom voiced itself in two
movements. The slaves in the South, aroused undoubtedly by vague rumors of the Haytian revolt,
made three fierce attempts at insurrection,—in 1800
under Gabriel in Virginia, in 1822 under Vesey in
Carolina, and in 1831 again in Virginia under the ter-

rible Nat Turner. In the Free States, on the other hand, a new and curious attempt at self-development was made. In Philadelphia and New York color-pre-scription led to a withdrawal of Negro communicants from white churches and the formation of a peculiar socio-religious institution among the Negroes known as the African Church,—an organization still living and controlling in its various branches over a million of men.

Walker's wild appeal against the trend of the times showed how the world was changing after the coming of the cotton-gin. By 1830 slavery seemed hopelessly fastened on the South, and the slaves thoroughly cowed into submission. The free Negroes of the North, inspired by the mulatto immigrants from the West Indies, began to change the basis of their de-mands; they recognized the slavery of slaves, but in-sisted that they themselves were freemen, and sought assimilation and amalgamation with the nation on the same terms with other men. Thus, Forten and Purvis of Philadelphia, Shad of Wilmington, Du Bois of New Haven, Barbadoes of Boston, and others, strove singly and together as men, they said, not as slaves; as "peo-ple of color," not as "Negroes." The trend of the times, however, refused them recognition save in indi-vidual and exceptional cases, considered them as one with all the despised blacks, and they soon found themselves striving to keep even the rights they for-merly had of voting and working and moving as free-men. Schemes of migration and colonization arose among them; but these they refused to entertain, and they eventually turned to the Abolition movement as a final refuge.

Here, led by Remond, Nell, Wells-Brown, and Douglass, a new period of self-assertion and self-de-velopment dawned. To be sure, ultimate freedom and assimilation was the ideal before the leaders, but the assertion of the manhood rights of the Negro by himself was the main reliance, and John Brown's raid was the extreme of its logic. After the war and emancipation, the great form of Frederick Douglass, the greatest of American Negro leaders, still led the host. Self-assertion, especially in political lines, was the main programme, and behind Douglass came Elliot, Bruce, and Langston, and the Reconstruction politicians, and, less conspicuous but of greater social significance, Alexander Crummell and Bishop Daniel Payne.

Then came the Revolution of 1876, the suppression of the Negro votes, the changing and shifting of ideals, and the seeking of new lights in the great night. Douglass, in his old age, still bravely stood for the ideals of his early manhood,—ultimate assimilation *through* self-assertion, and on no other terms. For a time Price arose as a new leader, destined, it seemed, not to give up, but to re-state the old ideals in a form less repugnant to the white South. But he passed away in his prime. Then came the new leader. Nearly all the former ones had become leaders by the silent suffrage of their fellows, had sought to lead their own people alone, and were usually, save Douglass, little known outside their race. But Booker T. Washington arose as essentially the leader not of one race but of two,—a compromiser between the South, the North, and the Negro. Naturally the Negroes resented, at first bitterly, signs of compromise which surrendered their civil and political rights, even though this was to be exchanged for larger chances of economic development. The rich and dominating North, however, was not only weary of the race problem, but was investing largely in Southern enterprises, and welcomed any method of peaceful coöperation. Thus, by national opinion, the Negroes began to recognize Mr. Washington's leadership; and the voice of criticism was hushed.

Mr. Washington represents in Negro thought the old attitude of adjustment and submission; but adjustment at such a peculiar time as to make his programme unique. This is an age of unusual economic development, and Mr. Washington's programme naturally takes an economic cast, becoming a gospel of Work and Money to such an extent as apparently almost completely to overshadow the higher aims of life. Moreover, this is an age when the more advanced races are coming in closer contact with the less developed races, and the race-feeling is therefore intensified; and Mr. Washington's programme practically accepts the alleged inferiority of the Negro races. Again, in our own land, the reaction from the sentiment of war time has given impetus to race-prejudice against Negroes, and Mr. Washington withdraws many of the high demands of Negroes as men and American citizens. In other periods of intensified prejudice all the Negro's tendency to self-assertion has been called forth; at this period a policy of submission is advocated. In the history of nearly all other races and peoples the doctrine preached at such crises has been that manly self-respect is worth more than lands and houses, and that a people who voluntarily surrender such respect, or cease striving for it, are not worth civilizing.

In answer to this, it has been claimed that the Negro can survive only through submission. Mr. Washington distinctly asks that black people give up, at least for the present, three things,—

First, political power,

Second, insistence on civil rights,

Third, higher education of Negro youth,—

and concentrate all their energies on industrial education, and accumulation of wealth, and the conciliation of the South. This policy has been courageously and insistently advocated for over fifteen years, and has been triumphant for perhaps ten years. As a result of this tender of the palm-branch, what has been the return? In these years there have occurred:

1. The disfranchisement of the Negro.

2. The legal creation of a distinct status of civil inferiority for the Negro.

3. The steady withdrawal of aid from institutions for the higher training of the Negro.

These movements are not, to be sure, direct results of Mr. Washington's teachings; but his propaganda has, without a shadow of doubt, helped their speedier accomplishment. The question then comes: Is it possible, and probable, that nine millions of men can make effective progress in economic lines if they are deprived of political rights, made a servile caste, and allowed only the most meagre chance for developing their exceptional men? If history and reason give any distinct answer to these questions, it is an emphatic *No*. And Mr. Washington thus faces the triple paradox of his career:

1. He is striving nobly to make Negro artisans business men and property-owners; but it is utterly impossible, under modern competitive methods, for workingmen and property-owners to defend their rights and exist without the right of suffrage.

2. He insists on thrift and self-respect, but at the same time counsels a silent submission to civic inferiority such as is bound to sap the manhood of any race in the long run.

3. He advocates common-school and industrial training, and depreciates institutions of higher learning; but neither the Negro common-schools, nor

Tuskegee itself, could remain open a day were it not for teachers trained in Negro colleges, or trained by their graduates.

This triple paradox in Mr. Washington's position is the object of criticism by two classes of colored Americans. One class is spiritually descended from Toussaint the Savior, through Gabriel, Vesey, and Turner, and they represent the attitude of revolt and revenge; they hate the white South blindly and distrust the white race generally, and so far as they agree on definite action, think that the Negro's only hope lies in emigration beyond the borders of the United States. And yet, by the irony of fate, nothing has more effectually made this programme seem hopeless than the recent course of the United States toward weaker and darker peoples in the West Indies, Hawaii, and the Philippines,—for where in the world may we go and be safe from lying and brute force?

The other class of Negroes who cannot agree with Mr. Washington has hitherto said little aloud. They deprecate the sight of scattered counsels, of internal disagreement; and especially they dislike making their just criticism of a useful and earnest man an excuse for a general discharge of venom from small-minded opponents. Nevertheless, the questions involved are so fundamental and serious that it is difficult to see how men like the Grimkes, Kelly Miller, J. W. E. Bowen, and other representatives of this group, can much longer be silent. Such men feel in conscience bound to ask of this nation three things:

1. The right to vote.
2. Civic equality.
3. The education of youth according to ability.

They acknowledge Mr. Washington's invaluable service in counselling patience and courtesy in such demands; they do not ask that ignorant black men vote when ignorant whites are debarred, or that any reasonable restrictions in the suffrage should not be applied; they know that the low social level of the mass of the race is responsible for much discrimination against it, but they also know, and the nation knows, that relentless color-prejudice is more often a cause than a result of the Negro's degradation; they seek the abatement of this relic of barbarism, and not its systematic encouragement and pampering by all agencies of social power from the Associated Press to the Church of Christ. They advocate, with Mr. Washington, a broad system of Negro common schools supplemented by thorough industrial training; but they are surprised that a man of Mr. Washington's insight cannot see that no such educational system ever has rested or can rest on any other basis than that of the well-equipped college and university, and they insist that there is a demand for a few such institutions throughout the South to train the best of the Negro youth as teachers, professional men, and leaders.

This group of men honor Mr. Washington for his attitude of conciliation toward the white South; they accept the "Atlanta Compromise" in its broadest interpretation; they recognize, with him, many signs of promise, many men of high purpose and fair judgment, in this section; they know that no easy task has been laid upon a region already tottering under heavy burdens. But, nevertheless, they insist that the way to truth and right lies in straightforward honesty, not in indiscriminate flattery; in praising those of the South who do well and criticising uncompromisingly those who do ill; in taking advantage of the opportunities at hand and urging their fellows to do the same, but at the same time in remembering that only a firm adherence to their higher ideals and aspirations will ever keep those ideals within the realm of possibility. They do not expect that the free right to vote, to enjoy civic rights, and to be educated, will come in a moment; they do not expect to see the bias and prejudices of years disappear at the blast of a trumpet; but they are absolutely certain that the way for a people to gain their reasonable rights is not by voluntarily throwing them away and insisting that they do not want them; that the way for a people to gain respect is not by continually belittling and ridiculing themselves; that, on the contrary, Negroes must insist continually, in season and out of season, that voting is necessary to modern manhood, that color discrimination is barbarism, and that black boys need education as well as white boys.

In failing thus to state plainly and unequivocally the legitimate demands of their people, even at the cost of opposing an honored leader, the thinking classes of American Negroes would shirk a heavy responsibility,—a responsibility to themselves, a responsibility to the struggling masses, a responsibility to the darker races of men whose future depends so largely on this American experiment, but especially a responsibility to this nation,—this common Fatherland. It is wrong to encourage a man or a people in evil-doing; it is wrong to aid and abet a national crime simply because it is unpopular not to do so. The growing spirit of kindliness and reconciliation between the North and South after the frightful difference of a generation ago ought to be a source of deep congratulation to all, and especially to those whose mistreatment caused the war; but if that reconciliation is to be marked by the industrial slavery and civic death of those same black men, with permanent legislation into a position of inferiority, then those black men, if they are really men, are called upon by every consideration of patriotism and loyalty to oppose such a course by all civilized methods, even though such opposition involves disagreement with Mr. Booker T. Washington. We have no right to sit silently by while the inevitable seeds are sown for a harvest of disaster to our children, black and white.

First, it is the duty of black men to judge the South discriminatingly. The present generation of Southerners are not responsible for the past, and they should not be blindly hated or blamed for it. Furthermore, to no class is the indiscriminate endorsement of the recent course of the South toward Negroes more nauseating than to the best thought of the South. The South is not "solid"; it is a land in the ferment of social change, wherein forces of all kinds are fighting for supremacy; and to praise the ill the South is to-day perpetrating is just as wrong as to condemn the good. Discriminating and broad-minded criticism is what the South needs,—needs it for the sake of her own white sons and daughters, and for the insurance of robust, healthy mental and moral development.

To-day even the attitude of the Southern whites toward the blacks is not, as so many assume, in all cases the same; the ignorant Southerner hates the Negro, the workingmen fear his competition, the money-makers wish to use him as a laborer, some of the educated see a menace in his upward development, while others—usually the sons of the masters—wish to help him to rise. National opinion has enabled this last class to maintain the Negro common schools, and to protect the Negro partially in property, life, and limb. Through the pressure of the money-makers, the Negro is in danger of being reduced to semi-slavery, especially in the country districts; the workingmen, and those of the educated who fear the Negro, have united to disfranchise him, and some have urged his deportation; while the passions of the ignorant are easily aroused to lynch and abuse any black man. To praise this intricate whirl of thought and prejudice is nonsense; to inveigh indiscriminately against "the South" is unjust; but to use the same breath in praising Governor Aycock, exposing Senator Morgan, arguing with Mr. Thomas Nelson Page, and denouncing Senator Ben Tillman, is not only sane, but the imperative duty of thinking black men.

It would be unjust to Mr. Washington not to acknowledge that in several instances he has opposed movements in the South which were unjust to the Negro; he sent memorials to the Louisiana and Alabama constitutional conventions, he has spoken against lynching, and in other ways has openly or silently set his influence against sinister schemes and unfortunate happenings. Notwithstanding this, it is equally true to assert that on the whole the distinct impression left by Mr. Washington's propaganda is, first, that the South is justified in its present attitude toward the Negro because of the Negro's degradation; secondly, that the prime cause of the Negro's failure to rise more quickly is his wrong education in the past; and, thirdly, that his future rise depends primarily on his own efforts. Each of these propositions is a dangerous half-truth. The supplementary truths must never be lost sight of: first, slavery and race-prejudice are potent if not sufficient causes of the Negro's position; second, industrial and common-school training were necessarily slow in planting because they had to await the black teachers trained by higher institutions,—it being extremely doubtful if any essentially different development was possible, and certainly a Tuskegee was unthinkable before 1880; and, third, while it is a great truth to say that the Negro must strive and strive mightily to help himself, it is equally true that unless his striving be not simply

seconded, but rather aroused and encouraged, by the
initiative of the richer and wiser environing group, he
cannot hope for great success.

In his failure to realize and impress this last point,
Mr. Washington is especially to be criticised. His doctrine has tended to make the whites, North and
South, shift the burden of the Negro problem to the
Negro's shoulders and stand aside as critical and
rather pessimistic spectators; when in fact the burden
belongs to the nation, and the hands of none of us are
clean if we bend not our energies to righting these
great wrongs.

The South ought to be led, by candid and honest
criticism, to assert her better self and do her full duty
to the race she has cruelly wronged and is still wrong-
ing. The North—her co-partner in guilt—cannot salve
her conscience by plastering it with gold. We cannot
settle this problem by diplomacy and suaveness, by
"policy" alone. If worse come to worst, can the moral
fibre of this country survive the slow throttling and
murder of nine millions of men?

The black men of America have a duty to perform,
a duty stern and delicate,—a forward movement to
oppose a part of the work of their greatest leader. So
far as Mr. Washington preaches Thrift, Patience, and
Industrial Training for the masses, we must hold up
his hands and strive with him, rejoicing in his honors
and glorying in the strength of this Joshua called of
God and of man to lead the headless host. But so far
as Mr. Washington apologizes for injustice, North or
South, does not rightly value the privilege and duty
of voting, belittles the emasculating effects of caste
distinctions, and opposes the higher training and ambition of our brighter minds,—so far as he, the South,
or the Nation, does this,—we must unceasingly and
firmly oppose them. By every civilized and peaceful

method we must strive for the rights which the world accords to men, clinging unwaveringly to those great words which the sons of the Fathers would fain forget: "We hold these truths to be self-evident: That all men are created equal; that they are endowed by their Creator with certain unalienable rights; that among these are life, liberty, and the pursuit of happiness."

IV

Of the Meaning of Progress

Willst Du Deine Macht verkünden,
Wähle sie die frei von Sünden,
Steh'n in Deinem ew'gen Haus!
Deine Geister sende aus!
Die Unsterblichen, die Reinen,
Die nicht fühlen, die nicht weinen!
Nicht die zarte Jungfrau wähle,
Nicht der Hirtin weiche Seele!

SCHILLER.

ONCE upon a time I taught school in the hills of
Tennessee, where the broad dark vale of the Mississippi begins to roll and crumple to greet the Alleghanies. I was a Fisk student then, and all Fisk men
thought that Tennessee—beyond the Veil—was theirs
alone, and in vacation time they sallied forth in lusty
bands to meet the county school-commissioners.
Young and happy, I too went, and I shall not soon
forget that summer, seventeen years ago.

First, there was a Teachers' Institute at the county-
seat; and there distinguished guests of the superintendent taught the teachers fractions and spelling and

other mysteries,—white teachers in the morning,
Negroes at night. A picnic now and then, and a supper, and the rough world was softened by laughter and
song. I remember how— But I wander.

There came a day when all the teachers left the Institute and began the hunt for schools. I learn from
hearsay (for my mother was mortally afraid of
firearms) that the hunting of ducks and bears and men
is wonderfully interesting, but I am sure that the man
who has never hunted a country school has something to learn of the pleasures of the chase. I see now
the white, hot roads lazily rise and fall and wind before me under the burning July sun; I feel the deep
weariness of heart and limb as ten, eight, six miles
stretch relentlessly ahead; I feel my heart sink heavily
as I hear again and again, "Got a teacher? Yes." So I
walked on and on—horses were too expensive—until I
had wandered beyond railways, beyond stage lines, to
a land of "varmints" and rattlesnakes, where the coming of a stranger was an event, and men lived and
died in the shadow of one blue hill.

Sprinkled over hill and dale lay cabins and farm-
houses, shut out from the world by the forests and the
rolling hills toward the east. There I found at last a
little school. Josie told me of it; she was a thin,
homely girl of twenty, with a dark-brown face and
thick, hard hair. I had crossed the stream at Water-
town, and rested under the great willows; then I had
gone to the little cabin in the lot where Josie was resting on her way to town. The gaunt farmer made me
welcome, and Josie, hearing my errand, told me anx-
iously that they wanted a school over the hill; that
but once since the war had a teacher been there; that
she herself longed to learn,—and thus she ran on, talking fast and loud, with much earnestness and energy.

Next morning I crossed the tall round hill, lingered

to look at the blue and yellow mountains stretching toward the Carolinas, then plunged into the wood, and came out at Josie's home. It was a dull frame cottage with four rooms, perched just below the brow of the hill, amid peach-trees. The father was a quiet, simple soul, calmly ignorant, with no touch of vulgarity. The mother was different,—strong, bustling, and energetic, with a quick, restless tongue, and an ambition to live "like folks." There was a crowd of children. Two boys had gone away. There remained two growing girls; a shy midget of eight; John, tall, awkward, and eighteen; Jim, younger, quicker, and better looking; and two babies of indefinite age. Then there was Josie herself. She seemed to be the centre of the family: always busy at service, or at home, or berrypicking; a little nervous and inclined to scold, like her mother, yet faithful, too, like her father. She had about her a certain fineness, the shadow of an unconscious moral heroism that would willingly give all of life to make life broader, deeper, and fuller for her and hers. I saw much of this family afterwards, and grew to love them for their honest efforts to be decent and comfortable, and for their knowledge of their own ignorance. There was with them no affectation. The mother would scold the father for being so "easy"; Josie would roundly berate the boys for carelessness; and all knew that it was a hard thing to dig a living out of a rocky side-hill.

I secured the school. I remember the day I rode horseback out to the commissioner's house with a pleasant young white fellow who wanted the white school. The road ran down the bed of a stream; the sun laughed and the water jingled, and we rode on. "Come in," said the commissioner,—"come in. Have a seat. Yes, that certificate will do. Stay to dinner. What do you want a month?" "Oh," thought I, "this is lucky"; but even then fell the awful shadow of the Veil, for they ate first, then I—alone.

The schoolhouse was a log hut, where Colonel Wheeler used to shelter his corn. It sat in a lot behind a rail fence and thorn bushes, near the sweetest of springs. There was an entrance where a door once was, and within, a massive rickety fireplace; great chinks between the logs served as windows. Furniture was scarce. A pale blackboard crouched in the corner. My desk was made of three boards, reinforced at critical points, and my chair, borrowed from the landlady, had to be returned every night. Seats for the children—these puzzled me much. I was haunted by a New England vision of neat little desks and chairs, but, alas! the reality was rough plank benches without backs, and at times without legs. They had the one virtue of making naps dangerous,—possibly fatal, for the floor was not to be trusted.

It was a hot morning late in July when the school opened. I trembled when I heard the patter of little feet down the dusty road, and saw the growing row of dark solemn faces and bright eager eyes facing me. First came Josie and her brothers and sisters. The longing to know, to be a student in the great school at Nashville, hovered like a star above this child-woman amid her work and worry, and she studied doggedly. There were the Dowells from their farm over toward Alexandria,—Fanny, with her smooth black face and wondering eyes; Martha, brown and dull; the pretty girl-wife of a brother, and the younger brood.

There were the Burkes,—two brown and yellow lads, and a tiny haughty-eyed girl. Fat Reuben's little chubby girl came, with golden face and old-gold hair, faithful and solemn. 'Thenie was on hand early,—a jolly, ugly, good-hearted girl, who slyly dipped snuff and looked after her little bow-legged brother. When her mother could spare her, 'Tildy came,—a midnight beauty, with starry eyes and tapering limbs; and her brother, correspondingly homely. And then the big boys,—the hulking Lawrences; the lazy Neills, unfathered sons of mother and daughter; Hickman, with a stoop in his shoulders; and the rest.

There they sat, nearly thirty of them, on the rough benches, their faces shading from a pale cream to a deep brown, the little feet bare and swinging, the eyes full of expectation, with here and there a twinkle of mischief, and the hands grasping Webster's blue-black spelling-book. I loved my school, and the fine faith the children had in the wisdom of their teacher was truly marvellous. We read and spelled together, wrote a little, picked flowers, sang, and listened to stories of the world beyond the hill. At times the school would dwindle away, and I would start out. I would visit Mun Eddings, who lived in two very dirty rooms, and ask why little Lugene, whose flaming face seemed ever ablaze with the dark-red hair uncombed, was absent all last week, or why I missed so often the inimitable rags of Mack and Ed. Then the father, who worked Colonel Wheeler's farm on shares, would tell me how the crops needed the boys; and the thin, slovenly mother, whose face was pretty when washed, assured me that Lugene must mind the baby. "But we'll start them again next week." When the Lawrences stopped, I knew that the doubts of the old folks about book-learning had conquered again, and so, toiling up the hill, and getting as far into the cabin as possible, I put Cicero "pro Archia Poeta" into the simplest English with local applications, and usually convinced them—for a week or so.

On Friday nights I often went home with some of the children,—sometimes to Doc Burke's farm. He was a great, loud, thin Black, ever working, and trying to buy the seventy-five acres of hill and dale where he lived; but people said that he would surely fail, and the "white folks would get it all." His wife was a magnificent Amazon, with saffron face and shining hair, uncorseted and barefooted, and the children were strong and beautiful. They lived in a one-and-a-half-room cabin in the hollow of the farm, near the spring. The front room was full of great fat white beds, scrupulously neat; and there were bad chromos on the walls, and a tired centre-table. In the tiny back kitchen I was often invited to "take out and help" myself to fried chicken and wheat biscuit, "meat" and corn pone, string-beans and berries. At first I used to be a little alarmed at the approach of bedtime in the one lone bedroom, but embarrassment was very deftly avoided. First, all the children nodded and slept, and were stowed away in one great pile of goose feathers; next, the mother and the father discreetly slipped away to the kitchen while I went to bed; then, blowing out the dim light, they retired in the dark. In the morning all were up and away before I thought of awaking. Across the road, where fat Reuben lived, they all went outdoors while the teacher retired, because they did not boast the luxury of a kitchen.

I liked to stay with the Dowells, for they had four rooms and plenty of good country fare. Uncle Bird had a small, rough farm, all woods and hills, miles from the big road; but he was full of tales,—he preached now and then,—and with his children, berries, horses, and wheat he was happy and prosperous. Often, to keep the peace, I must go where life was less lovely; for instance, 'Tildy's mother was incorrigibly dirty, Reuben's larder was limited seriously, and herds of untamed insects wandered over the Eddingses' beds. Best of all I loved to go to Josie's, and

sit on the porch, eating peaches, while the mother
bustled and talked: how Josie had bought the sew-
ing-machine; how Josie worked at service in winter,
but that four dollars a month was "mighty little"
wages; how Josie longed to go away to school, but
that it "looked like" they never could get far enough
ahead to let her; how the crops failed and the well
was yet unfinished; and, finally, how "mean" some of
the white folks were.

For two summers I lived in this little world; it was
dull and humdrum. The girls looked at the hill in
wistful longing, and the boys fretted and haunted Alexandria. Alexandria was "town,"—a straggling, lazy
village of houses, churches, and shops, and an aristocracy of Toms, Dicks, and Captains. Cuddled on the
hill to the north was the village of the colored folks,
who lived in three- or four-room unpainted cottages,
some neat and homelike, and some dirty. The dwellings were scattered rather aimlessly, but they centred
about the twin temples of the hamlet, the Methodist,
and the Hard-Shell Baptist churches. These, in turn,
leaned gingerly on a sad-colored schoolhouse. Hither
my little world wended its crooked way on Sunday to
meet other worlds, and gossip, and wonder, and make
the weekly sacrifice with frenzied priest at the altar of
the "old-time religion." Then the soft melody and
mighty cadences of Negro song fluttered and thundered.

I have called my tiny community a world, and so
its isolation made it; and yet there was among us but
a half-awakened common consciousness, sprung from
common joy and grief, at burial, birth, or wedding;
from a common hardship in poverty, poor land, and
low wages; and, above all, from the sight of the Veil
that hung between us and Opportunity. All this
caused us to think some thoughts together; but these,

when ripe for speech, were spoken in various languages. Those whose eyes twenty-five and more years before had seen "the glory of the coming of the Lord," saw in every present hindrance or help a dark fatalism bound to bring all things right in His own good time. The mass of those to whom slavery was a dim recollection of childhood found the world a puzzling thing: it asked little of them, and they answered with little, and yet it ridiculed their offering. Such a paradox they could not understand, and therefore sank into listless indifference, or shiftlessness, or reckless bravado. There were, however, some—such as Josie, Jim, and Ben—to whom War, Hell, and Slavery were but childhood tales, whose young appetites had been whetted to an edge by school and story and half-awakened thought. Ill could they be content, born without and beyond the World. And their weak wings beat against their barriers,—barriers of caste, of youth, of life; at last, in dangerous moments, against everything that opposed even a whim.

The ten years that follow youth, the years when first the realization comes that life is leading somewhere,—these were the years that passed after I left my little school. When they were past, I came by chance once more to the walls of Fisk University, to the halls of the chapel of melody. As I lingered there in the joy and pain of meeting old school-friends, there swept over me a sudden longing to pass again beyond the blue hill, and to see the homes and the school of other days, and to learn how life had gone with my school-children; and I went.

Josie was dead, and the gray-haired mother said simply, "We've had a heap of trouble since you've been away." I had feared for Jim. With a cultured parentage and a social caste to uphold him, he might have made a venturesome merchant or a West Point cadet. But here he was, angry with life and reckless; and when Farmer Durham charged him with stealing wheat, the old man had to ride fast to escape the stones which the furious fool hurled after him. They told Jim to run away; but he would not run, and the constable came that afternoon. It grieved Josie, and great awkward John walked nine miles every day to see his little brother through the bars of Lebanon jail. At last the two came back together in the dark night. The mother cooked supper, and Josie emptied her purse, and the boys stole away. Josie grew thin and silent, yet worked the more. The hill became steep for the quiet old father, and with the boys away there was little to do in the valley. Josie helped them to sell the old farm, and they moved nearer town. Brother Dennis, the carpenter, built a new house with six rooms; Josie toiled a year in Nashville, and brought back ninety dollars to furnish the house and change it to a home.

When the spring came, and the birds twittered, and the stream ran proud and full, little sister Lizzie, bold and thoughtless, flushed with the passion of youth, bestowed herself on the tempter, and brought home a nameless child. Josie shivered and worked on, with the vision of schooldays all fled, with a face wan and tired,—worked until, on a summer's day, some one married another; then Josie crept to her mother like a hurt child, and slept—and sleeps.

I paused to scent the breeze as I entered the valley. The Lawrences have gone,—father and son forever,— and the other son lazily digs in the earth to live. A new young widow rents out their cabin to fat Reuben. Reuben is a Baptist preacher now, but I fear as lazy as ever, though his cabin has three rooms; and little Ella has grown into a bouncing woman, and is ploughing corn on the hot hillside. There are babies a-plenty, and one half-witted girl. Across the valley is a house I did not know before, and there I found, rocking one baby and expecting another, one of my schoolgirls, a daughter of Uncle Bird Dowell. She looked somewhat worried with her new duties, but soon bristled into pride over her neat cabin and the tale of her thrifty husband, and the horse and cow, and the farm they were planning to buy.

My log schoolhouse was gone. In its place stood Progress; and Progress, I understand, is necessarily ugly. The crazy foundation stones still marked the former site of my poor little cabin, and not far away, on six weary boulders, perched a jaunty board house, perhaps twenty by thirty feet, with three windows and a door that locked. Some of the window-glass was broken, and part of an old iron stove lay mournfully under the house. I peeped through the window half reverently, and found things that were more familiar. The blackboard had grown by about two feet, and the seats were still without backs. The county owns the lot now, I hear, and every year there is a session of school. As I sat by the spring and looked on the Old and the New I felt glad, very glad, and yet—

After two long drinks I started on. There was the great double log-house on the corner. I remembered the broken, blighted family that used to live there. The strong, hard face of the mother, with its wilderness of hair, rose before me. She had driven her husband away, and while I taught school a strange man lived there, big and jovial, and people talked. I felt sure that Ben and 'Tildy would come to naught from such a home. But this is an odd world; for Ben is a busy farmer in Smith County, "doing well, too," they say, and he had cared for little 'Tildy until last spring, when a lover married her. A hard life the lad had led,

toiling for meat, and laughed at because he was
homely and crooked. There was Sam Carlon, an im-
pudent old skinflint, who had definite notions about
"niggers," and hired Ben a summer and would not
pay him. Then the hungry boy gathered his sacks together, and in broad daylight went into Carlon's corn;
and when the hard-fisted farmer set upon him, the
angry boy flew at him like a beast. Doc Burke saved a
murder and a lynching that day.

The story reminded me again of the Burkes, and an
impatience seized me to know who won in the battle,
Doc or the seventy-five acres. For it is a hard thing to
make a farm out of nothing, even in fifteen years. So I
hurried on, thinking of the Burkes. They used to have
a certain magnificent barbarism about them that I
liked. They were never vulgar, never immoral, but
rather rough and primitive, with an unconventionality
that spent itself in loud guffaws, slaps on the back,
and naps in the corner. I hurried by the cottage of
the misborn Neill boys. It was empty, and they were
grown into fat, lazy farm-hands. I saw the home of
the Hickmans, but Albert, with his stooping shoulders,
had passed from the world. Then I came to the
Burkes' gate and peered through; the inclosure looked
rough and untrimmed, and yet there were the same
fences around the old farm save to the left, where lay
twenty-five other acres. And lo! the cabin in the hollow had climbed the hill and swollen to a half-fin-
ished six-room cottage.

The Burkes held a hundred acres, but they were
still in debt. Indeed, the gaunt father who toiled
night and day would scarcely be happy out of debt,
being so used to it. Some day he must stop, for his
massive frame is showing decline. The mother wore
shoes, but the lion-like physique of other days was
broken. The children had grown up. Rob, the image

of his father, was loud and rough with laughter.
Birdie, my school baby of six, had grown to a picture
of maiden beauty, tall and tawny. "Edgar is gone,"
said the mother, with head half bowed,—"gone to
work in Nashville; he and his father couldn't agree."

Little Doc, the boy born since the time of my
school, took me horseback down the creek next morning toward Farmer Dowell's. The road and the stream
were battling for mastery, and the stream had the
better of it. We splashed and waded, and the merry
boy, perched behind me, chattered and laughed. He
showed me where Simon Thompson had bought a bit
of ground and a home; but his daughter Lana, a
plump, brown, slow girl, was not there. She had married a man and a farm twenty miles away. We
wound on down the stream till we came to a gate that
I did not recognize, but the boy insisted that it was
"Uncle Bird's." The farm was fat with the growing
crop. In that little valley was a strange stillness as I
rode up; for death and marriage had stolen youth and
left age and childhood there. We sat and talked that
night after the chores were done. Uncle Bird was
grayer, and his eyes did not see so well, but he was
still jovial. We talked of the acres bought,—one hundred and twenty-five,—of the new guest-chamber
added, of Martha's marrying. Then we talked of
death: Fanny and Fred were gone; a shadow hung
over the other daughter, and when it lifted she was to
go to Nashville to school. At last we spoke of the
neighbors, and as night fell, Uncle Bird told me how,
on a night like that, 'Thenie came wandering back to
her home over yonder, to escape the blows of her
husband. And next morning she died in the home that
her little bow-legged brother, working and saving,
had bought for their widowed mother.

My journey was done, and behind me lay hill and

dale, and Life and Death. How shall man measure Progress there where the dark-faced Josie lies? How many heartfuls of sorrow shall balance a bushel of wheat? How hard a thing is life to the lowly, and yet how human and real! And all this life and love and strife and failure,—is it the twilight of nightfall or the flush of some faint-dawning day?

Thus sadly musing, I rode to Nashville in the Jim Crow car.

V

Of the Wings of Atalanta

O black boy of Atlanta!
  But half was spoken;
The slave's chains and the master's
  Alike are broken;
The one curse of the races
  Held both in tether;
They are rising—all are rising—
  The black and white together.

WHITTIER.

SOUTH of the North, yet north of the South, lies the City of a Hundred Hills, peering out from the shadows of the past into the promise of the future. I have seen her in the morning, when the first flush of day had half-roused her; she lay gray and still on the crimson soil of Georgia; then the blue smoke began to curl from her chimneys, the tinkle of bell and scream of whistle broke the silence, the rattle and roar of busy life slowly gathered and swelled, until the seething whirl of the city seemed a strange thing in a sleepy land.

Once, they say, even Atlanta slept dull and drowsy at the foot-hills of the Alleghanies, until the iron baptism of war awakened her with its sullen waters, aroused and maddened her, and left her listening to the sea. And the sea cried to the hills and the hills answered the sea, till the city rose like a widow and cast away her weeds, and toiled for her daily bread; toiled steadily, toiled cunningly,—perhaps with some bitterness, with a touch of *réclame*,—and yet with real earnestness, and real sweat.

It is a hard thing to live haunted by the ghost of an untrue dream; to see the wide vision of empire fade into real ashes and dirt; to feel the pang of the conquered, and yet know that with all the Bad that fell on one black day, something was vanquished that deserved to live, something killed that in justice had not dared to die; to know that with the Right that triumphed, triumphed something of Wrong, something sordid and mean, something less than the broadest and best. All this is bitter hard; and many a man and city and people have found in it excuse for sulking, and brooding, and listless waiting.

Such are not men of the sturdier make; they of Atlanta turned resolutely toward the future; and that future held aloft vistas of purple and gold:—Atlanta, Queen of the cotton kingdom; Atlanta, Gateway to the Land of the Sun; Atlanta, the new Lachesis, spinner of web and woof for the world. So the city crowned her hundred hills with factories, and stored her shops with cunning handiwork, and stretched long iron ways to greet the busy Mercury in his coming. And the Nation talked of her striving.

Perhaps Atlanta was not christened for the winged maiden of dull Bœotia; you know the tale,—how swarthy Atalanta, tall and wild, would marry only him who out-raced her; and how the wily Hippomenes laid three apples of gold in the way. She fled like a shadow, paused, startled over the first apple, but even as he stretched his hand, fled again; hovered over the second, then, slipping from his hot grasp, flew over river, vale, and hill; but as she lingered over the third, his arms fell round her, and looking on each other, the blazing passion of their love profaned the sanctuary of Love, and they were cursed. If Atlanta be not named for Atalanta, she ought to have been.

Atalanta is not the first or the last maiden whom greed of gold has led to defile the temple of Love; and not maids alone, but men in the race of life, sink from the high and generous ideals of youth to the gambler's code of the Bourse; and in all our Nation's striving is not the Gospel of Work befouled by the Gospel of Pay? So common is this that one-half think it normal; so unquestioned, that we almost fear to question if the end of racing is not gold, if the aim of man is not rightly to be rich. And if this is the fault of America, how dire a danger lies before a new land and a new city, lest Atlanta, stooping for mere gold, shall find that gold accursed!

It was no maiden's idle whim that started this hard racing; a fearful wilderness lay about the feet of that city after the War,—feudalism, poverty, the rise of the Third Estate, serfdom, the re-birth of Law and Order, and above and between all, the Veil of Race. How heavy a journey for weary feet! what wings must Atalanta have to flit over all this hollow and hill, through sour wood and sullen water, and by the red waste of sun-baked clay! How fleet must Atalanta be if she will not be tempted by gold to profane the Sanctuary!

The Sanctuary of our fathers has, to be sure, few Gods,—some sneer, "all too few." There is the thrifty Mercury of New England, Pluto of the North, and Ceres of the West; and there, too, is the half-forgotten Apollo of the South, under whose aegis the maiden ran,—and as she ran she forgot him, even as there in

Bœotia Venus was forgot. She forgot the old ideal of
the Southern gentleman,—that new-world heir of the
grace and courtliness of patrician, knight, and noble;
forgot his honor with his foibles, his kindliness with
his carelessness, and stooped to apples of gold,—to
men busier and sharper, thriftier and more unscrupulous. Golden apples are beautiful—I remember the
lawless days of boyhood, when orchards in crimson
and gold tempted me over fence and field—and, too,
the merchant who has dethroned the planter is no
despicable *parvenu*. Work and wealth are the mighty
levers to lift this old new land; thrift and toil and saving are the highways to new hopes and new possibilities; and yet the warning is needed lest the wily Hippomenes tempt Atalanta to thinking that golden apples are the goal of racing, and not mere incidents by
the way.

Atlanta must not lead the South to dream of material prosperity as the touchstone of all success; already the fatal might of this idea is beginning to
spread; it is replacing the finer type of Southerner
with vulgar money-getters; it is burying the sweeter
beauties of Southern life beneath pretence and osten-
tation. For every social ill the panacea of Wealth has
been urged,—wealth to overthrow the remains of the
slave feudalism; wealth to raise the "cracker" Third
Estate; wealth to employ the black serfs, and the
prospect of wealth to keep them working; wealth as
the end and aim of politics, and as the legal tender
for law and order; and, finally, instead of Truth,
Beauty, and Goodness, wealth as the ideal of the
Public School.

Not only is this true in the world which Atlanta
typifies, but it is threatening to be true of a world beneath and beyond that world,—the Black World beyond the Veil. Today it makes little difference to At-

lanta, to the South, what the Negro thinks or dreams or wills. In the soul-life of the land he is to-day, and naturally will long remain, unthought of, half forgotten; and yet when he does come to think and will and do for himself,—and let no man dream that day will never come,—then the part he plays will not be one of sudden learning, but words and thoughts he has been taught to lisp in his race-childhood. To-day the ferment of his striving toward self-realization is to the strife of the white world like a wheel within a wheel: beyond the Veil are smaller but like problems of ideals, of leaders and the led, of serfdom, of poverty, of order and subordination, and, through all, the Veil of Race. Few know of these problems, few who know notice them; and yet there they are, awaiting student, artist, and seer,—a field for somebody sometime to discover. Hither has the temptation of Hippomenes penetrated; already in this smaller world, which now indirectly and anon directly must influence the larger for good or ill, the habit is forming of interpreting the world in dollars. The old leaders of Negro opinion, in the little groups where there is a Negro social consciousness, are being replaced by new; neither the black preacher nor the black teacher leads as he did two decades ago. Into their places are pushing the farmers and gardeners, the well-paid porters and artisans, the business-men,—all those with property and money. And with all this change, so curiously parallel to that of the Other-world, goes too the same inevitable change in ideals. The South laments to-day the slow, steady disappearance of a certain type of Negro, —the faithful, courteous slave of other days, with his incorruptible honesty and dignified humility. He is passing away just as surely as the old type of Southern gentleman is passing, and from not dissimilar causes,—the sudden transformation of a fair far-off ideal of Freedom into the hard reality of bread-winning and the consequent deification of Bread.

In the Black World, the Preacher and Teacher embodied once the ideals of this people—the strife for another and a juster world, the vague dream of righteousness, the mystery of knowing; but to-day the danger is that these ideals, with their simple beauty and weird inspiration, will suddenly sink to a question of cash and a lust for gold. Here stands this black young Atalanta, girding herself for the race that must be run; and if her eyes be still toward the hills and sky as in the days of old, then we may look for noble running; but what if some ruthless or wily or even thoughtless Hippomenes lay golden apples before her? What if the Negro people be wooed from a strife for righteousness, from a love of knowing, to regard dollars as the be-all and end-all of life? What if to the Mammonism of America be added the rising Mammonism of the re-born South, and the Mammonism of this South be reinforced by the budding Mammonism of its half-wakened black millions? Whither, then, is the new-world quest of Goodness and Beauty and Truth gone glimmering? Must this, and that fair flower of Freedom which, despite the jeers of latter-day striplings, sprung from our fathers' blood, must that too degenerate into a dusty quest of gold,—into lawless lust with Hippomenes?

The hundred hills of Atlanta are not all crowned with factories. On one, toward the west, the setting sun throws three buildings in bold relief against the sky. The beauty of the group lies in its simple unity:
—a broad lawn of green rising from the red street and mingled roses and peaches; north and south, two plain and stately halls; and in the midst, half hidden in ivy, a larger building, boldly graceful, sparingly

decorated, and with one low spire. It is a restful group,—one never looks for more; it is all here, all intelligible. There I live, and there I hear from day to day the low hum of restful life. In winter's twilight, when the red sun glows, I can see the dark figures pass between the halls to the music of the night-bell. In the morning, when the sun is golden, the clang of the day-bell brings the hurry and laughter of three hundred young hearts from hall and street, and from the busy city below,—children all dark and heavy-haired,—to join their clear young voices in the music of the morning sacrifice. In a half-dozen class-rooms they gather then,—here to follow the love-song of Dido, here to listen to the tale of Troy divine; there to wander among the stars, there to wander among men and nations,—and elsewhere other well-worn ways of knowing this queer world. Nothing new, no time-saving devices,—simply old time-glorified methods of delving for Truth, and searching out the hidden beauties of life, and learning the good of living. The riddle of existence is the college curriculum that was laid before the Pharaohs, that was taught in the groves by Plato, that formed the *trivium* and *quadrivium*, and is to-day laid before the freedmen's sons by Atlanta University. And this course of study will not change; its methods will grow more deft and effectual, its content richer by toil of scholar and sight of seer; but the true college will ever have one goal,—not to earn meat, but to know the end and aim of that life which meat nourishes.

The vision of life that rises before these dark eyes has in it nothing mean or selfish. Not at Oxford or at Leipsic, not at Yale or Columbia, is there an air of higher resolve or more unfettered striving; the determination to realize for men, both black and white, the broadest possibilities of life, to seek the better and the

best, to spread with their own hands the Gospel of
Sacrifice,—all this is the burden of their talk and
dream. Here, amid a wide desert of caste and proscription, amid the heart-hurting slights and jars and
vagaries of a deep race-dislike, lies this green oasis,
where hot anger cools, and the bitterness of disappointment is sweetened by the springs and breezes of
Parnassus; and here men may lie and listen, and learn
of a future fuller than the past, and hear the voice of
Time:

"Entbehren sollst du, sollst entbehren."

They made their mistakes, those who planted Fisk
and Howard and Atlanta before the smoke of battle
had lifted; they made their mistakes, but those mistakes were not the things at which we lately laughed
somewhat uproariously. They were right when they
sought to found a new educational system upon the
University: where, forsooth, shall we ground knowledge save on the broadest and deepest knowledge?
The roots of the tree, rather than the leaves, are the
sources of its life; and from the dawn of history, from
Academus to Cambridge, the culture of the University has been the broad foundation-stone on which is
built the kindergarten's A B C.

But these builders did make a mistake in minimiz-
ing the gravity of the problem before them; in thinking it a matter of years and decades; in therefore
building quickly and laying their foundation care-
lessly, and lowering the standard of knowing, until
they had scattered haphazard through the South some
dozen poorly equipped high schools and miscalled
them universities. They forgot, too, just as their suc-
cessors are forgetting, the rule of inequality:—that of
the million black youth, some were fitted to know and

some to dig; that some had the talent and capacity of university men, and some the talent and capacity of blacksmiths; and that true training meant neither that all should be college men nor all artisans, but that the one should be made a missionary of culture to an untaught people, and the other a free workman among serfs. And to seek to make the blacksmith a scholar is almost as silly as the more modern scheme of making the scholar a blacksmith; almost, but not quite.

The function of the university is not simply to teach bread-winning, or to furnish teachers for the public schools or to be a centre of polite society; it is, above all, to be the organ of that fine adjustment between real life and the growing knowledge of life, an adjustment which forms the secret of civilization. Such an institution the South of to-day sorely needs. She has religion, earnest, bigoted:—religion that on both sides the Veil often omits the sixth, seventh, and eighth commandments, but substitutes a dozen supplementary ones. She has, as Atlanta shows, growing thrift and love of toil, but she lacks that broad knowledge of what the world knows and knew of human living and doing, which she may apply to the thousand problems of real life to-day confronting her. The need of the South is knowledge and culture, —not in dainty limited quantity, as before the war, but in broad busy abundance in the world of work; and until she has this, not all the Apples of Hesperides, be they golden and bejewelled, can save her from the curse of the Bœotian lovers.

The Wings of Atalanta are the coming universities of the South. They alone can bear the maiden past the temptation of golden fruit. They will not guide her flying feet away from the cotton and gold; for— ah, thoughtful Hippomenes!—do not the apples lie in

the very Way of Life? But they will guide her over
and beyond them, and leave her kneeling in the Sanctuary of Truth and Freedom and broad Humanity,
virgin and undefiled. Sadly did the Old South err in
human education, despising the education of the
masses, and niggardly in the support of colleges. Her
ancient university foundations dwindled and withered
under the foul breath of slavery; and even since the
war they have fought a failing fight for life in the
tainted air of social unrest and commercial selfishness,
stunted by the death of criticism, and starving for
lack of broadly cultured men. And if this is the white
South's need and danger, how much heavier the danger and need of the freedmen's sons! how pressing
here the need of broad ideals and true culture, the
conservation of soul from sordid aims and petty passions! Let us build the Southern university—William
and Mary, Trinity, Georgia, Texas, Tulane, Vander-
bilt, and the others—fit to live; let us build, too, the
Negro universities:—Fisk, whose foundation was ever
broad; Howard, at the heart of the Nation; Atlanta at
Atlanta, whose ideal of scholarship has been held
above the temptation of numbers. Why not here, and
perhaps elsewhere, plant deeply and for all time centres of learning and living, colleges that yearly would
send into the life of the South a few white men and a
few black men of broad culture, catholic tolerance,
and trained ability, joining their hands to other hands,
and giving to this squabble of the Races a decent and
dignified peace?

Patience, Humility, Manners, and Taste, common
schools and kindergartens, industrial and technical
schools, literature and tolerance,—all these spring
from knowledge and culture, the children of the university. So must men and nations build, not otherwise,
not upside down.

Teach workers to work,—a wise saying; wise when applied to German boys and American girls; wiser when said of Negro boys, for they have less knowledge of working and none to teach them. Teach thinkers to think,—a needed knowledge in a day of loose and careless logic; and they whose lot is gravest must have the carefulest training to think aright. If these things are so, how foolish to ask what is the best education for one or seven or sixty million souls! shall we teach them trades, or train them in liberal arts? Neither and both: teach the workers to work and the thinkers to think; make carpenters of carpenters, and philosophers of philosophers, and fops of fools. Nor can we pause here. We are training not isolated men but a living group of men,—nay, a group within a group. And the final product of our training must be neither a psychologist nor a brickmason, but a man. And to make men, we must have ideals, broad, pure, and inspiring ends of living,—not sordid money-getting, not apples of gold. The worker must work for the glory of his handiwork, not simply for pay; the thinker must think for truth, not for fame. And all this is gained only by human strife and longing; by ceaseless training and education; by founding Right on righteousness and Truth on the unhampered search for Truth; by founding the common school on the university, and the industrial school on the common school; and weaving thus a system, not a distortion, and bringing a birth, not an abortion.

When night falls on the City of a Hundred Hills, a wind gathers itself from the seas and comes murmuring westward. And at its bidding, the smoke of the drowsy factories sweeps down upon the mighty city and covers it like a pall, while yonder at the University the stars twinkle above Stone Hall. And they say that yon gray mist is the tunic of Atalanta pausing over her golden apples. Fly, my maiden, fly, for yonder comes Hippomenes!

VI

Of the Training of Black Men

Why, if the Soul can fling the Dust aside,
And naked on the Air of Heaven ride,
 Were't not a Shame—were't not a Shame for him
In this clay carcase crippled to abide?
                OMAR KHAYYÁM (FITZGERALD).

FROM the shimmering swirl of waters where many, many thoughts ago the slave-ship first saw the square tower of Jamestown, have flowed down to our day three streams of thinking: one swollen from the larger world here and over-seas, saying, the multiplying of human wants in culture-lands calls for the world-wide coöperation of men in satisfying them. Hence arises a new human unity, pulling the ends of earth nearer, and all men, black, yellow, and white. The larger humanity strives to feel in this contact of living Nations and sleeping hordes a thrill of new life in the world, crying, "If the contact of Life and Sleep be Death, shame on such Life." To be sure, behind this thought lurks the afterthought of force and dominion,—the

121

making of brown men to delve when the temptation
of beads and red calico cloys.

The second thought streaming from the death-ship
and the curving river is the thought of the older
South,—the sincere and passionate belief that somewhere between men and cattle, God created a *tertium
quid*, and called it a Negro,—a clownish, simple crea-
ture, at times even lovable within its limitations, but
straitly foreordained to walk within the Veil. To be
sure, behind the thought lurks the afterthought,—
some of them with favoring chance might become
men, but in sheer self-defence we dare not let them,
and we build about them walls so high, and hang between them and the light a veil so thick, that they
shall not even think of breaking through.

And last of all there trickles down that third and
darker thought,—the thought of the things themselves,
the confused, half-conscious mutter of men who are
black and whitened, crying "Liberty, Freedom, Opportunity—vouchsafe to us, O boastful World, the
chance of living men!" To be sure, behind the
thought lurks the afterthought,—suppose, after all, the
World is right and we are less than men? Suppose
this mad impulse within is all wrong, some mock mi-
rage from the untrue?

So here we stand among thoughts of human unity,
even through conquest and slavery; the inferiority of
black men, even if forced by fraud; a shriek in the
night for the freedom of men who themselves are not
yet sure of their right to demand it. This is the tangle
of thought and afterthought wherein we are called to
solve the problem of training men for life.

Behind all its curiousness, so attractive alike to sage
and *dilettante*, lie its dim dangers, throwing across us
shadows at once grotesque and awful. Plain it is to us
that what the world seeks through desert and wild we

have within our threshold,—a stalwart laboring force, suited to the semi-tropics; if, deaf to the voice of the Zeitgeist, we refuse to use and develop these men, we risk poverty and loss. If, on the other hand, seized by the brutal afterthought, we debauch the race thus caught in our talons, selfishly sucking their blood and brains in the future as in the past, what shall save us from national decadence? Only that saner selfishness, which Education teaches, can find the rights of all in the whirl of work.

Again, we may decry the color-prejudice of the South, yet it remains a heavy fact. Such curious kinks of the human mind exist and must be reckoned with soberly. They cannot be laughed away, nor always successfully stormed at, nor easily abolished by act of legislature. And yet they must not be encouraged by being let alone. They must be recognized as facts, but unpleasant facts; things that stand in the way of civilization and religion and common decency. They can be met in but one way,—by the breadth and broadening of human reason, by catholicity of taste and culture. And so, too, the native ambition and aspiration of men, even though they be black, backward, and ungraceful, must not lightly be dealt with. To stimulate wildly weak and untrained minds is to play with mighty fires; to flout their striving idly is to welcome a harvest of brutish crime and shameless lethargy in our very laps. The guiding of thought and the deft coordination of deed is at once the path of honor and humanity.

And so, in this great question of reconciling three vast and partially contradictory streams of thought, the one panacea of Education leaps to the lips of all:— such human training as will best use the labor of all men without enslaving or brutalizing; such training as will give us poise to encourage the prejudices that bulwark society, and to stamp out those that in sheer barbarity deafen us to the wail of prisoned souls within the Veil, and the mounting fury of shackled men.

But when we have vaguely said that Education will set this tangle straight, what have we uttered but a truism? Training for life teaches living; but what training for the profitable living together of black men and white? A hundred and fifty years ago our task would have seemed easier. Then Dr. Johnson blandly assured us that education was needful solely for the embellishments of life, and was useless for ordinary vermin. To-day we have climbed to heights where we would open at least the outer courts of knowledge to all, display its treasures to many, and select the few to whom its mystery of Truth is revealed, not wholly by birth or the accidents of the stock market, but at least in part according to deftness and aim, talent and character. This programme, however, we are sorely puzzled in carrying out through that part of the land where the blight of slavery fell hardest, and where we are dealing with two backward peoples. To make here in human education that ever necessary combination of the permanent and the contingent—of the ideal and the practical in workable equilibrium—has been there, as it ever must be in every age and place, a matter of infinite experiment and frequent mistakes.

In rough approximation we may point out four varying decades of work in Southern education since the Civil War. From the close of the war until 1876, was the period of uncertain groping and temporary relief. There were army schools, mission schools, and schools of the Freedman's Bureau in chaotic disarrangement seeking system and coöperation. Then followed ten years of constructive definite effort toward the building of complete school systems in the South. Normal schools and colleges were founded for the freedmen, and teachers trained there to man the public schools. There was the inevitable tendency of war to underestimate the prejudices of the master and the ignorance of the slave, and all seemed clear sailing out of the wreckage of the storm. Meantime, starting in this decade yet especially developing from 1885 to 1895, began the industrial revolution of the South. The land saw glimpses of a new destiny and the stirring of new ideals. The educational system striving to complete itself saw new obstacles and a field of work ever broader and deeper. The Negro colleges, hurriedly founded, were inadequately equipped, illogically distributed, and of varying efficiency and grade; the normal and high schools were doing little more than common-school work, and the common schools were training but a third of the children who ought to be in them, and training these too often poorly. At the same time the white South, by reason of its sudden conversion from the slavery ideal, by so much the more became set and strengthened in its racial prejudice, and crystallized it into harsh law and harsher custom; while the marvellous pushing forward of the poor white daily threatened to take even bread and butter from the mouths of the heavily handicapped sons of the freedmen. In the midst, then, of the larger problem of Negro education sprang up the more practical question of work, the inevitable economic quandary that faces a people in the transition from slavery to freedom, and especially those who make that change amid hate and prejudice, lawlessness and ruthless competition.

The industrial school springing to notice in this decade, but coming to full recognition in the decade beginning with 1895, was the proffered answer to this

combined educational and economic crisis, and an
answer of singular wisdom and timeliness. From the
very first in nearly all the schools some attention had
been given to training in handiwork, but now was
this training first raised to a dignity that brought it in
direct touch with the South's magnificent industrial
development, and given an emphasis which reminded
black folk that before the Temple of Knowledge
swing the Gates of Toil.

Yet after all they are but gates, and when turning
our eyes from the temporary and the contingent in
the Negro problem to the broader question of the
permanent uplifting and civilization of black men in
America, we have a right to inquire, as this enthusiasm for material advancement mounts to its height,
if after all the industrial school is the final and sufficient answer in the training of the Negro race; and to
ask gently, but in all sincerity, the ever-recurring
query of the ages, Is not life more than meat, and the
body more than raiment? And men ask this to-day all
the more eagerly because of sinister signs in recent
educational movements. The tendency is here, born of
slavery and quickened to renewed life by the crazy
imperialism of the day, to regard human beings as
among the material resources of a land to be trained
with an eye single to future dividends. Race-preju-
dices, which keep brown and black men in their
"places," we are coming to regard as useful allies with
such a theory, no matter how much they may dull the
ambition and sicken the hearts of struggling human
beings. And above all, we daily hear that an education that encourages aspiration, that sets the loftiest of
ideals and seeks as an end culture and character
rather than bread-winning, is the privilege of white
men and the danger and delusion of black.

Especially has criticism been directed against the

former educational efforts to aid the Negro. In the four periods I have mentioned, we find first, boundless, planless enthusiasm and sacrifice; then the preparation of teachers for a vast public-school system; then the launching and expansion of that school system amid increasing difficulties; and finally the training of workmen for the new and growing industries. This development has been sharply ridiculed as a logical anomaly and flat reversal of nature. Soothly we have been told that first industrial and manual training should have taught the Negro to work, then simple schools should have taught him to read and write, and finally, after years, high and normal schools could have completed the system, as intelligence and wealth demanded.

That a system logically so complete was historically impossible, it needs but a little thought to prove. Progress in human affairs is more often a pull than a push, a surging forward of the exceptional man, and the lifting of his duller brethren slowly and painfully to his vantage-ground. Thus it was no accident that gave birth to universities centuries before the common schools, that made fair Harvard the first flower of our wilderness. So in the South: the mass of the freedmen at the end of the war lacked the intelligence so necessary to modern workingmen. They must first have the common school to teach them to read, write, and cipher; and they must have higher schools to teach teachers for the common schools. The white teachers who flocked South went to establish such a common-school system. Few held the idea of founding colleges; most of them at first would have laughed at the idea. But they faced, as all men since them have faced, that central paradox of the South,— the social separation of the races. At that time it was the sudden volcanic rupture of nearly all relations be-

tween black and white, in work and government and
family life. Since then a new adjustment of relations
in economic and political affairs has grown up,—an
adjustment subtle and difficult to grasp, yet singularly
ingenious, which leaves still that frightful chasm at
the color-line across which men pass at their peril.
Thus, then and now, there stand in the South two
separate worlds; and separate not simply in the
higher realms of social intercourse, but also in church
and school, on railway and street-car, in hotels and
theatres, in streets and city sections, in books and
newspapers, in asylums and jails, in hospitals and
graveyards. There is still enough of contact for large
economic and group coöperation, but the separation
is so thorough and deep that it absolutely precludes
for the present between the races anything like that
sympathetic and effective group-training and leadership of the one by the other, such as the American
Negro and all backward peoples must have for effectual progress.

This the missionaries of '68 soon saw; and if effective industrial and trade schools were impracticable
before the establishment of a common-school system,
just as certainly no adequate common schools could
be founded until there were teachers to teach them.
Southern whites would not teach them; Northern
whites in sufficient numbers could not be had. If the
Negro was to learn, he must teach himself, and the
most effective help that could be given him was the
establishment of schools to train Negro teachers. This
conclusion was slowly but surely reached by every
student of the situation until simultaneously, in
widely separated regions, without consultation or systematic plan, there arose a series of institutions designed to furnish teachers for the untaught. Above the
sneers of critics at the obvious defects of this proce-

dure must ever stand its one crushing rejoinder: in a single generation they put thirty thousand black teachers in the South; they wiped out the illiteracy of the majority of the black people of the land, and they made Tuskegee possible.

Such higher training-schools tended naturally to deepen broader development: at first they were common and grammar schools, then some became high schools. And finally, by 1900, some thirty-four had one year or more of studies of college grade. This development was reached with different degrees of speed in different institutions: Hampton is still a high school, while Fisk University started her college in 1871, and Spelman Seminary about 1896. In all cases the aim was identical,—to maintain the standards of the lower training by giving teachers and leaders the best practicable training; and above all, to furnish the black world with adequate standards of human culture and lofty ideals of life. It was not enough that the teachers of teachers should be trained in technical normal methods; they must also, so far as possible, be broad-minded, cultured men and women, to scatter civilization among a people whose ignorance was not simply of letters, but of life itself.

It can thus be seen that the work of education in the South began with higher institutions of training, which threw off as their foliage common schools, and later industrial schools, and at the same time strove to shoot their roots ever deeper toward college and university training. That this was an inevitable and necessary development, sooner or later, goes without saying; but there has been, and still is, a question in many minds if the natural growth was not forced, and if the higher training was not either overdone or done with cheap and unsound methods. Among white Southerners this feeling is widespread and positive. A prominent Southern journal voiced this in a recent editorial.

"The experiment that has been made to give the colored students classical training has not been satisfactory. Even though many were able to pursue the course, most of them did so in a parrot-like way, learning what was taught, but not seeming to appropriate the truth and import of their instruction, and graduating without sensible aim or valuable occupation for their future. The whole scheme has proved a waste of time, efforts, and the money of the state."

While most fair-minded men would recognize this as extreme and overdrawn, still without doubt many are asking, Are there a sufficient number of Negroes ready for college training to warrant the undertaking? Are not too many students prematurely forced into this work? Does it not have the effect of dissatisfying the young Negro with his environment? And do these graduates succeed in real life? Such natural questions cannot be evaded, nor on the other hand must a Nation naturally skeptical as to Negro ability assume an unfavorable answer without careful inquiry and patient openness to conviction. We must not forget that most Americans answer all queries regarding the Negro *a priori*, and that the least that human courtesy can do is to listen to evidence.

The advocates of the higher education of the Negro would be the last to deny the incompleteness and glaring defects of the present system: too many institutions have attempted to do college work, the work in some cases has not been thoroughly done, and quantity rather than quality has sometimes been sought. But all this can be said of higher education throughout the land; it is the almost inevitable incident of educational growth, and leaves the deeper question of the legitimate demand for the higher training of Negroes untouched. And this latter question can be settled in but one way,—by a first-hand study of the facts. If we leave out of view all institutions which have not actually graduated students from a course higher than that of a New England high school, even though they be called colleges; if then we take the thirty-four remaining institutions, we may clear up many misapprehensions by asking searchingly, What kind of institutions are they? what do they teach? and what sort of men do they graduate?

And first we may say that this type of college, including Atlanta, Fisk, and Howard, Wilberforce and Claflin, Shaw, and the rest, is peculiar, almost unique. Through the shining trees that whisper before me as I write, I catch glimpses of a boulder of New England granite, covering a grave, which graduates of Atlanta University have placed there,—

"GRATEFUL MEMORY OF THEIR FORMER TEACHER AND FRIEND AND OF THE UNSELFISH LIFE HE LIVED, AND THE NOBLE WORK HE WROUGHT; THAT THEY, THEIR CHILDREN, AND THEIR CHILDREN'S CHILDREN MIGHT BE BLESSED."

This was the gift of New England to the freed Negro: not alms, but a friend; not cash, but character. It was not and is not money these seething millions want, but love and sympathy, the pulse of hearts beating with red blood;—a gift which to-day only their own kindred and race can bring to the masses, but which once saintly souls brought to their favored children in the crusade of the sixties, that finest thing

in American history, and one of the few things un-
tainted by sordid greed and cheap vainglory. The
teachers in these institutions came not to keep the
Negroes in their place, but to raise them out of the
defilement of the places where slavery had wallowed
them. The colleges they founded were social settlements; homes where the best of the sons of the freedmen came in close and sympathetic touch with the
best traditions of New England. They lived and ate
together, studied and worked, hoped and harkened in
the dawning light. In actual formal content their curriculum was doubtless old-fashioned, but in educational power it was supreme, for it was the contact of
living souls.

From such schools about two thousand Negroes
have gone forth with the bachelor's degree. The number in itself is enough to put at rest the argument that
too large a proportion of Negroes are receiving higher
training. If the ratio to population of all Negro students throughout the land, in both college and secon-
dary training, be counted, Commissioner Harris as-
sures us "it must be increased to five times its present
average" to equal the average of the land.

Fifty years ago the ability of Negro students in any
appreciable numbers to master a modern college
course would have been difficult to prove. To-day it is
proved by the fact that four hundred Negroes, many
of whom have been reported as brilliant students,
have received the bachelor's degree from Harvard,
Yale, Oberlin, and seventy other leading colleges.
Here we have, then, nearly twenty-five hundred
Negro graduates, of whom the crucial query must be
made, How far did their training fit them for life? It
is of course extremely difficult to collect satisfactory
data on such a point,—difficult to reach the men, to
get trustworthy testimony, and to gauge that testi-

mony by any generally acceptable criterion of success. In 1900, the Conference at Atlanta University undertook to study these graduates, and published the results. First they sought to know what these graduates were doing, and succeeded in getting answers from nearly two-thirds of the living. The direct testimony was in almost all cases corroborated by the reports of the colleges where they graduated, so that in the main the reports were worthy of credence. Fifty-three per cent of these graduates were teachers,— presidents of institutions, heads of normal schools, principals of city school-systems, and the like. Seventeen per cent were clergymen; another seventeen per cent were in the professions, chiefly as physicians. Over six per cent were merchants, farmers, and artisans, and four per cent were in the government civil-service. Granting even that a considerable proportion of the third unheard from are unsuccessful, this is a record of usefulness. Personally I know many hundreds of these graduates, and have corresponded with more than a thousand; through others I have followed carefully the life-work of scores; I have taught some of them and some of the pupils whom they have taught, lived in homes which they have builded, and looked at life through their eyes. Comparing them as a class with my fellow students in New England and in Europe, I cannot hesitate in saying that nowhere have I met men and women with a broader spirit of helpfulness, with deeper devotion to their life-work, or with more consecrated determination to succeed in the face of bitter difficulties than among Negro college-bred men. They have, to be sure, their proportion of ne'er-do-weels, their pedants and lettered fools, but they have a surprisingly small proportion of them; they have not that culture of manner which we instinctively associate with university men, forgetting that in reality it is the heritage from cultured homes, and that no people a generation removed from slavery can escape a certain unpleasant rawness and *gaucherie*, despite the best of training.

With all their larger vision and deeper sensibility, these men have usually been conservative, careful leaders. They have seldom been agitators, have withstood the temptation to head the mob, and have worked steadily and faithfully in a thousand communities in the South. As teachers, they have given the South a commendable system of city schools and large numbers of private normal-schools and academies. Colored college-bred men have worked side by side with white college graduates at Hampton; almost from the beginning the backbone of Tuskegee's teaching force has been formed of graduates from Fisk and Atlanta. And to-day the institute is filled with college graduates, from the energetic wife of the principal down to the teacher of agriculture, including nearly half of the executive council and a majority of the heads of departments. In the professions, college men are slowly but surely leavening the Negro church, are healing and preventing the devastations of disease, and beginning to furnish legal protection for the liberty and property of the toiling masses. All this is needful work. Who would do it if Negroes did not? How could Negroes do it if they were not trained carefully for it? If white people need colleges to furnish teachers, ministers, lawyers, and doctors, do black people need nothing of the sort?

If it is true that there are an appreciable number of Negro youth in the land capable by character and talent to receive that higher training, the end of which is culture, and if the two and a half thousand who have had something of this training in the past have in the main proved themselves useful to their race and generation, the question then comes, What place in the future development of the South ought the Negro college and college-bred man to occupy? That the present social separation and acute race-sensitiveness must eventually yield to the influences of culture, as the South grows civilized, is clear. But such transformation calls for singular wisdom and patience. If, while the healing of this vast sore is progressing, the races are to live for many years side by side, united in economic effort, obeying a common government, sensitive to mutual thought and feeling, yet subtly and silently separate in many matters of deeper human intimacy,—if this unusual and dangerous development is to progress amid peace and order, mutual respect and growing intelligence, it will call for social surgery at once the delicatest and nicest in modern history. It will demand broad-minded, upright men, both white and black, and in its final accomplishment American civilization will triumph. So far as white men are concerned, this fact is to-day being recognized in the South, and a happy renaissance of university education seems imminent. But the very voices that cry hail to this good work are, strange to relate, largely silent or antagonistic to the higher education of the Negro.

Strange to relate! for this is certain, no secure civilization can be built in the South with the Negro as an ignorant, turbulent proletariat. Suppose we seek to remedy this by making them laborers and nothing more: they are not fools, they have tasted of the Tree of Life, and they will not cease to think, will not cease attempting to read the riddle of the world. By taking away their best equipped teachers and leaders, by slamming the door of opportunity in the faces of their bolder and brighter minds, will you make them satisfied with their lot? or will you not rather transfer their leading from the hands of men taught to think to the hands of untrained demagogues? We ought not to forget that despite the pressure of poverty, and despite the active discouragement and even ridicule of friends, the demand for higher training steadily increases among Negro youth: there were, in the years from 1875 to 1880, 22 Negro graduates from Northern colleges; from 1885 to 1890 there were 43, and from 1895 to 1900, nearly 100 graduates. From Southern Negro colleges there were, in the same three periods, 143, 413, and over 500 graduates. Here, then, is the plain thirst for training; by refusing to give this Talented Tenth the key to knowledge, can any sane man imagine that they will lightly lay aside their yearning and contentedly become hewers of wood and drawers of water?

No. The dangerously clear logic of the Negro's position will more and more loudly assert itself in that day when increasing wealth and more intricate social organization preclude the South from being, as it so largely is, simply an armed camp for intimidating black folk. Such waste of energy cannot be spared if the South is to catch up with civilization. And as the black third of the land grows in thrift and skill, unless skilfully guided in its larger philosophy, it must more and more brood over the red past and the creeping, crooked present, until it grasps a gospel of revolt and revenge and throws its new-found energies athwart the current of advance. Even to-day the masses of the Negroes see all too clearly the anomalies of their position and the moral crookedness of yours. You may marshal strong indictments against them, but their counter-cries, lacking though they be in formal logic, have burning truths within them which you may not wholly ignore, O Southern Gentlemen! If you deplore their presence here, they ask, Who brought us? When you cry, Deliver us from the vision of intermarriage, they answer that legal marriage is infinitely better than systematic concubinage and prostitution. And if in just fury you accuse their vagabonds of violating women, they also in fury quite as just may reply: The rape which your gentlemen have done against helpless black women in defiance of your own laws is written on the foreheads of two millions of mulattoes, and written in ineffaceable blood. And finally, when you fasten crime upon this race as its peculiar trait, they answer that slavery was the arch-crime, and lynching and lawlessness its twin abortions; that color and race are not crimes, and yet it is they which in this land receive most unceasing condemnation, North, East, South, and West.

I will not say such arguments are wholly justified, —I will not insist that there is no other side to the shield; but I do say that of the nine millions of Negroes in this nation, there is scarcely one out of the cradle to whom these arguments do not daily present themselves in the guise of terrible truth. I insist that the question of the future is how best to keep these millions from brooding over the wrongs of the past and the difficulties of the present, so that all their energies may be bent toward a cheerful striving and coöperation with their white neighbors toward a larger, juster, and fuller future. That one wise method of doing this lies in the closer knitting of the Negro to the great industrial possibilities of the South is a great truth. And this the common schools and the manual training and trade schools are working to accomplish. But these alone are not enough. The foundations of knowledge in this race, as in others, must be sunk deep in the college and university if we would build a solid, permanent structure. Internal problems of social advance must inevitably come,—problems of work and wages, of families and homes, of morals and the

true valuing of the things of life; and all these and
other inevitable problems of civilization the Negro
must meet and solve largely for himself, by reason of
his isolation; and can there be any possible solution
other than by study and thought and an appeal to the
rich experience of the past? Is there not, with such a
group and in such a crisis, infinitely more danger to
be apprehended from half-trained minds and shallow
thinking than from over-education and over-refine-
ment? Surely we have wit enough to found a Negro
college so manned and equipped as to steer successfully between the *dilettante* and the fool. We shall
hardly induce black men to believe that if their stom-
achs be full, it matters little about their brains. They
already dimly perceive that the paths of peace winding between honest toil and dignified manhood call
for the guidance of skilled thinkers, the loving, rever-
ent comradeship between the black lowly and the
black men emancipated by training and culture.

The function of the Negro college, then, is clear: it
must maintain the standards of popular education, it
must seek the social regeneration of the Negro, and it
must help in the solution of problems of race contact
and coöperation. And finally, beyond all this, it must
develop men. Above our modern socialism, and out of
the worship of the mass, must persist and evolve that
higher individualism which the centres of culture protect; there must come a loftier respect for the sover-
eign human soul that seeks to know itself and the
world about it; that seeks a freedom for expansion
and self-development; that will love and hate and
labor in its own way, untrammeled alike by old and
new. Such souls aforetime have inspired and guided
worlds, and if we be not wholly bewitched by our
Rhinegold, they shall again. Herein the longing of
black men must have respect: the rich and bitter

depth of their experience, the unknown treasures of their inner life, the strange rendings of nature they have seen, may give the world new points of view and make their loving, living, and doing precious to all human hearts. And to themselves in these the days that try their souls, the chance to soar in the dim blue air above the smoke is to their finer spirits boon and guerdon for what they lose on earth by being black.

I sit with Shakespeare and he winces not. Across the color line I move arm in arm with Balzac and Dumas, where smiling men and welcoming women glide in gilded halls. From out the caves of evening that swing between the strong-limbed earth and the tracery of the stars, I summon Aristotle and Aurelius and what soul I will, and they come all graciously with no scorn nor condescension. So, wed with Truth, I dwell above the Veil. Is this the life you grudge us, O knightly America? Is this the life you long to change into the dull red hideousness of Georgia? Are you so afraid lest peering from this high Pisgah, between Philistine and Amalekite, we sight the Promised Land?

VII

Of the Black Belt

I am black but comely, O ye daughters of Jerusalem,
As the tents of Kedar, as the curtains of Solomon.
Look not upon me, because I am black,
Because the sun hath looked upon me:
My mother's children were angry with me;
They made me the keeper of the vineyards;
But mine own vineyard have I not kept.

THE SONG OF SOLOMON.

OUT of the North the train thundered, and we woke to see the crimson soil of Georgia stretching away bare and monotonous right and left. Here and there lay straggling, unlovely villages, and lean men loafed leisurely at the depots; then again came the stretch of pines and clay. Yet we did not nod, nor weary of the scene; for this is historic ground. Right across our track, three hundred and sixty years ago, wandered

140

the cavalcade of Hernando de Soto, looking for gold and the Great Sea; and he and his foot-sore captives disappeared yonder in the grim forests to the west. Here sits Atlanta, the city of a hundred hills, with something Western, something Southern, and something quite its own, in its busy life. Just this side Atlanta is the land of the Cherokees and to the southwest, not far from where Sam Hose was crucified, you may stand on a spot which is to-day the centre of the Negro problem,—the centre of those nine million men who are America's dark heritage from slavery and the slave-trade.

Not only is Georgia thus the geographical focus of our Negro population, but in many other respects, both now and yesterday, the Negro problems have seemed to be centered in this State. No other State in the Union can count a million Negroes among its citizens,—a population as large as the slave population of the whole Union in 1800; no other State fought so long and strenuously to gather this host of Africans. Oglethorpe thought slavery against law and gospel; but the circumstances which gave Georgia its first inhabitants were not calculated to furnish citizens over-nice in their ideas about rum and slaves. Despite the prohibitions of the trustees, these Georgians, like some of their descendants, proceeded to take the law into their own hands; and so pliant were the judges, and so flagrant the smuggling, and so earnest were the prayers of Whitefield, that by the middle of the eighteenth century all restrictions were swept away, and the slave-trade went merrily on for fifty years and more.

Down in Darien, where the Delegal riots took place some summers ago, there used to come a strong protest against slavery from the Scotch Highlanders; and the Moravians of Ebenezer did not like the system.

But not till the Haytian Terror of Toussaint was the trade in men even checked; while the national statute of 1808 did not suffice to stop it. How the Africans poured in!—fifty thousand between 1790 and 1810, and then, from Virginia and from smugglers, two thousand a year for many years more. So the thirty thousand Negroes of Georgia in 1790 doubled in a decade,—were over a hundred thousand in 1810, had reached two hundred thousand in 1820, and half a million at the time of the war. Thus like a snake the black population writhed upward.

But we must hasten on our journey. This that we pass as we near Atlanta is the ancient land of the Cherokees,—that brave Indian nation which strove so long for its fatherland, until Fate and the United States Government drove them beyond the Mississippi. If you wish to ride with me you must come into the "Jim Crow Car." There will be no objection,—already four other white men, and a little white girl with her nurse, are in there. Usually the races are mixed in there; but the white coach is all white. Of course this car is not so good as the other, but it is fairly clean and comfortable. The discomfort lies chiefly in the hearts of those four black men yonder—and in mine.

We rumble south in quite a business-like way. The bare red clay and pines of Northern Georgia begin to disappear, and in their place appears a rich rolling land, luxuriant, and here and there well tilled. This is the land of the Creek Indians; and a hard time the Georgians had to seize it. The towns grow more frequent and more interesting, and brand-new cotton mills rise on every side. Below Macon the world grows darker; for now we approach the Black Belt,—that strange land of shadows, at which even slaves paled in the past, and whence come now only faint and half-intelligible murmurs to the world beyond. The "Jim Crow Car" grows larger and a shade better; three rough field-hands and two or three white loafers accompany us, and the newsboy still spreads his wares at one end. The sun is setting, but we can see the great cotton country as we enter it,—the soil now dark and fertile, now thin and gray, with fruit-trees and dilapidated buildings,—all the way to Albany.

At Albany, in the heart of the Black Belt, we stop. Two hundred miles south of Atlanta, two hundred miles west of the Atlantic, and one hundred miles north of the Great Gulf lies Dougherty County, with ten thousand Negroes and two thousand whites. The Flint River winds down from Andersonville, and, turning suddenly at Albany, the county-seat, hurries on to join the Chattahoochee and the sea. Andrew Jackson knew the Flint well, and marched across it once to avenge the Indian Massacre at Fort Mims. That was in 1814, not long before the battle of New Orleans; and by the Creek treaty that followed this campaign, all Dougherty County, and much other rich land, was ceded to Georgia. Still, settlers fought shy of this land, for the Indians were all about, and they were unpleasant neighbors in those days. The panic of 1837, which Jackson bequeathed to Van Buren, turned the planters from the impoverished lands of Virginia, the Carolinas, and east Georgia, toward the West. The Indians were removed to Indian Territory, and settlers poured into these coveted lands to retrieve their broken fortunes. For a radius of a hundred miles about Albany, stretched a great fertile land, luxuriant with forests of pine, oak, ash, hickory, and poplar; hot with the sun and damp with the rich black swamp-land; and here the corner-stone of the Cotton Kingdom was laid.

Albany is to-day a wide-streeted, placid, Southern

town, with a broad sweep of stores and saloons, and flanking rows of homes,—whites usually to the north, and blacks to the south. Six days in the week the town looks decidedly too small for itself, and takes frequent and prolonged naps. But on Saturday suddenly the whole county disgorges itself upon the place, and a perfect flood of black peasantry pours through the streets, fills the stores, blocks the sidewalks, chokes the thoroughfares, and takes full possession of the town. They are black, sturdy, uncouth country folk, good-natured and simple, talkative to a degree, and yet far more silent and brooding than the crowds of the Rhine-pfalz, or Naples, or Cracow. They drink considerable quantities of whiskey, but do not get very drunk; they talk and laugh loudly at times, but seldom quarrel or fight. They walk up and down the streets, meet and gossip with friends, stare at the shop windows, buy coffee, cheap candy, and clothes, and at dusk drive home—happy? well no, not exactly happy, but much happier than as though they had not come.

Thus Albany is a real capital,—a typical Southern county town, the centre of the life of ten thousand souls; their point of contact with the outer world, their centre of news and gossip, their market for buying and selling, borrowing and lending, their fountain of justice and law. Once upon a time we knew country life so well and city life so little, that we illustrated city life as that of a closely crowded country district. Now the world has well-nigh forgotten what the country is, and we must imagine a little city of black people scattered far and wide over three hundred lonesome square miles of land, without train or trolley, in the midst of cotton and corn, and wide patches of sand and gloomy soil.

It gets pretty hot in Southern Georgia in July,—a

sort of dull, determined heat that seems quite independent of the sun; so it took us some days to muster
courage enough to leave the porch and venture out
on the long country roads, that we might see this unknown world. Finally we started. It was about ten in
the morning, bright with a faint breeze, and we
jogged leisurely southward in the valley of the Flint.
We passed the scattered box-like cabins of the brick-
yard hands, and the long tenement-row facetiously
called "The Ark," and were soon in the open country,
and on the confines of the great plantations of other
days. There is the "Joe Fields place"; a rough old fellow was he, and had killed many a "nigger" in his
day. Twelve miles his plantation used to run,—a regular barony. It is nearly all gone now; only straggling
bits belong to the family, and the rest has passed to
Jews and Negroes. Even the bits which are left are
heavily mortgaged, and, like the rest of the land,
tilled by tenants. Here is one of them now,—a tall
brown man, a hard worker and a hard drinker, illiter-
ate, but versed in farmlore, as his nodding crops declare. This distressingly new board house is his, and
he has just moved out of yonder moss-grown cabin
with its one square room.

From the curtains in Benton's house, down the
road, a dark comely face is staring at the strangers;
for passing carriages are not every-day occurrences
here. Benton is an intelligent yellow man with a
good-sized family, and manages a plantation blasted
by the war and now the broken staff of the widow.
He might be well-to-do, they say; but he carouses too
much in Albany. And the half-desolate spirit of neglect born of the very soil seems to have settled on
these acres. In times past there were cotton-gins and
machinery here; but they have rotted away.

The whole land seems forlorn and forsaken. Here

are the remnants of the vast plantations of the Shel-
dons, the Pellots, and the Rensons; but the souls of
them are passed. The houses lie in half ruin, or have
wholly disappeared; the fences have flown, and the
families are wandering in the world. Strange vicissi-
tudes have met these whilom masters. Yonder stretch
the wide acres of Bildad Reasor; he died in war-time,
but the upstart overseer hastened to wed the widow.
Then he went, and his neighbors too, and now only
the black tenant remains; but the shadow-hand of the
master's grand-nephew or cousin or creditor stretches
out of the gray distance to collect the rack-rent re-
morselessly, and so the land is uncared-for and poor.
Only black tenants can stand such a system, and they
only because they must. Ten miles we have ridden
to-day and have seen no white face.

A resistless feeling of depression falls slowly upon
us, despite the gaudy sunshine and the green cotton-
fields. This, then, is the Cotton Kingdom,—the shadow
of a marvellous dream. And where is the King? Perhaps this is he,—the sweating ploughman, tilling his
eighty acres with two lean mules, and fighting a hard
battle with debt. So we sit musing, until, as we turn a
corner on the sandy road, there comes a fairer scene
suddenly in view,—a neat cottage snugly ensconced
by the road, and near it a little store. A tall bronzed
man rises from the porch as we hail him, and comes
out to our carriage. He is six feet in height, with a
sober face that smiles gravely. He walks too straight
to be a tenant,—yes, he owns two hundred and forty
acres. "The land is run down since the boom-days of
eighteen hundred and fifty," he explains, and cotton is
low. Three black tenants live on his place, and in his
little store he keeps a small stock of tobacco, snuff,
soap, and soda, for the neighborhood. Here is his
gin-house with new machinery just installed. Three

hundred bales of cotton went through it last year. Two children he has sent away to school. Yes, he says sadly, he is getting on, but cotton is down to four cents; I know how Debt sits staring at him.

Wherever the King may be, the parks and palaces of the Cotton Kingdom have not wholly disappeared. We plunge even now into great groves of oak and towering pine, with an undergrowth of myrtle and shrubbery. This was the "home-house" of the Thompsons,—slave-barons who drove their coach and four in the merry past. All is silence now, and ashes, and tangled weeds. The owner put his whole fortune into the rising cotton industry of the fifties, and with the falling prices of the eighties he packed up and stole away. Yonder is another grove, with unkempt lawn, great magnolias, and grass-grown paths. The Big House stands in half-ruin, its great front door staring blankly at the street, and the back part grotesquely restored for its black tenant. A shabby, well-built Negro he is, unlucky and irresolute. He digs hard to pay rent to the white girl who owns the remnant of the place. She married a policeman, and lives in Savannah.

Now and again we come to churches. Here is one now,—Shepherds, they call it,—a great whitewashed barn of a thing, perched on stilts of stone, and looking for all the world as though it were just resting here a moment and might be expected to waddle off down the road at almost any time. And yet it is the centre of a hundred cabin homes; and sometimes, of a Sunday, five hundred persons from far and near gather here and talk and eat and sing. There is a schoolhouse near,—a very airy, empty shed; but even this is an improvement, for usually the school is held in the church. The churches vary from log-huts to those like Shepherd's, and the schools from nothing to this little

house that sits demurely on the county line. It is a
tiny plank-house, perhaps ten by twenty, and has
within a double row of rough unplaned benches, resting mostly on legs, sometimes on boxes. Opposite the
door is a square home-made desk. In one corner are
the ruins of a stove, and in the other a dim blackboard. It is the cheerfulest schoolhouse I have seen in
Dougherty, save in town. Back of the schoolhouse is a
lodgehouse two stories high and not quite finished.
Societies meet there,—societies "to care for the sick
and bury the dead"; and these societies grow and
flourish.

We had come to the boundaries of Dougherty, and
were about to turn west along the county-line, when
all these sights were pointed out to us by a kindly old
man, black, white-haired, and seventy. Forty-five
years he had lived here, and now supports himself
and his old wife by the help of the steer tethered
yonder and the charity of his black neighbors. He
shows us the farm of the Hills just across the county
line in Baker,—a widow and two strapping sons, who
raised ten bales (one need not add "cotton" down
here) last year. There are fences and pigs and cows,
and the soft-voiced, velvet-skinned young Memnon,
who sauntered half-bashfully over to greet the strangers, is proud of his home. We turn now to the west
along the county line. Great dismantled trunks of
pines tower above the green cotton-fields, cracking
their naked gnarled fingers toward the border of living forest beyond. There is little beauty in this region,
only a sort of crude abandon that suggests power,—a
naked grandeur, as it were. The houses are bare and
straight; there are no hammocks or easy-chairs, and
few flowers. So when, as here at Rawdon's, one sees a
vine clinging to a little porch, and home-like windows
peeping over the fences, one takes a long breath. I

think I never before quite realized the place of the
Fence in civilization. This is the Land of the Unfenced, where crouch on either hand scores of ugly
one-room cabins, cheerless and dirty. Here lies the
Negro problem in its naked dirt and penury. And
here are no fences. But now and then the criss-cross
rails or straight palings break into view, and then we
know a touch of culture is near. Of course Harrison
Gohagen,—a quiet yellow man, young, smooth-faced,
and diligent,—of course he is lord of some hundred
acres, and we expect to see a vision of well-kept
rooms and fat beds and laughing children. For has he
not fine fences? And those over yonder, why should
they build fences on the rack-rented land? It will only
increase their rent.

On we wind, through sand and pines and glimpses
of old plantations, till there creeps into sight a cluster
of buildings,—wood and brick, mills and houses, and
scattered cabins. It seemed quite a village. As it came
nearer and nearer, however, the aspect changed: the
buildings were rotten, the bricks were falling out, the
mills were silent, and the store was closed. Only in
the cabins appeared now and then a bit of lazy life. I
could imagine the place under some weird spell, and
was half-minded to search out the princess. An old
ragged black man, honest, simple, and improvident,
told us the tale. The Wizard of the North—the Capi-
talist—had rushed down in the seventies to woo this
coy dark soil. He bought a square mile or more, and
for a time the field-hands sang, the gins groaned, and
the mills buzzed. Then came a change. The agent's
son embezzled the funds and ran off with them. Then
the agent himself disappeared. Finally the new agent
stole even the books, and the company in wrath
closed its business and its houses, refused to sell, and
let houses and furniture and machinery rust and rot.

So the Waters-Loring plantation was stilled by the
spell of dishonesty, and stands like some gaunt rebuke
to a scarred land.

Somehow that plantation ended our day's journey;
for I could not shake off the influence of that silent
scene. Back toward town we glided, past the straight
and thread-like pines, past a dark tree-dotted pond
where the air was heavy with a dead sweet perfume.
White slender-legged curlews flitted by us, and the
garnet blooms of the cotton looked gay against the
green and purple stalks. A peasant girl was hoeing in
the field, white-turbaned and black-limbed. All this
we saw, but the spell still lay upon us.

How curious a land is this,—how full of untold
story, of tragedy and laughter, and the rich legacy of
human life; shadowed with a tragic past, and big
with future promise! This is the Black Belt of Georgia. Dougherty County is the west end of the Black
Belt, and men once called it the Egypt of the Confederacy. It is full of historic interest. First there is the
Swamp, to the west, where the Chickasawhatchee
flows sullenly southward. The shadow of an old plantation lies at its edge, forlorn and dark. Then comes
the pool; pendent gray moss and brackish waters appear, and forests filled with wildfowl. In one place
the wood is on fire, smouldering in dull red anger;
but nobody minds. Then the swamp grows beautiful;
a raised road, built by chained Negro convicts, dips
down into it, and forms a way walled and almost covered in living green. Spreading trees spring from a
prodigal luxuriance of undergrowth; great dark green
shadows fade into the black background, until all is
one mass of tangled semi-tropical foliage, marvellous
in its weird savage splendor. Once we crossed a black
silent stream, where the sad trees and writhing creep-
ers, all glinting fiery yellow and green, seemed like

some vast cathedral,—some green Milan builded of wildwood. And as I crossed, I seemed to see again that fierce tragedy of seventy years ago. Osceola, the Indian-Negro chieftain, had risen in the swamps of Florida, vowing vengeance. His war-cry reached the red Creeks of Dougherty, and their war-cry rang from the Chattahoochee to the sea. Men and women and children fled and fell before them as they swept into Dougherty. In yonder shadows a dark and hideously painted warrior glided stealthily on,—another and another, until three hundred had crept into the treacherous swamp. Then the false slime closing about them called the white men from the east. Waist-deep, they fought beneath the tall trees, until the war-cry was hushed and the Indians glided back into the west. Small wonder the wood is red.

Then came the black slaves. Day after day the clank of chained feet marching from Virginia and Carolina to Georgia was heard in these rich swamp lands. Day after day the songs of the callous, the wail of the motherless, and the muttered curses of the wretched echoed from the Flint to the Chickasawhatchee, until by 1860 there had risen in West Dougherty perhaps the richest slave kingdom the modern world ever knew. A hundred and fifty barons commanded the labor of nearly six thousand Negroes, held sway over farms with ninety thousand acres tilled land, valued even in times of cheap soil at three millions of dollars. Twenty thousand bales of ginned cotton went yearly to England, New and Old; and men that came there bankrupt made money and grew rich. In a single decade the cotton output increased four-fold and the value of lands was tripled. It was the heyday of the *nouveau riche*, and a life of careless extravagance among the masters. Four and six bobtailed thoroughbreds rolled their coaches to town;

open hospitality and gay entertainment were the rule.
Parks and groves were laid out, rich with flower and
vine, and in the midst stood the low wide-halled "big
house," with its porch and columns and great fireplaces.

And yet with all this there was something sordid,
something forced,—a certain feverish unrest and reck-
lessness; for was not all this show and tinsel built
upon a groan? "This land was a little Hell," said a
ragged, brown, and grave-faced man to me. We were
seated near a roadside blacksmith-shop, and behind
was the bare ruin of some master's home. "I've seen
niggers drop dead in the furrow, but they were
kicked aside, and the plough never stopped. Down in
the guard-house, there's where the blood ran."

With such foundations a kingdom must in time
sway and fall. The masters moved to Macon and Au-
gusta, and left only the irresponsible overseers on the
land. And the result is such ruin as this, the Lloyd
"home-place":—great waving oaks, a spread of lawn,
myrtles and chestnuts, all ragged and wild; a solitary
gate-post standing where once was a castle entrance;
an old rusty anvil lying amid rotting bellows and
wood in the ruins of a blacksmith shop; a wide rambling old mansion, brown and dingy, filled now with
the grandchildren of the slaves who once waited on
its tables; while the family of the master has dwindled to two lone women, who live in Macon and feed
hungrily off the remnants of an earldom. So we ride
on, past phantom gates and falling homes,—past the
once flourishing farms of the Smiths, the Gandys, and
the Lagores,—and find all dilapidated and half ruined,
even there where a solitary white woman, a relic of
other days, sits alone in state among miles of Negroes and rides to town in her ancient coach each day.

This was indeed the Egypt of the Confederacy,—

the rich granary whence potatoes and corn and cotton
poured out to the famished and ragged Confederate
troops as they battled for a cause lost long before
1861. Sheltered and secure, it became the place of refuge for families, wealth, and slaves. Yet even then the
hard ruthless rape of the land began to tell. The red-
clay sub-soil already had begun to peer above the
loam. The harder the slaves were driven the more
careless and fatal was their farming. Then came the
revolution of war and Emancipation, the bewilderment of Reconstruction,—and now, what is the Egypt
of the Confederacy, and what meaning has it for the
nation's weal or woe?

It is a land of rapid contrasts and of curiously mingled hope and pain. Here sits a pretty blue-eyed
quadroon hiding her bare feet; she was married only
last week, and yonder in the field is her dark young
husband, hoeing to support her, at thirty cents a day
without board. Across the way is Gatesby, brown and
tall, lord of two thousand acres shrewdly won and
held. There is a store conducted by his black son, a
blacksmith shop, and a ginnery. Five miles below
here is a town owned and controlled by one white
New Englander. He owns almost a Rhode Island
county, with thousands of acres and hundreds of
black laborers. Their cabins look better than most,
and the farm, with machinery and fertilizers, is much
more business-like than any in the county, although
the manager drives hard bargains in wages. When
now we turn and look five miles above, there on the
edge of town are five houses of prostitutes,—two of
blacks and three of whites; and in one of the houses
of the whites a worthless black boy was harbored too
openly two years ago; so he was hanged for rape.
And here, too, is the high whitewashed fence of the
"stockade," as the county prison is called; the white

folks say it is ever full of black criminals,—the black folks say that only colored boys are sent to jail, and they not because they are guilty, but because the State needs criminals to eke out its income by their forced labor.

Immigrants are heirs of the slave baron in Dougherty; and as we ride westward, by wide stretching cornfields and stubby orchards of peach and pear, we see on all sides within the circle of dark forest a Land of Canaan. Here and there are tales of projects for money-getting, born in the swift days of Reconstruction,—"improvement" companies, wine companies, mills and factories; most failed, and foreigners fell heir. It is a beautiful land, this Dougherty, west of the Flint. The forests are wonderful, the solemn pines have disappeared, and this is the "Oakey Woods," with its wealth of hickories, beeches, oaks and palmettos. But a pall of debt hangs over the beautiful land; the merchants are in debt to the wholesalers, the planters are in debt to the merchants, the tenants owe the planters, and laborers bow and bend beneath the burden of it all. Here and there a man has raised his head above these murky waters. We passed one fenced stock-farm with grass and grazing cattle, that looked very home-like after endless corn and cotton. Here and there are black free-holders: there is the gaunt dull-black Jackson, with his hundred acres. "I says, 'Look up! If you don't look up you can't get up,'" remarks Jackson, philosophically. And he's gotten up. Dark Carter's neat barns would do credit to New England. His master helped him to get a start, but when the black man died last fall the master's sons immediately laid claim to the estate. "And them white folks will get it, too," said my yellow gossip.

I turn from these well-tended acres with a comfortable feeling that the Negro is rising. Even then, however, the fields, as we proceed, begin to redden and the trees disappear. Rows of old cabins appear filled with renters and laborers,—cheerless, bare, and dirty, for the most part, although here and there the very age and decay makes the scene picturesque. A young black fellow greets us. He is twenty-two, and just married. Until last year he had good luck renting; then cotton fell, and the sheriff seized and sold all he had. So he moved here, where the rent is higher, the land poorer, and the owner inflexible; he rents a forty-dollar mule for twenty dollars a year. Poor lad!—a slave at twenty-two. This plantation, owned now by a foreigner, was a part of the famous Bolton estate. After the war it was for many years worked by gangs of Negro convicts,—and black convicts then were even more plentiful than now; it was a way of making Negroes work, and the question of guilt was a minor one. Hard tales of cruelty and mistreatment of the chained freemen are told, but the county authorities were deaf until the free-labor market was nearly ruined by wholesale migration. Then they took the convicts from the plantations, but not until one of the fairest regions of the "Oakey Woods" had been ruined and ravished into a red waste, out of which only a Yankee or an immigrant could squeeze more blood from debt-cursed tenants.

No wonder that Luke Black, slow, dull, and discouraged, shuffles to our carriage and talks hopelessly. Why should he strive? Every year finds him deeper in debt. How strange that Georgia, the world-heralded refuge of poor debtors, should bind her own to sloth and misfortune as ruthlessly as ever England did! The poor land groans with its birth-pains, and brings forth scarcely a hundred pounds of cotton to the acre, where fifty years ago it yielded eight times as much. Of his meagre yield the tenant pays from a quarter to a third in rent, and most of the rest in interest on food and supplies bought on credit. Twenty years yonder sunken-cheeked, old black man has labored under that system, and now, turned day-laborer, is supporting his wife and boarding himself on his wages of a dollar and a half a week, received only part of the year.

The Bolton convict farm formerly included the neighboring plantation. Here it was that the convicts were lodged in the great log prison still standing. A dismal place it still remains, with rows of ugly huts filled with surly ignorant tenants. "What rent do you pay here?" I inquired. "I don't know,—what is it, Sam?" "All we make," answered Sam. It is a depressing place,—bare, unshaded, with no charm of past association, only a memory of forced human toil,—now, then, and before the war. They are not happy, these black men whom we meet throughout this region. There is little of the joyous abandon and playfulness which we are wont to associate with the plantation Negro. At best, the natural good-nature is edged with complaint or has changed into sullenness and gloom. And now and then it blazes forth in veiled but hot anger. I remember one big red-eyed black whom we met by the roadside. Forty-five years he had labored on this farm, beginning with nothing, and still having nothing. To be sure, he had given four children a common-school training, and perhaps if the new fence-law had not allowed unfenced crops in West Dougherty he might have raised a little stock and kept ahead. As it is, he is hopelessly in debt, disappointed, and embittered. He stopped us to inquire after the black boy in Albany, whom it was said a policeman had shot and killed for loud talking on the sidewalk. And then he said slowly: "Let a white man touch me, and he dies; I don't boast this,—I don't say it around loud, or before the children,—but I mean it. I've seen them whip my father and my old mother in them cotton-rows till the blood ran; by—" and we passed on.

Now Sears, whom we met next lolling under the chubby oak-trees, was of quite different fibre. Happy? —Well, yes; he laughed and flipped pebbles, and thought the world was as it was. He had worked here twelve years and has nothing but a mortgaged mule. Children? Yes, seven; but they hadn't been to school this year,—couldn't afford books and clothes, and couldn't spare their work. There go part of them to the fields now,—three big boys astride mules, and a strapping girl with bare brown legs. Careless ignorance and laziness here, fierce hate and vindictiveness there; —these are the extremes of the Negro problem which we met that day, and we scarce knew which we preferred.

Here and there we meet distinct characters quite out of the ordinary. One came out of a piece of newly cleared ground, making a wide detour to avoid the snakes. He was an old, hollow-cheeked man, with a drawn and characterful brown face. He had a sort of self-contained quaintness and rough humor impossible to describe; a certain cynical earnestness that puzzled one. "The niggers were jealous of me over on the other place," he said, "and so me and the old woman begged this piece of woods, and I cleared it up myself. Made nothing for two years, but I reckon I've got a crop now." The cotton looked tall and rich, and we praised it. He curtsied low, and then bowed almost to the ground, with an imperturbable gravity that seemed almost suspicious. Then he continued, "My mule died last week,"—a calamity in this land equal to a devastating fire in town,—"but a white man loaned me another." Then he added, eyeing us, "Oh, I gets along with white folks." We turned the conversation. "Bears? deer?" he answered, "well, I should say there were," and he let fly a string of brave oaths, as he told hunting-tales of the swamp. We left him standing still in the middle of the road looking after us, and yet apparently not noticing us.

The Whistle place, which includes his bit of land, was bought soon after the war by an English syndicate, the "Dixie Cotton and Corn Company." A marvellous deal of style their factor put on, with his servants and coach-and-six; so much so that the concern soon landed in inextricable bankruptcy. Nobody lives in the old house now, but a man comes each winter out of the North and collects his high rents. I know not which are the more touching,—such old empty houses, or the homes of the masters' sons. Sad and bitter tales lie hidden back of those white doors,— tales of poverty, of struggle, of disappointment. A revolution such as that of '63 is a terrible thing; they that rose rich in the morning often slept in paupers' beds. Beggars and vulgar speculators rose to rule over them, and their children went astray. See yonder sad-colored house, with its cabins and fences and glad crops! It is not glad within; last month the prodigal son of the struggling father wrote home from the city for money. Money! Where was it to come from? And so the son rose in the night and killed his baby, and killed his wife, and shot himself dead. And the world passed on.

I remember wheeling around a bend in the road beside a graceful bit of forest and a singing brook. A long low house faced us, with porch and flying pillars, great oaken door, and a broad lawn shining in the evening sun. But the window-panes were gone, the pillars were worm-eaten, and the moss-grown roof was falling in. Half curiously I peered through the unhinged door, and saw where, on the wall across the hall, was written in once gay letters a faded "Welcome."

Quite a contrast to the southwestern part of Dougherty County is the northwest. Soberly timbered in oak and pine, it has none of that half-tropical luxuriance of the southwest. Then, too, there are fewer signs of a romantic past, and more of systematic modern land-grabbing and money-getting. White people are more in evidence here, and farmer and hired labor replace to some extent the absentee landlord and rack-rented tenant. The crops have neither the luxuriance of the richer land nor the signs of neglect so often seen, and there were fences and meadows here and there. Most of this land was poor, and beneath the notice of the slave-baron, before the war. Since then his poor relations and foreign immigrants have seized it. The returns of the farmer are too small to allow much for wages, and yet he will not sell off small farms. There is the Negro Sanford; he has worked fourteen years as overseer on the Ladson place, and "paid out enough for fertilizers to have bought a farm," but the owner will not sell off a few acres.

Two children—a boy and a girl—are hoeing sturdily in the fields on the farm where Corliss works. He is smooth-faced and brown, and is fencing up his pigs. He used to run a successful cotton-gin, but the Cotton Seed Oil Trust has forced the price of ginning so low that he says it hardly pays him. He points out a stately old house over the way as the home of "Pa Willis." We eagerly ride over, for "Pa Willis" was the tall and powerful black Moses who led the Negroes for a generation, and led them well. He was a Baptist preacher, and when he died, two thousand black people followed him to the grave; and now they preach

his funeral sermon each year. His widow lives here,—
a weazened, sharp-featured little woman, who curtsied quaintly as we greeted her. Further on lives Jack
Delson, the most prosperous Negro farmer in the
county. It is a joy to meet him,—a great broad-shouldered, handsome black man, intelligent and jovial. Six
hundred and fifty acres he owns, and has eleven black
tenants. A neat and tidy home nestled in a flower-gar-
den, and a little store stands beside it.

We pass the Munson place, where a plucky white
widow is renting and struggling; and the eleven hundred acres of the Sennet plantation, with its Negro
overseer. Then the character of the farms begins to
change. Nearly all the lands belong to Russian Jews;
the overseers are white, and the cabins are bare
board-houses scattered here and there. The rents are
high, and day-laborers and "contract" hands abound.
It is a keen, hard struggle for living here, and few
have time to talk. Tired with the long ride, we gladly
drive into Gillonsville. It is a silent cluster of farm-
houses standing on the crossroads, with one of its
stores closed and the other kept by a Negro preacher.
They tell great tales of busy times at Gillonsville before all the railroads came to Albany; now it is chiefly
a memory. Riding down the street, we stop at the
preacher's and seat ourselves before the door. It was
one of those scenes one cannot soon forget:—a wide,
low, little house, whose motherly roof reached over
and sheltered a snug little porch. There we sat, after
the long hot drive, drinking cool water,—the talkative
little storekeeper who is my daily companion; the silent old black woman patching pantaloons and saying
never a word; the ragged picture of helpless misfortune who called in just to see the preacher; and
finally the neat matronly preacher's wife, plump, yellow, and intelligent. "Own land?" said the wife; "well,

only this house." Then she added quietly, "We did buy seven hundred acres across up yonder, and paid for it; but they cheated us out of it. Sells was the owner." "Sells!" echoed the ragged misfortune, who was leaning against the balustrade and listening, "he's a regular cheat. I worked for him thirty-seven days this spring, and he paid me in cardboard checks which were to be cashed at the end of the month. But he never cashed them,—kept putting me off. Then the sheriff came and took my mule and corn and furniture—" "Furniture? But furniture is exempt from seizure by law." "Well, he took it just the same," said the hard-faced man.

VIII

Of the Quest of the Golden Fleece

But the Brute said in his breast, "Till the mills I grind have
    ceased,
The riches shall be dust of dust, dry ashes be the feast!

    "On the strong and cunning few
      Cynic favors I will strew;
I will stuff their maw with overplus until their spirit dies;
    From the patient and the low
      I will take the joys they know;
    They shall hunger after vanities and still an-hungered go.
Madness shall be on the people, ghastly jealousies arise;
Brother's blood shall cry on brother up the dead and empty skies."
                    WILLIAM VAUGHN MOODY.

HAVE you ever seen a cotton-field white with the harvest,—its golden fleece hovering above the black earth
like a silvery cloud edged with dark green, its bold
white signals waving like the foam of billows from
Carolina to Texas across that Black and human Sea? I
have sometimes half suspected that here the winged
ram Chrysomallus left that Fleece after which Jason
and his Argonauts went vaguely wandering into the

shadowy East three thousand years ago; and certainly one might frame a pretty and not far-fetched analogy of witchery and dragon's teeth, and blood and armed men, between the ancient and the modern quest of the Golden Fleece in the Black Sea.

And now the golden fleece is found; not only found, but, in its birthplace, woven. For the hum of the cotton-mills is the newest and most significant thing in the New South to-day. All through the Carolinas and Georgia, away down to Mexico, rise these gaunt red buildings, bare and homely, and yet so busy and noisy withal that they scarce seem to belong to the slow and sleepy land. Perhaps they sprang from dragons' teeth. So the Cotton Kingdom still lives; the world still bows beneath her sceptre. Even the markets that once defied the *parvenu* have crept one by one across the seas, and then slowly and reluctantly, but surely, have started toward the Black Belt.

To be sure, there are those who wag their heads knowingly and tell us that the capital of the Cotton Kingdom has moved from the Black to the White Belt,—that the Negro of to-day raises not more than half of the cotton crop. Such men forget that the cotton crop has doubled, and more than doubled, since the era of slavery, and that, even granting their contention, the Negro is still supreme in a Cotton Kingdom larger than that on which the Confederacy builded its hopes. So the Negro forms to-day one of the chief figures in a great world-industry; and this, for its own sake, and in the light of historic interest, makes the field-hands of the cotton country worth studying.

We seldom study the condition of the Negro to-day honestly and carefully. It is so much easier to assume that we know it all. Or perhaps, having already reached conclusions in our own minds, we are loth to have them disturbed by facts. And yet how little we really know of these millions,—of their daily lives and longings, of their homely joys and sorrows, of their real shortcomings and the meaning of their crimes! All this we can only learn by intimate contact with the masses, and not by wholesale arguments covering millions separate in time and space, and differing widely in training and culture. To-day, then, my reader, let us turn our faces to the Black Belt of Georgia and seek simply to know the condition of the black farm-laborers of one county there.

Here in 1890 lived ten thousand Negroes and two thousand whites. The country is rich, yet the people are poor. The keynote of the Black Belt is debt; not commercial credit, but debt in the sense of continued inability on the part of the mass of the population to make income cover expense. This is the direct heritage of the South from the wasteful economies of the slave *régime;* but it was emphasized and brought to a crisis by the Emancipation of the slaves. In 1860, Dougherty County had six thousand slaves, worth at least two and a half millions of dollars; its farms were estimated at three millions,—making five and a half millions of property, the value of which depended largely on the slave system, and on the speculative demand for land once marvellously rich but already partially devitalized by careless and exhaustive culture. The war then meant a financial crash; in place of the five and a half millions of 1860, there remained in 1870 only farms valued at less than two millions. With this came increased competition in cotton culture from the rich lands of Texas; a steady fall in the normal price of cotton followed, from about fourteen cents a pound in 1860 until it reached four cents in 1898. Such a financial revolution was it that involved the owners of the cotton-belt in debt. And if things went ill with the master, how fared it with the man?

The plantations of Dougherty County in slavery days were not as imposing and aristocratic as those of Virginia. The Big House was smaller and usually one-storied, and sat very near the slave cabins. Sometimes these cabins stretched off on either side like wings; sometimes only on one side, forming a double row, or edging the road that turned into the plantation from the main thoroughfare. The form and disposition of the laborers' cabins throughout the Black Belt is to-day the same as in slavery days. Some live in the self-same cabins, others in cabins rebuilt on the sites of the old. All are sprinkled in little groups over the face of the land, centering about some dilapidated Big House where the head-tenant or agent lives. The general character and arrangement of these dwellings remains on the whole unaltered. There were in the county, outside the corporate town of Albany, about fifteen hundred Negro families in 1898. Out of all these, only a single family occupied a house with seven rooms; only fourteen have five rooms or more. The mass live in one- and two-room homes.

The size and arrangements of a people's homes are no unfair index of their condition. If, then, we inquire more carefully into these Negro homes, we find much that is unsatisfactory. All over the face of the land is the one-room cabin,—now standing in the shadow of the Big House, now staring at the dusty road, now rising dark and sombre amid the green of the cotton-fields. It is nearly always old and bare, built of rough boards, and neither plastered nor ceiled. Light and ventilation are supplied by the single door and by the square hole in the wall with its wooden shutter. There is no glass, porch, or ornamentation without. Within is a fireplace, black and smoky, and usually unsteady with age. A bed or two, a table, a wooden chest, and a few chairs compose the furniture; while a stray show-bill or a newspaper makes up the decorations for the walls. Now and then one may find such a cabin kept scrupulously neat, with merry steaming fireplaces and hospitable door; but the majority are dirty and dilapidated, smelling of eating and sleeping, poorly ventilated, and anything but homes.

Above all, the cabins are crowded. We have come to associate crowding with homes in cities almost exclusively. This is primarily because we have so little accurate knowledge of country life. Here in Dougherty County one may find families of eight and ten occupying one or two rooms, and for every ten rooms of house accommodation for the Negroes there are twenty-five persons. The worst tenement abominations of New York do not have above twenty-two persons for every ten rooms. Of course, one small, close room in a city, without a yard, is in many respects worse than the larger single country room. In other respects it is better; it has glass windows, a decent chimney, and a trustworthy floor. The single great advantage of the Negro peasant is that he may spend most of his life outside his hovel, in the open fields.

There are four chief causes of these wretched homes: First, long custom born of slavery has assigned such homes to Negroes; white laborers would be offered better accommodations, and might, for that and similar reasons, give better work. Secondly, the Negroes, used to such accommodations, do not as a rule demand better; they do not know what better houses mean. Thirdly, the landlords as a class have not yet come to realize that it is a good business investment to raise the standard of living among labor by slow and judicious methods; that a Negro laborer who demands three rooms and fifty cents a day would give more efficient work and leave a larger profit than a discouraged toiler herding his family in one room and working for thirty cents. Lastly, among such conditions of life there are few incentives to make the laborer become a better farmer. If he is ambitious, he moves to town or tries other labor; as a tenant-farmer his outlook is almost hopeless, and following it as a makeshift, he takes the house that is given him without protest.

In such homes, then, these Negro peasants live. The families are both small and large; there are many single tenants,—widows and bachelors, and remnants of broken groups. The system of labor and the size of the houses both tend to the breaking up of family groups: the grown children go away as contract hands or migrate to town, the sister goes into service; and so one finds many families with hosts of babies, and many newly married couples, but comparatively few families with half-grown and grown sons and daughters. The average size of Negro families has undoubtedly decreased since the war, primarily from economic stress. In Russia over a third of the bridegrooms and over half the brides are under twenty; the same was true of the ante-bellum Negroes. To-day, however, very few of the boys and less than a fifth of the Negro girls under twenty are married. The young men marry between the ages of twenty-five and thirty-five; the young women between twenty and thirty. Such postponement is due to the difficulty of earning sufficient to rear and support a family; and it undoubtedly leads, in the country districts, to sexual immorality. The form of this immorality, however, is very seldom that of prostitution, and less frequently that of illegitimacy than one would imagine. Rather, it takes the form of separation and desertion after a family group has been formed. The number of sepa-

rated persons is thirty-five to the thousand,—a very
large number. It would of course be unfair to com-
pare this number with divorce statistics, for many of
these separated women are in reality widowed, were
the truth known, and in other cases the separation is
not permanent. Nevertheless, here lies the seat of
greatest moral danger. There is little or no prostitution among these Negroes, and over three-forths of
the families, as found by house-to-house investigation,
deserve to be classed as decent people with considerable regard for female chastity. To be sure, the
ideas of the mass would not suit New England, and
there are many loose habits and notions. Yet the rate
of illegitimacy is undoubtedly lower than in Austria
or Italy, and the women as a class are modest. The
plague-spot in sexual relations is easy marriage and
easy separation. This is no sudden development, nor
the fruit of Emancipation. It is the plain heritage
from slavery. In those days Sam, with his master's
consent, "took up" with Mary. No ceremony was necessary, and in the busy life of the great plantations of
the Black Belt it was usually dispensed with. If now
the master needed Sam's work in another plantation
or in another part of the same plantation, or if he took
a notion to sell the slave, Sam's married life with
Mary was usually unceremoniously broken, and then
it was clearly to the master's interest to have both of
them take new mates. This widespread custom of
two centuries has not been eradicated in thirty years.
To-day Sam's grandson "takes up" with a woman
without license or ceremony; they live together de-
cently and honestly, and are, to all intents and purposes, man and wife. Sometimes these unions are
never broken until death; but in too many cases family quarrels, a roving spirit, a rival suitor, or perhaps
more frequently the hopeless battle to support a fam-

ily, lead to separation, and a broken household is the result. The Negro church has done much to stop this practice, and now most marriage ceremonies are performed by the pastors. Nevertheless, the evil is still deep seated, and only a general raising of the standard of living will finally cure it.

Looking now at the county black population as a whole, it is fair to characterize it as poor and ignorant. Perhaps ten per cent compose the well-to-do and the best of the laborers, while at least nine per cent are thoroughly lewd and vicious. The rest, over eighty per cent, are poor and ignorant, fairly honest and well meaning, plodding, and to a degree shiftless, with some but not great sexual looseness. Such class lines are by no means fixed; they vary, one might almost say, with the price of cotton. The degree of ignorance cannot easily be expressed. We may say, for instance, that nearly two-thirds of them cannot read or write. This but partially expresses the fact. They are ignorant of the world about them, of modern economic organization, of the function of government, of individual worth and possibilities,—of nearly all those things which slavery in self-defence had to keep them from learning. Much that the white boy imbibes from his earliest social atmosphere forms the puzzling problems of the black boy's mature years. America is not another world for Opportunity to *all* her sons.

It is easy for us to lose ourselves in details in endeavoring to grasp and comprehend the real condition of a mass of human beings. We often forget that each unit in the mass is a throbbing human soul. Ignorant it may be, and poverty stricken, black and curious in limb and ways and thought; and yet it loves and hates, it toils and tires, it laughs and weeps its bitter tears, and looks in vague and awful longing at the grim horizon of its life,—all this, even as you and

I. These black thousands are not in reality lazy; they are improvident and careless; they insist on breaking the monotony of toil with a glimpse at the great town-world on Saturday; they have their loafers and their rascals; but the great mass of them work continuously and faithfully for a return, and under circumstances that would call forth equal voluntary effort from few if any other modern laboring class. Over eighty-eight per cent of them—men, women, and children—are farmers. Indeed, this is almost the only industry. Most of the children get their schooling after the "crops are laid by," and very few there are that stay in school after the spring work has begun. Child-labor is to be found here in some of its worst phases, as fostering ignorance and stunting physical development. With the grown men of the county there is little variety in work: thirteen hundred are farmers, and two hundred are laborers, teamsters, etc., including twenty-four artisans, ten merchants, twenty-one preachers, and four teachers. This narrowness of life reaches its maximum among the women: thirteen hundred and fifty of these are farm laborers, one hundred are servants and washerwomen, leaving sixty-five housewives, eight teachers, and six seamstresses.

Among this people there is no leisure class. We often forget that in the United States over half the youth and adults are not in the world earning incomes, but are making homes, learning of the world, or resting after the heat of the strife. But here ninety-six per cent are toiling; no one with leisure to turn the bare and cheerless cabin into a home, no old folks to sit beside the fire and hand down traditions of the past; little of careless happy childhood and dreaming youth. The dull monotony of daily toil is broken only by the gayety of the thoughtless and the Saturday trip to town. The toil, like all farm toil, is monotonous, and here there are little machinery and few tools to relieve its burdensome drudgery. But with all this, it is work in the pure open air, and this is something in a day when fresh air is scarce.

The land on the whole is still fertile, despite long abuse. For nine or ten months in succession the crops will come if asked: garden vegetables in April, grain in May, melons in June and July, hay in August, sweet potatoes in September, and cotton from then to Christmas. And yet on two-thirds of the land there is but one crop, and that leaves the toilers in debt. Why is this?

Away down the Baysan road, where the broad flat fields are flanked by great oak forests, is a plantation; many thousands of acres it used to run, here and there, and beyond the great wood. Thirteen hundred human beings here obeyed the call of one,—were his in body, and largely in soul. One of them lives there yet,—a short, stocky man, his dull-brown face seamed and drawn, and his tightly curled hair gray-white. The crops? Just tolerable, he said; just tolerable. Getting on? No—he wasn't getting on at all. Smith of Albany "furnishes" him, and his rent is eight hundred pounds of cotton. Can't make anything at that. Why didn't he buy land! Humph! Takes money to buy land. And he turns away. Free! The most piteous thing amid all the black ruin of war-time, amid the broken fortunes of the masters, the blighted hopes of mothers and maidens, and the fall of an empire,—the most piteous thing amid all this was the black freedman who threw down his hoe because the world called him free. What did such a mockery of freedom mean? Not a cent of money, not an inch of land, not a mouthful of victuals,—not even ownership of the rags on his back. Free! On Saturday, once or twice a

month, the old master, before the war, used to dole
out bacon and meal to his Negroes. And after the first
flush of freedom wore off, and his true helplessness
dawned on the freedman, he came back and picked
up his hoe, and old master still doled out his bacon
and meal. The legal form of service was theoretically
far different; in practice, task-work or "cropping" was
substituted for daily toil in gangs; and the slave gradually became a metayer, or tenant on shares, in name,
but a laborer with indeterminate wages in fact.

Still the price of cotton fell, and gradually the landlords deserted their plantations, and the reign of the
merchant began. The merchant of the Black Belt is a
contractor, and part despot. His store, which used
most frequently to stand at the cross-roads and become the centre of a weekly village, has now moved
to town; and thither the Negro tenant follows him.
The merchant keeps everything,—clothes and shoes,
coffee and sugar, pork and meal, canned and dried
goods, wagons and ploughs, seed and fertilizer,—and
what he has not in stock he can give you an order for
at the store across the way. Here, then, comes the tenant, Sam Scott, after he has contracted with some absent landlord's agent for hiring forty acres of land; he
fingers his hat nervously until the merchant finishes
his morning chat with Colonel Saunders, and calls
out, "Well, Sam, what do you want?" Sam wants him
to "furnish" him,—*i.e.*, to advance him food and clothing for the year, and perhaps seed and tools, until his
crop is raised and sold. If Sam seems a favorable subject, he and the merchant go to a lawyer, and Sam ex-
ecutes a chattel mortgage on his mule and wagon in
return for seed and a week's rations. As soon as the
green cotton-leaves appear above the ground, another
mortgage is given on the "crop." Every Saturday, or
at longer intervals, Sam calls upon the merchant for

his "rations"; a family of five usually gets about thirty pounds of fat side-pork and a couple of bushels of cornmeal a month. Besides this, clothing and shoes must be furnished; if Sam or his family is sick, there are orders on the druggist and doctor; if the mule wants shoeing, an order on the blacksmith, etc. If Sam is a hard worker and crops promise well, he is often encouraged to buy more,—sugar, extra clothes, perhaps a buggy. But he is seldom encouraged to save. When cotton rose to ten cents last fall, the shrewd merchants of Dougherty County sold a thousand buggies in one season, mostly to black men.

The security offered for such transactions—a crop and chattel mortgage—may at first seem slight. And, indeed, the merchants tell many a true tale of shiftlessness and cheating; of cotton picked at night, mules disappearing, and tenants absconding. But on the whole the merchant of the Black Belt is the most prosperous man in the section. So skilfully and so closely has he drawn the bonds of the law about the tenant, that the black man has often simply to choose between pauperism and crime; he "waives" all homestead exemptions in his contract; he cannot touch his own mortgaged crop, which the laws put almost in the full control of the land-owner and of the merchant. When the crop is growing the merchant watches it like a hawk; as soon as it is ready for market he takes possession of it, sells it, pays the landowner his rent, subtracts his bill for supplies, and if, as sometimes happens, there is anything left, he hands it over to the black serf for his Christmas celebration.

The direct result of this system is an all-cotton scheme of agriculture and the continued bankruptcy of the tenant. The currency of the Black Belt is cotton. It is a crop always salable for ready money, not usually subject to great yearly fluctuations in price, and one which the Negroes know how to raise. The land-lord therefore demands his rent in cotton, and the merchant will accept mortgages on no other crop. There is no use asking the black tenant, then, to di-versify his crops,—he cannot under this system. More-over, the system is bound to bankrupt the tenant. I remember once meeting a little one-mule wagon on the River road. A young black fellow sat in it driving listlessly, his elbows on his knees. His dark-faced wife sat beside him, stolid, silent.

"Hello!" cried my driver,—he has a most imprudent way of addressing these people, though they seem used to it,—"what have you got there?"

"Meat and meal," answered the man, stopping. The meat lay uncovered in the bottom of the wagon,—a great thin side of fat pork covered with salt; the meal was in a white bushel bag.

"What did you pay for that meat?"

"Ten cents a pound." It could have been bought for six or seven cents cash.

"And the meal?"

"Two dollars." One dollar and ten cents is the cash price in town. Here was a man paying five dollars for goods which he could have bought for three dollars cash, and raised for one dollar or one dollar and a half.

Yet it is not wholly his fault. The Negro farmer started behind,—started in debt. This was not his choosing, but the crime of this happy-go-lucky nation which goes blundering along with its Reconstruction tragedies, its Spanish war interludes and Philippine matinees, just as though God really were dead. Once in debt, it is no easy matter for a whole race to emerge.

In the year of low-priced cotton, 1898, out of three hundred tenant families one hundred and seventy-five

ended their year's work in debt to the extent of fourteen thousand dollars; fifty cleared nothing, and the
remaining seventy-five made a total profit of sixteen
hundred dollars. The net indebtedness of the black
tenant families of the whole county must have been
at least sixty thousand dollars. In a more prosperous
year the situation is far better; but on the average the
majority of tenants end the year even, or in debt,
which means that they work for board and clothes.
Such an economic organization is radically wrong.
Whose is the blame?

The underlying causes of this situation are complicated but discernible. And one of the chief, outside
the carelessness of the nation in letting the slave start
with nothing, is the widespread opinion among the
merchants and employers of the Black Belt that only
by the slavery of debt can the Negro be kept at work.
Without doubt, some pressure was necessary at the
beginning of the free-labor system to keep the listless
and lazy at work; and even to-day the mass of the
Negro laborers need stricter guardianship than most
Northern laborers. Behind this honest and widespread
opinion dishonesty and cheating of the ignorant laborers have a good chance to take refuge. And to all
this must be added the obvious fact that a slave ancestry and a system of unrequited toil has not im-
proved the efficiency or temper of the mass of black
laborers. Nor is this peculiar to Sambo; it has in history
been just as true of John and Hans, of Jacques and
Pat, of all ground-down peasantries. Such is the situation of the mass of the Negroes in the Black Belt to-
day; and they are thinking about it. Crime, and a
cheap and dangerous socialism, are the inevitable results of this pondering. I see now that ragged black
man sitting on a log, aimlessly whittling a stick. He
muttered to me with the murmur of many ages, when

he said: "White man sit down whole year; Nigger
work day and night and make crop; Nigger hardly
gits bread and meat; white man sittin' down gits all.
It's wrong." And what do the better classes of
Negroes do to improve their situation? One of two
things: if any way possible, they buy land; if not, they
migrate to town. Just as centuries ago it was no
easy thing for the serf to escape into the freedom of
town-life, even so to-day there are hindrances laid in
the way of county laborers. In considerable parts of
all the Gulf States, and especially in Mississippi,
Louisiana, and Arkansas, the Negroes on the plantations in the back-country districts are still held at
forced labor practically without wages. Especially is
this true in districts where the farmers are composed
of the more ignorant class of poor whites, and the
Negroes are beyond the reach of schools and intercourse with their advancing fellows. If such a peon
should run away, the sheriff, elected by white suffrage,
can usually be depended on to catch the fugitive, return him, and ask no questions. If he escape to another
country, a charge of petty thieving, easily true, can be
depended upon to secure his return. Even if some un-
duly officious person insist upon a trial, neighborly
comity will probably make his conviction sure, and
then the labor due the county can easily be bought by
the master. Such a system is impossible in the more
civilized parts of the South, or near the large towns
and cities; but in those vast stretches of land beyond
the telegraph and the newspaper the spirit of the Thirteenth Amendment is sadly broken. This represents
the lowest economic depths of the black American
peasant; and in a study of the rise and condition of the
Negro freeholder we must trace his economic progress
from the modern serfdom.

Even in the better-ordered country districts of the

South the free movement of agricultural laborers is
hindered by the migration-agent laws. The "Associated Press" recently informed the world of the ar-
rest of a young white man in Southern Georgia who
represented the "Atlantic Naval Supplies Company,"
and who "was caught in the act of enticing hands
from the turpentine farm of Mr. John Greer." The
crime for which this young man was arrested is taxed
five hundred dollars for each county in which the employment agent proposes to gather laborers for work
outside the State. Thus the Negroes' ignorance of the
labor-market outside his own vicinity is increased
rather than diminished by the laws of nearly every
Southern State.

Similar to such measures is the unwritten law of the
back districts and small towns of the South, that the
character of all Negroes unknown to the mass of the
community must be vouched for by some white man.
This is really a revival of the old Roman idea of the
patron under whose protection the new-made freedman was put. In many instances this system has been
of great good to the Negro, and very often under the
protection and guidance of the former master's family, or other white friends, the freedman progressed in
wealth and morality. But the same system has in
other cases resulted in the refusal of whole communities to recognize the right of a Negro to change his
habitation and to be master of his own fortunes. A
black stranger in Baker County, Georgia, for instance,
is liable to be stopped anywhere on the public highway and made to state his business to the satisfaction
of any white interrogator. If he fails to give a suitable
answer, or seems too independent or "sassy," he may
be arrested or summarily driven away.

Thus it is that in the country districts of the South,
by written or unwritten law, peonage, hindrances to

the migration of labor, and a system of white patronage exists over large areas. Besides this, the chance
for lawless oppression and illegal exactions is vastly
greater in the country than in the city, and nearly all
the more serious race disturbances of the last decade
have arisen from disputes in the county between master and man,—as, for instance, the Sam Hose affair. As
a result of such a situation, there arose, first, the Black
Belt; and, second, the Migration to Town. The Black
Belt was not, as many assumed, a movement toward
fields of labor under more genial climatic conditions;
it was primarily a huddling for self-protection,—a
massing of the black population for mutual defence in
order to secure the peace and tranquillity necessary
to economic advance. This movement took place between Emancipation and 1880, and only partially accomplished the desired results. The rush to town
since 1880 is the counter-movement of men disappointed in the economic opportunities of the Black
Belt.

In Dougherty County, Georgia, one can see easily
the results of this experiment in huddling for protection. Only ten per cent of the adult population was
born in the county, and yet the blacks outnumber the
whites four or five to one. There is undoubtedly a security to the blacks in their very numbers,—a personal freedom from arbitrary treatment, which makes
hundreds of laborers cling to Dougherty in spite of
low wages and economic distress. But a change is
coming, and slowly but surely even here the agricultural laborers are drifting to town and leaving the
broad acres behind. Why is this? Why do not the
Negroes become land-owners, and build up the black
landed peasantry, which has for a generation and
more been the dream of philanthropist and states-
man?

To the car-window sociologist, to the man who seeks to understand and know the South by devoting the few leisure hours of a holiday trip to unravelling the snarl of centuries,—to such men very often the whole trouble with the black field-hand may be summed up by Aunt Ophelia's word, "Shiftless!" They have noted repeatedly scenes like one I saw last summer. We were riding along the highroad to town at the close of a long hot day. A couple of young black fellows passed us in a muleteam, with several bushels of loose corn in the ear. One was driving, listlessly bent forward, his elbows on his knees,—a happy-go-lucky, careless picture of irresponsibility. The other was fast asleep in the bottom of the wagon. As we passed we noticed an ear of corn fall from the wagon. They never saw it,—not they. A rod farther on we noted another ear on the ground; and between that creeping mule and town we counted twenty-six ears of corn. Shiftless? Yes, the personification of shiftlessness. And yet follow those boys: they are not lazy; to-morrow morning they'll be up with the sun; they work hard when they do work, and they work willingly. They have no sordid, selfish, money-getting ways, but rather a fine disdain for mere cash. They'll loaf before your face and work behind your back with good-natured honesty. They'll steal a watermelon, and hand you back your lost purse intact. Their great defect as laborers lies in their lack of incentive beyond the mere pleasure of physical exertion. They are careless because they have not found that it pays to be careful; they are improvident because the improvident ones of their acquaintance get on about as well as the provident. Above all, they cannot see why they should take unusual pains to make the white man's land better, or to fatten his mule, or save his corn. On the other hand, the white land-owner argues

that any attempt to improve these laborers by increased responsibility, or higher wages, or better
homes, or land of their own, would be sure to result
in failure. He shows his Northern visitor the scarred
and wretched land; the ruined mansions, the worn-
out soil and mortgaged acres, and says, This is Negro
freedom!

Now it happens that both master and man have
just enough argument on their respective sides to
make it difficult for them to understand each other.
The Negro dimly personifies in the white man all his
ills and misfortunes; if he is poor, it is because the
white man seizes the fruit of his toil; if he is ignorant,
it is because the white man gives him neither time
nor facilities to learn; and, indeed, if any misfortune
happens to him, it is because of some hidden machinations of "white folks." On the other hand, the masters and the masters' sons have never been able to see
why the Negro, instead of settling down to be day-laborers for bread and clothes, are infected with a silly
desire to rise in the world, and why they are sulky,
dissatisfied, and careless, where their fathers were
happy and dumb and faithful. "Why, you niggers
have an easier time than I do," said a puzzled Albany
merchant to his black customer. "Yes," he replied,
"and so does yo' hogs."

Taking, then, the dissatisfied and shiftless field-
hand as a starting-point, let us inquire how the black
thousands of Dougherty have struggled from him up
toward their ideal, and what that ideal is. All social
struggle is evidenced by the rise, first of economic,
then of social classes, among a homogeneous population. To-day the following economic classes are
plainly differentiated among these Negroes.

A "submerged tenth" of croppers, with a few paupers; forty per cent who are metayers and thirty-nine

per cent of semi-metayers and wage-laborers. There are left five per cent of money-renters and six per cent of freeholders,—the "Upper Ten" of the land. The croppers are entirely without capital, even in the limited sense of food or money to keep them from seed-time to harvest. All they furnish is their labor; the land-owner furnishes land, stock, tools, seed, and house; and at the end of the year the laborer gets from a third to a half of the crop. Out of his share, however, comes pay and interest for food and clothing advanced him during the year. Thus we have a laborer without capital and without wages, and an employer whose capital is largely his employees' wages. It is an unsatisfactory arrangement, both for hirer and hired, and is usually in vogue on poor land with hard-pressed owners.

Above the croppers come the great mass of the black population who work the land on their own responsibility, paying rent in cotton and supported by the crop-mortgage system. After the war this system was attractive to the freedmen on account of its larger freedom and its possibility for making a surplus. But with the carrying out of the crop-lien system, the deterioration of the land, and the slavery of debt, the position of the metayers has sunk to a dead level of practically unrewarded toil. Formerly all tenants had some capital, and often considerable; but absentee landlordism, rising rack-rent, and falling cotton have stripped them well-nigh of all, and probably not over half of them to-day own their mules. The change from cropper to tenant was accomplished by fixing the rent. If, now, the rent fixed was reasonable, this was an incentive to the tenant to strive. On the other hand, if the rent was too high, or if the land deteriorated, the result was to discourage and check the efforts of the black peasantry. There is no doubt that the latter case is true; that in Dougherty County every economic advantage of the price of cotton in market and of the strivings of the tenant has been taken advantage of by the landlords and merchants, and swallowed up in rent and interest. If cotton rose in price, the rent rose even higher; if cotton fell, the rent remained or followed reluctantly. If the tenant worked hard and raised a large crop, his rent was raised the next year; if that year the crop failed, his corn was confiscated and his mule sold for debt. There were, of course, exceptions to this,—cases of personal kindness and forbearance; but in the vast majority of cases the rule was to extract the uttermost farthing from the mass of the black farm laborers.

The average metayer pays from twenty to thirty per cent of his crop in rent. The result of such rack-rent can only be evil,—abuse and neglect of the soil, deterioration in the character of the laborers, and a widespread sense of injustice. "Wherever the country is poor," cried Arthur Young, "it is in the hands of metayers," and "their condition is more wretched than that of day-laborers." He was talking of Italy a century ago; but he might have been talking of Dougherty County to-day. And especially is that true to-day which he declares was true in France before the Revolution: "The metayers are considered as little better than menial servants, removable at pleasure, and obliged to conform in all things to the will of the landlords." On this low plane half the black population of Dougherty County—perhaps more than half the black millions of this land—are to-day struggling.

A degree above these we may place those laborers who receive money wages for their work. Some receive a house with perhaps a garden-spot; then supplies of food and clothing are advanced, and certain fixed wages are given at the end of the year, varying from thirty to sixty dollars, out of which the supplies must be paid for, with interest. About eighteen per cent of the population belong to this class of semi-metayers, while twenty-two per cent are laborers paid by the month or year, and are either "furnished" by their own savings or perhaps more usually by some merchant who takes his chances of payment. Such laborers receive from thirty-five to fifty cents a day during the working season. They are usually young unmarried persons, some being women; and when they marry they sink to the class of metayers, or, more seldom, become renters.

The renters for fixed money rentals are the first of the emerging classes, and form five per cent of the families. The sole advantage of this small class is their freedom to choose their crops, and the increased responsibility. which comes through having money transactions. While some of the renters differ little in condition from the metayers, yet on the whole they are more intelligent and responsible persons, and are the ones who eventually become land-owners. Their better character and greater shrewdness enable them to gain, perhaps to demand, better terms in rents; rented farms, varying from forty to a hundred acres, bear an average rental of about fifty-four dollars a year. The men who conduct such farms do not long remain renters; either they sink to metayers, or with a successful series of harvests rise to be land-owners.

In 1870 the tax-books of Dougherty report no Negroes as landholders. If there were any such at that time,—and there may have been a few,—their land was probably held in the name of some white patron, —a method not uncommon during slavery. In 1875 ownership of land had begun with seven hundred and fifty acres; ten years later this had increased to over sixty-five hundred acres, to nine thousand acres in

1890 and ten thousand in 1900. The total assessed
property has in this same period risen from eighty
thousand dollars in 1875 to two hundred and forty
thousand dollars in 1900.

Two circumstances complicate this development
and make it in some respects difficult to be sure of the
real tendencies; they are the panic of 1893, and the
low price of cotton in 1898. Besides this, the system of
assessing property in the country districts of Georgia
is somewhat antiquated and of uncertain statistical
value; there are no assessors, and each man makes a
sworn return to a tax-receiver. Thus public opinion
plays a large part, and the returns vary strangely from
year to year. Certainly these figures show the small
amount of accumulated capital among the Negroes,
and the consequent large dependence of their property on temporary prosperity. They have little to tide
over a few years of economic depression, and are at
the mercy of the cotton-market far more than the
whites. And thus the land-owners, despite their marvellous efforts, are really a transient class, continually
being depleted by those who fall back into the class
of renters or metayers, and augmented by newcomers
from the masses. Of one hundred land-owners in 1898,
half had bought their land since 1893, a fourth between 1890 and 1893, a fifth between 1884 and 1890,
and the rest between 1870 and 1884. In all, one hundred and eighty-five Negroes have owned land in this
county since 1875.

If all the black land-owners who had ever held land
here had kept it or left it in the hands of black men,
the Negroes would have owned nearer thirty thousand
acres than the fifteen thousand they now hold. And yet
these fifteen thousand acres are a creditable showing,
—a proof of no little weight of the worth and ability of
the Negro people. If they had been given an economic

start at Emancipation, if they had been in an enlightened and rich community which really desired their best good, then we might perhaps call such a result small or even insignificant. But for a few thousand poor ignorant field-hands, in the face of poverty, a falling market, and social stress, to save and capitalize two hundred thousand dollars in a generation has meant a tremendous effort. The rise of a nation, the pressing forward of a social class, means a bitter struggle, a hard and soul-sickening battle with the world such as few of the more favored classes know or appreciate.

Out of the hard economic conditions of this portion of the Black Belt, only six per cent of the population have succeeded in emerging into peasant proprietorship; and these are not all firmly fixed, but grow and shrink in number with the wavering of the cotton-market. Fully ninety-four per cent have struggled for land and failed, and half of them sit in hopeless serfdom. For these there is one other avenue of escape toward which they have turned in increasing numbers, namely, migration to town. A glance at the distribution of land among the black owners curiously reveals this fact. In 1898 the holdings were as follows: Under forty acres, forty-nine families; forty to two hundred and fifty acres, seventeen families; two hundred and fifty to one thousand acres, thirteen families; one thousand or more acres, two families. Now in 1890 there were forty-four holdings, but only nine of these were under forty acres. The great increase of holdings, then, has come in the buying of small homesteads near town, where their owners really share in the town life; this is a part of the rush to town. And for every land-owner who has thus hurried away from the narrow and hard conditions of country life, how many field-hands, how many tenants, how many ruined renters, have joined that long procession? Is it not strange compensation? The sin of the country districts is visited on the town, and the social sores of city life to-day may, here in Dougherty County, and perhaps in many places near and far, look for their final healing without the city walls.

IX

Of the Sons of Master and Man

Life treads on life, and heart on heart;
We press too close in church and mart
To keep a dream or grave apart.
MRS. BROWNING.

THE world-old phenomenon of the contact of diverse races of men is to have new exemplification during the new century. Indeed, the characteristic of our age is the contact of European civilization with the world's undeveloped peoples. Whatever we may say of the results of such contact in the past, it certainly forms a chapter in human action not pleasant to look back upon. War, murder, slavery, extermination, and debauchery,—this has again and again been the result of carrying civilization and the blessed gospel to the isles of the sea and the heathen without the law. Nor does it altogether satisfy the conscience of the modern world to be told complacently that all this has been right and proper, the fated triumph of strength over weakness, of righteousness over evil, of superiors over inferiors. It would certainly be soothing if one could readily believe all this; and yet there are too many ugly facts for everything to be thus easily explained away. We feel and know that there are many delicate differences in race psychology, numberless changes that our crude social measurements are not yet able to follow minutely, which explain much of history and social development. At the same time, too, we know that these considerations have never adequately explained or excused the triumph of brute force and cunning over weakness and innocence.

It is, then, the strife of all honorable men of the twentieth century to see that in the future competition of races the survival of the fittest shall mean the triumph of the good, the beautiful, and the true; that we may be able to preserve for future civilization all that is really fine and noble and strong, and not continue to put a premium on greed and impudence and cruelty. To bring this hope to fruition, we are compelled daily to turn more and more to a conscientious study of the phenomena of race-contact,—to a study frank and fair, and not falsified and colored by our wishes or our fears. And we have in the South as fine a field for such a study as the world affords,—a field, to be sure, which the average American scientist deems somewhat beneath his dignity, and which the average man who is not a scientist knows all about, but nevertheless a line of study which by reason of the enormous race complications with which God seems about to punish this nation must increasingly claim our sober attention, study, and thought, we must ask, what are the actual relations of whites and blacks in the South? and we must be answered, not by apology or fault-finding, but by a plain, unvarnished tale.

In the civilized life of to-day the contact of men and their relations to each other fall in a few main lines of action and communication: there is, first, the physical proximity of home and dwelling-places, the way in which neighborhoods group themselves, and the contiguity of neighborhoods. Secondly, and in our age chiefest, there are the economic relations,—the methods by which individuals coöperate for earning a living, for the mutual satisfaction of wants, for the production of wealth. Next, there are the political relations, the coöperation in social control, in group government, in laying and paying the burden of taxation. In the fourth place there are the less tangible but highly important forms of intellectual contact and commerce, the interchange of ideas through conversation and conference, through periodicals and libraries; and, above all, the gradual formation for each community of that curious *tertium quid* which we call public opinion. Closely allied with this come the various forms of social contact in everyday life, in travel, in theatres, in house gatherings, in marrying and giving in marriage. Finally, there are the varying forms of religious enterprise, of moral teaching and benevolent endeavor. These are the principle ways in which men living in the same communities are brought into contact with each other. It is my present task, therefore, to indicate, from my point of view, how the black race in the South meet and mingle with the whites in these matters of everyday life.

First, as to physical dwelling. It is usually possible to draw in nearly every Southern community a physical color-line on the map, on the one side of which whites dwell and on the other Negroes. The winding and intricacy of the geographical color-line varies, of course, in different communities. I know some towns where a straight line drawn through the middle of the main street separates nine-tenths of the whites from nine-tenths of the blacks. In other towns the older settlement of whites has been encircled by a broad band of blacks; in still other cases little settlements or nuclei of blacks have sprung up amid surrounding whites. Usually in cities each street has its distinctive color, and only now and then do the colors meet in close proximity. Even in the country something of this segregation is manifest in the smaller areas, and of course in the larger phenomena of the Black Belt.

All this segregation by color is largely independent of that natural clustering by social grades common to all communities. A Negro slum may be in dangerous proximity to a white residence quarter, while it is quite common to find a white slum planted in the heart of a respectable Negro district. One thing, however, seldom occurs: the best of the whites and the best of the Negroes almost never live in anything like close proximity. It thus happens that in nearly every Southern town and city, both whites and blacks see commonly the worst of each other. This is a vast change from the situation in the past, when, through the close contact of master and house-servant in the patriarchal big house, one found the best of both races in close contact and sympathy, while at the same time the squalor and dull round of toil among the field-hands was removed from the sight and hearing of the family. One can easily see how a person who saw slavery thus from his father's parlors, and sees freedom on the streets of a great city, fails to grasp or comprehend the whole of the new picture. On the other hand, the settled belief of the mass of the Negroes that the Southern white people do not have the black man's best interests at heart has been intensified in later years by this continual daily contact of the better class of blacks with the worst representatives of the white race.

Coming now to the economic relations of the races, we are on ground made familiar by study, much discussion, and no little philanthropic effort. And yet with all this there are many essential elements in the coöperation of Negroes and whites for work and wealth that are too readily overlooked or not thoroughly understood. The average American can easily conceive of a rich land awaiting development and filled with black laborers. To him the Southern problem is simply that of making efficient workingmen out of this material, by giving them the requisite technical skill and the help of invested capital. The problem, however is by no means as simple as this, from the obvious fact that these workingmen have been trained for centuries as slaves. They exhibit, therefore, all the advantages and defects of such training; they are willing and good-natured, but not self-reliant, provident, or careful. If now the economic development of the South is to be pushed to the verge of exploitation, as seems probable, then we have a mass of workingmen thrown into relentless competition with the workingmen of the world, but handicapped by a training the very opposite to that of the modern self-reliant democratic laborer. What the black laborer needs is careful personal guidance, group leadership of men with hearts in their bosoms, to train them to foresight, carefulness, and honesty. Nor does it require any fine-spun theories of racial differences to prove the necessity of such group training after the brains of the race have been knocked out by two hundred and fifty years of assiduous education in submission, carelessness, and stealing. After Emancipation, it was the plain duty of some one to assume this group leadership and training of the Negro laborer. I will not stop here to inquire whose duty it was—whether that of the white ex-master who had profited by unpaid toil, or the Northern philanthropist whose persistence brought on the crisis, or the National Government whose edict freed the bondmen; I will not stop to ask whose duty it was, but I insist it was the duty of some one to see that these workingmen were not left alone and unguided, without capital, without land, without skill, without economic organization, without even the bald protection of law, order, and decency,—left in a great land, not to settle down to slow and careful internal development, but destined to be thrown almost immediately into relentless and sharp competition with the best of modern workingmen under an economic system where every participant is fighting for himself, and too often utterly regardless of the rights or welfare of his neighbor.

For we must never forget that the economic system of the South to-day which has succeeded the old regime is not the same system as that of the old industrial North, of England, or of France, with their trade-unions, their restrictive laws, their written and unwritten commercial customs, and their long experience. It is, rather, a copy of that England of the early nineteenth century, before the factory acts,—the England that wrung pity from thinkers and fired the wrath of Carlyle. The rod of empire that passed from the hands of Southern gentlemen in 1865, partly by force, partly by their own petulance, has never returned to them. Rather it has passed to those men who have come to take charge of the industrial exploitation of the New South,—the sons of poor whites fired with a new thirst for wealth and power, thrifty and avaricious Yankees, and unscrupulous immigrants. Into the hands of these men the Southern laborers, white and black, have fallen; and this to their sorrow. For the laborers as such, there is in these new captains of industry neither love nor hate, neither sympathy nor romance; it is a cold question of dollars and dividends. Under such a system all labor is bound to suffer. Even the white laborers are not yet intelligent, thrifty, and well trained enough to maintain themselves against the powerful inroads of organized capital. The results among them, even, are long hours of toil, low wages, child labor, and lack of protection against usury and cheating. But among the black laborers all this is aggravated, first, by a race prejudice which varies from a doubt and distrust among the best element of whites to a frenzied hatred among the worst; and, secondly, it is aggravated, as I have said before, by the wretched economic heritage of the freedmen from slavery. With this training it is difficult for the freedman to learn to grasp the opportunities already opened to him, and the new opportunities are seldom given him, but go by favor to the whites.

Left by the best elements of the South with little protection or oversight, he has been made in law and custom the victim of the worst and most unscrupulous men in each community. The crop-lien system which is depopulating the fields of the South is not simply the result of shiftlessness on the part of Negroes, but is also the result of cunningly devised laws as to mortgages, liens, and misdemeanors, which can be made by conscienceless men to entrap and snare the unwary until escape is impossible, further toil a farce, and protest a crime. I have seen, in the Black Belt of Georgia, an ignorant, honest Negro buy and pay for a farm in installments three separate times, and then in the face of law and decency the enterprising Ameri-

can who sold it to him pocketed the money and deed
and left the black man landless, to labor on his own
land at thirty cents a day. I have seen a black farmer
fall in debt to a white storekeeper, and that storekeeper go to his farm and strip it of every single
marketable article,—mules, ploughs, stored crops,
tools, furniture, bedding, clocks, looking-glass,—and
all this without a sheriff or officer, in the face of the
law for homestead exemptions, and without rendering
to a single responsible person any account or reckoning. And such proceedings can happen, and will happen, in any community where a class of ignorant toilers are placed by custom and race-prejudice beyond
the pale of sympathy and race-brotherhood. So long
as the best elements of a community do not feel in
duty bound to protect and train and care for the
weaker members of their group, they leave them to
be preyed upon by these swindlers and rascals.

This unfortunate economic situation does not mean
the hindrance of all advance in the black South, or
the absence of a class of black landlords and mechanics who, in spite of disadvantages, are accumulating
property and making good citizens. But it does mean
that this class is not nearly so large as a fairer economic system might easily make it, that those who
survive in the competition are handicapped so as to
accomplish much less than they deserve to, and that,
above all, the *personnel* of the successful class is left
to chance and accident, and not to any intelligent
culling or reasonable methods of selection. As a remedy for this, there is but one possible procedure.
We must accept some of the race prejudice in the
South as a fact,—deplorable in its intensity, unfortunate in results, and dangerous for the future, but nevertheless a hard fact which only time can efface. We
cannot hope, then, in this generation, or for several

generations, that the mass of the whites can be brought to assume that close sympathetic and self-sacrificing leadership of the blacks which their present situation so eloquently demands. Such leadership, such social teaching and example, must come from the blacks themselves. For some time men doubted as to whether the Negro could develop such leaders; but to-day no one seriously disputes the capability of individual Negroes to assimilate the culture and common sense of modern civilization, and to pass it on, to some extent at least, to their fellows. If this is true, then here is the path out of the economic situation, and here is the imperative demand for trained Negro leaders of character and intelligence,—men of skill, men of light and leading, college-bred men, black captains of industry, and missionaries of culture; men who thoroughly comprehend and know modern civilization, and can take hold of Negro communities and raise and train them by force of precept and example, deep sympathy, and the inspiration of common blood and ideals. But if such men are to be effective they must have some power,—they must be backed by the best public opinion of these communities, and able to wield for their objects and aims such weapons as the experience of the world has taught are indispensable to human progress.

Of such weapons the greatest, perhaps, in the modern world is the power of the ballot; and this brings me to a consideration of the third form of contact between whites and blacks in the South,—political activity.

In the attitude of the American mind toward Negro suffrage can be traced with unusual accuracy the prevalent conceptions of government. In the fifties we were near enough the echoes of the French Revolution to believe pretty thoroughly in universal suffrage.

We argued, as we thought then rather logically, that
no social class was so good, so true, and so disinter-
ested as to be trusted wholly with the political destiny of its neighbors; that in every state the best arbi-
ters of their own welfare are the persons directly
affected; consequently that it is only by arming every
hand with a ballot,—with the right to have a voice in
the policy of the state,—that the greatest good to the
greatest number could be attained. To be sure, there
were objections to these arguments, but we thought
we had answered them tersely and convincingly; if
some one complained of the ignorance of voters, we
answered, "Educate them." If another complained of
their venality, we replied, "Disfranchise them or put
them in jail." And, finally, to the men who feared demagogues and the natural perversity of some human
beings we insisted that time and bitter experience
would teach the most hardheaded. It was at this time
that the question of Negro suffrage in the South was
raised. Here was a defenceless people suddenly made
free. How were they to be protected from those who
did not believe in their freedom and were determined
to thwart it? Not by force, said the North; not by government guardianship, said the South; then by the
ballot, the sole and legitimate defence of a free people, said the Common Sense of the Nation. No one
thought, at the time, that the ex-slaves could use the
ballot intelligently or very effectively; but they did
think that the possession of so great power by a great
class in the nation would compel their fellows to educate this class to its intelligent use.

Meantime, new thoughts came to the nation: the
inevitable period of moral retrogression and political
trickery that ever follows in the wake of war overtook
us. So flagrant became the political scandals that reputable men began to leave politics alone, and poli-

tics consequently became disreputable. Men began to pride themselves on having nothing to do with their own government, and to agree tacitly with those who regarded public office as a private perquisite. In this state of mind it became easy to wink at the suppression of the Negro vote in the South, and to advise self-respecting Negroes to leave politics entirely alone. The decent and reputable citizens of the North who neglected their own civic duties grew hilarious over the exaggerated importance with which the Negro regarded the franchise. Thus it easily happened that more and more the better class of Negroes followed the advice from abroad and the pressure from home, and took no further interest in politics, leaving to the careless and the venal of their race the exercise of their rights as voters. The black vote that still remained was not trained and educated, but further debauched by open and unblushing bribery, or force and fraud; until the Negro voter was thoroughly inoculated with the idea that politics was a method of private gain by disreputable means.

And finally, now, to-day, when we are awakening to the fact that the perpetuity of republican institutions on this continent depends on the purification of the ballot, the civic training of voters, and the raising of voting to the plane of a solemn duty which a patriotic citizen neglects to his peril and to the peril of his children's children,—in this day, when we are striving for a renaissance of civic virtue, what are we going to say to the black voter of the South? Are we going to tell him still that politics is a disreputable and useless form of human activity? Are we going to induce the best class of Negroes to take less and less interest in government, and to give up their right to take such an interest, without a protest? I am not saying a word against all legitimate efforts to purge the ballot of ignorance, pauperism, and crime. But few have pretended that the present movement for disfranchisement in the South is for such a purpose; it has been plainly and frankly declared in nearly every case that the object of the disfranchising laws is the elimination of the black man from politics.

Now, is this a minor matter which has no influence on the main question of the industrial and intellectual development of the Negro? Can we establish a mass of black laborers and artisans and landholders in the South who, by law and public opinion, have absolutely no voice in shaping the laws under which they live and work? Can the modern organization of industry, assuming as it does free democratic government and the power and ability of the laboring classes to compel respect for their welfare,—can this system be carried out in the South when half its laboring force is voiceless in the public councils and powerless in its own defence? To-day the black man of the South has almost nothing to say as to how much he shall be taxed, or how those taxes shall be expended; as to who shall execute the laws, and how they shall do it; as to who shall make the laws, and how they shall be made. It is pitiable that frantic efforts must be made at critical times to get law-makers in some States even to listen to the respectful presentation of the black man's side of a current controversy. Daily the Negro is coming more and more to look upon law and justice, not as protecting safeguards, but as sources of humiliation and oppression. The laws are made by men who have little interest in him; they are executed by men who have absolutely no motive for treating the black people with courtesy or consideration; and, finally, the accused law-breaker is tried, not by his peers, but too often by men who would rather punish ten innocent Negroes than let one guilty one escape.

I should be the last one to deny the patent weaknesses and shortcomings of the Negro people; I should be the last to withhold sympathy from the white South in its efforts to solve its intricate social problems. I freely acknowledged that it is possible, and sometimes best, that a partially undeveloped people should be ruled by the best of their stronger and better neighbors for their own good, until such time as they can start and fight the world's battles alone. I have already pointed out how sorely in need of such economic and spiritual guidance the emancipated Negro was, and I am quite willing to admit that if the representatives of the best white Southern public opinion were the ruling and guiding powers in the South to-day the conditions indicated would be fairly well fulfilled. But the point I have insisted upon and now emphasize again, is that the best opinion of the South to-day is not the ruling opinion. That to leave the Negro helpless and without a ballot to-day is to leave him, not to the guidance of the best, but rather to the exploitation and debauchment of the worst; that this is no truer of the South than of the North,— of the North than of Europe: in any land, in any country under modern free competition, to lay any class of weak and despised people, be they white, black, or blue, at the political mercy of their stronger, richer, and more resourceful fellows, is a temptation which human nature seldom has withstood and seldom will withstand.

Moreover, the political status of the Negro in the South is closely connected with the question of Negro crime. There can be no doubt that crime among Negroes has sensibly increased in the last thirty years, and that there has appeared in the slums of great cities a distinct criminal class among the blacks. In explaining this unfortunate development, we must note

two things: (1) that the inevitable result of Emancipation was to increase crime and criminals, and (2)
that the police system of the South was primarily designed to control slaves. As to the first point, we must
not forget that under a strict slave system there can
scarcely be such a thing as crime. But when these
variously constituted human particles are suddenly
thrown broadcast on the sea of life, some swim, some
sink, and some hang suspended, to be forced up or
down by the chance currents of a busy hurrying
world. So great an economic and social revolution as
swept the South in '63 meant a weeding out among
the Negroes of the incompetents and vicious, the beginning of a differentiation of social grades. Now a
rising group of people are not lifted bodily from the
ground like an inert solid mass, but rather stretch upward like a living plant with its roots still clinging in
the mould. The appearance, therefore, of the Negro
criminal was a phenomenon to be awaited; and while
it causes anxiety, it should not occasion surprise.

Here again the hope for the future depended peculiarly on careful and delicate dealing with these criminals. Their offences at first were those of laziness,
carelessness, and impulse, rather than of malignity or
ungoverned viciousness. Such misdemeanors needed
discriminating treatment, firm but reformatory, with
no hint of injustice, and full proof of guilt. For such
dealing with criminals, white or black, the South had
no machinery, no adequate jails or reformatories; its
police system was arranged to deal with blacks alone,
and tacitly assumed that every white man was *ipso
facto* a member of that police. Thus grew up a double
system of justice, which erred on the white side by
undue leniency and the practical immunity of red-
handed criminals, and erred on the black side by
undue severity, injustice, and lack of discrimination.

For, as I have said, the police system of the South was originally designed to keep track of all Negroes, not simply of criminals; and when the Negroes were freed and the whole South was convinced of the impossibility of free Negro labor, the first and almost universal device was to use the courts as a means of reënslaving the blacks. It was not then a question of crime, but rather one of color, that settled a man's conviction on almost any charge. Thus Negroes came to look upon courts as instruments of injustice and oppression, and upon those convicted in them as martyrs and victims.

When, now, the real Negro criminal appeared, and instead of petty stealing and vagrancy we began to have highway robbery, burglary, murder, and rape, there was a curious effect on both sides the color-line: the Negroes refused to believe the evidence of white witnesses or the fairness of white juries, so that the greatest deterrent to crime, the public opinion of one's own social caste, was lost, and the criminal was looked upon as crucified rather than hanged. On the other hand, the whites, used to being careless as to the guilt or innocence of accused Negroes, were swept in moments of passion beyond law, reason, and decency. Such a situation is bound to increase crime, and has increased it. To natural viciousness and vagrancy are being daily added motives of revolt and revenge which stir up all the latent savagery of both races and make peaceful attention to economic development often impossible.

But the chief problem in any community cursed with crime is not the punishment of the criminals, but the preventing of the young from being trained to crime. And here again the peculiar conditions of the South have prevented proper precautions. I have seen twelve-year-old boys working in chains on the public

streets of Atlanta, directly in front of the schools, in
company with old and hardened criminals; and this
indiscriminate mingling of men and women and children makes the chain-gangs perfect schools of crime
and debauchery. The struggle for reformatories,
which has gone on in Virginia, Georgia, and other
States, is the one encouraging sign of the awakening
of some communities to the suicidal results of this
policy.

It is the public schools, however, which can be
made, outside the homes, the greatest means of training decent self-respecting citizens. We have been so
hotly engaged recently in discussing trade-schools
and the higher education that the pitiable plight of
the public-school system in the South has almost
dropped from view. Of every five dollars spent for
public education in the State of Georgia, the white
schools get four dollars and the Negro one dollar; and
even then the white public-school system, save in the
cities, is bad and cries for reform. If this is true of the
whites, what of the blacks? I am becoming more and
more convinced, as I look upon the system of common-school training in the South, that the national
government must soon step in and aid popular education in some way. To-day it has been only by the
most strenuous efforts on the part of the thinking men
of the South that the Negro's share of the school fund
has not been cut down to a pittance in some half-
dozen States; and that movement not only is not
dead, but in many communities is gaining strength.
What in the name of reason does this nation expect of
a people, poorly trained and hard pressed in severe
economic competition, without political rights, and
with ludicrously inadequate common-school facilities?
What can it expect but crime and listlessness, offset
here and there by the dogged struggles of the fortu-

nate and more determined who are themselves buoyed by the hope that in due time the country will come to its senses?

I have thus far sought to make clear the physical, economic, and political relations of the Negroes and whites in the South, as I have conceived them, including, for the reasons set forth, crime and education. But after all that has been said on these more tangible matters of human contact, there still remains a part essential to a proper description of the South which it is difficult to describe or fix in terms easily understood by strangers. It is, in fine, the atmosphere of the land, the thought and feeling, the thousand and one little actions which go to make up life. In any community or nation it is these little things which are most elusive to the grasp and yet most essential to any clear conception of the group life taken as a whole. What is thus true of all communities is peculiarly true of the South, where, outside of written history and outside of printed law, there has been going on for a generation as deep a storm and stress of human souls, as intense a ferment of feeling, as intricate a writhing of spirit, as ever a people experienced. Within and without the sombre veil of color vast social forces have been at work,—efforts for human betterment, movements toward disintegration and despair, tragedies and comedies in social and economic life, and a swaying and lifting and sinking of human hearts which have made this land a land of mingled sorrow and joy, of change and excitement and unrest.

The centre of this spiritual turmoil has ever been the millions of black freedmen and their sons, whose destiny is so fatefully bound up with that of the nation. And yet the casual observer visiting the South sees at first little of this. He notes the growing frequency of dark faces as he rides along,—but otherwise the days slip lazily on, the sun shines, and this little world seems as happy and contented as other worlds he has visited. Indeed, on the question of questions—the Negro problem—he hears so little that there almost seems to be a conspiracy of silence; the morning papers seldom mention it, and then usually in a far-fetched academic way, and indeed almost every one seems to forget and ignore the darker half of the land, until the astonished visitor is inclined to ask if after all there *is* any problem here. But if he lingers long enough there comes the awakening: perhaps in a sudden whirl of passion which leaves him gasping at its bitter intensity; more likely in a gradually dawning sense of things he had not at first noticed. Slowly but surely his eyes begin to catch the shadows of the color-line: here he meets crowds of Negroes and whites; then he is suddenly aware that he cannot discover a single dark face; or again at the close of a day's wandering he may find himself in some strange assembly, where all faces are tinged brown or black, and where he has the vague, uncomfortable feeling of the stranger. He realizes at last that silently, resistlessly, the world about flows by him in two great streams: they ripple on in the same sunshine, they approach and mingle their waters in seeming carelessness,—then they divide and flow wide apart. It is done quietly; no mistakes are made, or if one occurs, the swift arm of the law and of public opinion swings down for a moment, as when the other day a black man and a white woman were arrested for talking together on Whitehall Street in Atlanta.

Now if one notices carefully one will see that between these two worlds, despite much physical contact and daily intermingling, there is almost no community of intellectual life or point of transference where the thoughts and feelings of one race can come into direct contact and sympathy with the thoughts and feelings of the other. Before and directly after the war, when all the best of the Negroes were domestic servants in the best of the white families, there were bonds of intimacy, affection, and sometimes blood relationship, between the races. They lived in the same home, shared in the family life, often attended the same church, and talked and conversed with each other. But the increasing civilization of the Negro since then has naturally meant the development of higher classes: there are increasing numbers of ministers, teachers, physicians, merchants, mechanics, and independent farmers, who by nature and training are the aristocracy and leaders of the blacks. Between them, however, and the best element of the whites, there is little or no intellectual commerce. They go to separate churches, they live in separate sections, they are strictly separated in all public gatherings, they travel separately, and they are beginning to read different papers and books. To most libraries, lectures, concerts, and museums, Negroes are either not admitted at all, or on terms peculiarly galling to the pride of the very classes who might otherwise be attracted. The daily paper chronicles the doings of the black world from afar with no great regard for accuracy; and so on, throughout the category of means for intellectual communication,—schools, conferences, efforts for social betterment, and the like,—it is usually true that the very representatives of the two races, who for mutual benefit and the welfare of the land ought to be in complete understanding and sympathy, are so far strangers that one side thinks all whites are narrow and prejudiced, and the other thinks educated Negroes dangerous and insolent. Moreover, in a land where the tyranny of public opinion and the intolerance of criticism is for obvious historical reasons so strong as in the South, such a situation is extremely difficult to correct. The white man, as well as the Negro, is bound and barred by the color-line, and many a scheme of friendliness and philanthropy, of broad-minded sympathy and generous fellowship between the two has dropped still-born because some busybody has forced the color-question to the front and brought the tremendous force of unwritten law against the innovators.

It is hardly necessary for me to add very much in regard to the social contact between the races. Nothing has come to replace that finer sympathy and love between some masters and house servants which the radical and more uncompromising drawing of the color-line in recent years has caused almost completely to disappear. In a world where it means so much to take a man by the hand and sit beside him, to look frankly into his eyes and feel his heart beating with red blood; in a world where a social cigar or a cup of tea together means more than legislative halls and magazine articles and speeches,—one can imagine the consequences of the almost utter absence of such social amenities between estranged races, whose separation extends even to parks and streetcars.

Here there can be none of that social going down to the people,—the opening of heart and hand of the best to the worst, in generous acknowledgment of a common humanity and a common destiny. On the other hand, in matters of simple almsgiving, where there can be no question of social contact, and in the succor of the aged and sick, the South, as if stirred by a feeling of its unfortunate limitations, is generous to a fault. The black beggar is never turned away without a good deal more than a crust, and a call for help for the unfortunate meets quick response. I remember, one cold winter, in Atlanta, when I refrained from contributing to a public relief fund lest Negroes should be discriminated against, I afterward inquired of a friend: "Were any black people receiving aid?" "Why," said he, "they were *all* black."

And yet this does not touch the kernel of the problem. Human advancement is not a mere question of almsgiving, but rather of sympathy and coöperation among classes who would scorn charity. And here is a land where, in the higher walks of life, in all the higher striving for the good and noble and true, the color-line comes to separate natural friends and co-workers; while at the bottom of the social group, in the saloon, the gambling-hell, and the brothel, that same line wavers and disappears.

I have sought to paint an average picture of real relations between the sons of master and man in the South. I have not glossed over matters for policy's sake, for I fear we have already gone too far in that sort of thing. On the other hand, I have sincerely sought to let no unfair exaggerations creep in. I do not doubt that in some Southern communities conditions are better than those I have indicated; while I am no less certain that in other communities they are far worse.

Nor does the paradox and danger of this situation fail to interest and perplex the best conscience of the South. Deeply religious and intensely democratic as are the mass of the whites, they feel acutely the false position in which the Negro problems place them. Such an essentially honest-hearted and generous people cannot cite the caste-levelling precepts of Christianity, or believe in equality of opportunity for all men, without coming to feel more and more with each generation that the present drawing of the color-line is a flat contradiction to their beliefs and professions. But just as often as they come to this point, the present social condition of the Negro stands as a menace and a portent before even the most open-minded: if there were nothing to charge against the Negro but his blackness or other physical peculiarities, they argue, the problem would be comparatively simple; but what can we say to his ignorance, shiftlessness, poverty, and crime? can a self-respecting group hold anything but the least possible fellowship with such persons and survive? and shall we let a mawkish sentiment sweep away the culture of our fathers or the hope of our children? The argument so put is of great strength, but it is not a whit stronger than the argument of thinking Negroes: granted, they reply, that the condition of our masses is bad; there is certainly on the one hand adequate historical cause for this, and unmistakable evidence that no small number have, in spite of tremendous disadvantages, risen to the level of American civilization. And when, by proscription and prejudice, these same Negroes are classed with and treated like the lowest of their people, simply *because* they are Negroes, such a policy not only discourages thrift and intelligence among black men, but puts a direct premium on the very things you complain of,—inefficiency and crime. Draw lines of crime, of incompetency, of vice, as tightly and uncompromisingly as you will, for these things must be proscribed; but a color-line not only does not accomplish this purpose, but thwarts it.

In the face of two such arguments, the future of the South depends on the ability of the representatives of these opposing views to see and appreciate and sympathize with each other's position,—for the Negro to realize more deeply than he does at present the need of uplifting the masses of his people, for the white people to realize more vividly than they have yet done the deadening and disastrous effect of a color-prejudice that classes Phillis Wheatley and Sam Hose in the same despised class.

It is not enough for the Negroes to declare that color-prejudice is the sole cause of their social condition, nor for the white South to reply that their social condition is the main cause of prejudice. They both act as reciprocal cause and effect, and a change in neither alone will bring the desired effect. Both must change, or neither can improve to any great extent. The Negro cannot stand the present reactionary tendencies and unreasoning drawing of the color-line indefinitely without discouragement and retrogression. And the condition of the Negro is ever the excuse for further discrimination. Only by a union of intelligence and sympathy across the color-line in this critical period of the Republic shall justice and right triumph,

"That mind and soul according well,
May make one music as before,
But vaster."

X

Of the Faith of the Fathers

Dim face of Beauty haunting all the world,
  Fair face of Beauty all too fair to see,
Where the lost stars adown the heavens are hurled,—
    There, there alone for thee
    May white peace be.

Beauty, sad face of Beauty, Mystery, Wonder,
  What are these dreams to foolish babbling men
Who cry with little noises 'neath the thunder
    Of Ages ground to sand,
    To a little sand.

FIONA MACLEOD.

IT was out in the country, far from home, far from
my foster home, on a dark Sunday night. The road
wandered from our rambling log-house up the stony
bed of a creek, past wheat and corn, until we could
hear dimly across the fields a rhythmic cadence of
song,—soft, thrilling, powerful, that swelled and died
sorrowfully in our ears. I was a country school-
teacher then, fresh from the East, and had never seen
a Southern Negro revival. To be sure, we in Berkshire
were not perhaps as stiff and formal as they in Suffolk

of olden time; yet we were very quiet and subdued, and I know not what would have happened those clear Sabbath mornings had some one punctuated the sermon with a wild scream, or interrupted the long prayer with a loud Amen! And so most striking to me, as I approached the village and the little plain church perched aloft, was the air of intense excitement that possessed that mass of black folk. A sort of suppressed terror hung in the air and seemed to seize us, —a pythian madness, a demoniac possession, that lent terrible reality to song and word. The black and massive form of the preacher swayed and quivered as the words crowded to his lips and flew at us in singular eloquence. The people moaned and fluttered, and then the gaunt-cheeked brown woman beside me suddenly leaped straight into the air and shrieked like a lost soul, while round about came wail and groan and outcry, and a scene of human passion such as I had never conceived before.

Those who have not thus witnessed the frenzy of a Negro revival in the untouched backwoods of the South can but dimly realize the religious feeling of the slave; as described, such scenes appear grotesque and funny, but as seen they are awful. Three things characterized this religion of the slave,—the Preacher, the Music, and the Frenzy. The Preacher is the most unique personality developed by the Negro on American soil. A leader, a politician, an orator, a "boss," an intriguer, an idealist,—all these he is, and ever, too, the centre of a group of men, now twenty, now a thousand in number. The combination of a certain adroitness with deep-seated earnestness, of tact with consummate ability, gave him his preëminence, and helps him maintain it. The type, of course, varies according to time and place, from the West Indies in the sixteenth century to New England in the nineteenth, and from the Mississippi bottoms to cities like New Orleans or New York.

The Music of Negro religion is that plaintive rhythmic melody, with its touching minor cadences, which, despite caricature and defilement, still remains the most original and beautiful expression of human life and longing yet born on American soil. Sprung from the African forests, where its counterpart can still be heard, it was adapted, changed, and intensified by the tragic soul-life of the slave, until, under the stress of law and whip, it became the one true expression of a people's sorrow, despair, and hope.

Finally the Frenzy of "Shouting," when the Spirit of the Lord passed by, and, seizing the devotee, made him mad with supernatural joy, was the last essential of Negro religion and the one more devoutly believed in than all the rest. It varied in expression from the silent rapt countenance or the low murmur and moan to the mad abandon of physical fervor,—the stamping, shrieking, and shouting, the rushing to and fro and wild waving of arms, the weeping and laughing, the vision and the trance. All this is nothing new in the world, but old as religion, as Delphi and Endor. And so firm a hold did it have on the Negro, that many generations firmly believed that without this visible manifestation of the God there could be no true communion with the Invisible.

These were the characteristics of Negro religious life as developed up to the time of Emancipation. Since under the peculiar circumstances of the black man's environment they were the one expression of his higher life, they are of deep interest to the student of his development, both socially and psychologically. Numerous are the attractive lines of inquiry that here group themselves. What did slavery mean to the African savage? What was his attitude toward the World and Life? What seemed to him good and evil,—God and Devil? Whither went his longings and strivings, and wherefore were his heart-burnings and disappointments? Answers to such questions can come only from a study of Negro religion as a development, through its gradual changes from the heathenism of the Gold Coast to the institutional Negro church of Chicago.

Moreover, the religious growth of millions of men, even though they be slaves, cannot be without potent influence upon their contemporaries. The Methodists and Baptists of America owe much of their condition to the silent but potent influence of their millions of Negro converts. Especially is this noticeable in the South, where theology and religious philosophy are on this account a long way behind the North, and where the religion of the poor whites is a plain copy of Negro thought and methods. The mass of "gospel" hymns which has swept through American churches and well-nigh ruined our sense of song consists largely of debased imitations of Negro melodies made by ears that caught the jingle but not the music, the body but not the soul, of the Jubilee songs. It is thus clear that the study of Negro religion is not only a vital part of the history of the Negro in America, but an interesting part of American history.

The Negro church of to-day is the social centre of Negro life in the United States, and the most characteristic expression of African character. Take a typical church in a small Virginia town: it is the "First Baptist"—a roomy brick edifice seating five hundred or more persons, tastefully finished in Georgia pine, with a carpet, a small organ, and stained-glass windows. Underneath is a large assembly room with benches. This building is the central club-house of a community of a thousand or more Negroes. Various organi-

zations meet here,—the church proper, the Sunday-
school, two or three insurance societies, women's societies, secret societies, and mass meetings of various
kinds. Entertainments, suppers, and lectures are held
beside the five or six regular weekly religious services.
Considerable sums of money are collected and expended here, employment is found for the idle,
strangers are introduced, news is disseminated and
charity distributed. At the same time this social, intellectual, and economic centre is a religious centre of
great power. Depravity, Sin, Redemption, Heaven,
Hell, and Damnation are preached twice a Sunday
after the crops are laid by; and few indeed of the
community have the hardihood to withstand conversion. Back of this more formal religion, the Church
often stands as a real conserver of morals, a strength-
ener of family life, and the final authority on what is
Good and Right.

Thus one can see in the Negro church to-day, re-
produced in microcosm, all the great world from
which the Negro is cut off by color-prejudice and social condition. In the great city churches the same
tendency is noticeable and in many respects emphasized. A great church like the Bethel of Philadelphia
has over eleven hundred members, an edifice seating
fifteen hundred persons and valued at one hundred
thousand dollars, an annual budget of five thousand
dollars, and a government consisting of a pastor with
several assisting local preachers, an executive and legislative board, financial boards and tax collectors;
general church meetings for making laws; sub-divided
groups led by class leaders, a company of militia, and
twenty-four auxiliary societies. The activity of a
church like this is immense and far-reaching, and the
bishops who preside over these organizations

throughout the land are among the most powerful Negro rulers in the world.

Such churches are really governments of men, and consequently a little investigation reveals the curious fact that, in the South, at least, practically every American Negro is a church member. Some, to be sure, are not regularly enrolled, and a few do not habitually attend services; but, practically, a proscribed people must have a social centre, and that centre for this people is the Negro church. The census of 1890 showed nearly twenty-four thousand Negro churches in the country, with a total enrolled membership of over two and a half millions, or ten actual church members to every twenty-eight persons, and in some Southern States one in every two persons. Besides these there is the large number who, while not enrolled as members, attend and take part in many of the activities of the church. There is an organized Negro church for every sixty black families in the nation, and in some States for every forty families, owning, on an average, a thousand dollars' worth of property each, or nearly twenty-six million dollars in all.

Such, then, is the large development of the Negro church since Emancipation. The question now is, What have been the successive steps of this social history and what are the present tendencies? First, we must realize that no such institution as the Negro church could rear itself without definite historical foundations. These foundations we can find if we remember that the social history of the Negro did not start in America. He was brought from a definite social environment,—the polygamous clan life under the headship of the chief and the potent influence of the priest. His religion was nature-worship, with profound belief in invisible surrounding influences, good

and bad, and his worship was through incantation
and sacrifice. The first rude change in this life was the
slave ship and the West Indian sugar-fields. The plantation organization replaced the clan and tribe, and
the white master replaced the chief with far greater
and more despotic powers. Forced and long-contin-
ued toil became the rule of life, the old ties of blood
relationship and kinship disappeared, and instead of
the family appeared a new polygamy and polyandry,
which, in some cases, almost reached promiscuity. It
was a terrific social revolution, and yet some traces
were retained of the former group life, and the chief
remaining institution was the Priest or Medicine-man.
He early appeared on the plantation and found his
function as the healer of the sick, the interpreter of
the Unknown, the comforter of the sorrowing, the supernatural avenger of wrong, and the one who rudely
but picturesquely expressed the longing, disappointment, and resentment of a stolen and oppressed people. Thus, as bard, physician, judge, and priest,
within the narrow limits allowed by the slave system,
rose the Negro preacher, and under him the first
church was not at first by any means Christian nor
definitely organized; rather it was an adaptation and
mingling of heathen rites among the members of each
plantation, and roughly designated as Voodooism. Association with the masters, missionary effort and motives of expediency gave these rites an early veneer of
Christianity, and after the lapse of many generations
the Negro church became Christian.

Two characteristic things must be noticed in regard
to the church. First, it became almost entirely Baptist
and Methodist in faith; secondly, as a social institution it antedated by many decades the monogamic
Negro home. From the very circumstances of its beginning, the church was confined to the plantation,

and consisted primarily of a series of disconnected units; although, later on, some freedom of movement was allowed, still this geographical limitation was always important and was one cause of the spread of the decentralized and democratic Baptist faith among the slaves. At the same time, the visible rite of baptism appealed strongly to their mystic temperament. To-day the Baptist Church is still largest in membership among Negroes, and has a million and a half communicants. Next in popularity came the churches organized in connection with the white neighboring churches, chiefly Baptist and Methodist, with a few Episcopalian and others. The Methodists still form the second greatest denomination, with nearly a million members. The faith of these two leading denominations was more suited to the slave church from the prominence they gave to religious feeling and fervor. The Negro membership in other denominations has always been small and relatively unimportant, although the Episcopalians and Presbyterians are gaining among the more intelligent classes to-day, and the Catholic Church is making headway in certain sections. After Emancipation, and still earlier in the North, the Negro churches largely severed such affiliations as they had had with the white churches, either by choice or by compulsion. The Baptist churches became independent, but the Methodists were compelled early to unite for purposes of episcopal government. This gave rise to the great African Methodist Church, the greatest Negro organization in the world, to the Zion Church and the Colored Methodist, and to the black conferences and churches in this and other denominations.

The second fact noted, namely, that the Negro church antedates the Negro home, leads to an explanation of much that is paradoxical in this communistic institution and in the morals of its members. But especially it leads us to regard this institution as peculiarly the expression of the inner ethical life of a people in a sense seldom true elsewhere. Let us turn, then, from the outer physical development of the church to the more important inner ethical life of the people who compose it. The Negro has already been pointed out many times as a religious animal,—a being of that deep emotional nature which turns instinctively toward the supernatural. Endowed with a rich tropical imagination and a keen, delicate appreciation of Nature, the transplanted African lived in a world animate with gods and devils, elves and witches; full of strange influences,—of Good to be implored, of Evil to be propitiated. Slavery, then, was to him the dark triumph of Evil over him. All the hateful powers of the Under-world were striving against him, and a spirit of revolt and revenge filled his heart. He called up all the resources of heathenism to aid, —exorcism and witch-craft, the mysterious Obi worship with its barbarious rites, spells, and blood-sacrifice even, now and then, of human victims. Weird midnight orgies and mystic conjurations were invoked, the witch-woman and the voodoo-priest became the centre of Negro group life, and that vein of vague superstition which characterizes the unlettered Negro even to-day was deepened and strengthened.

In spite, however, of such success as that of the fierce Maroons, the Danish blacks, and others, the spirit of revolt gradually died away under the untiring energy and superior strength of the slave masters. By the middle of the eighteenth century the black slave had sunk, with hushed murmurs, to his place at the bottom of a new economic system, and was unconsciously ripe for a new philosophy of life. Nothing suited his condition then better than the doctrines of passive submission embodied in the newly learned Christianity. Slave masters early realized this, and cheerfully aided religious propaganda within certain bounds. The long system of repression and degradation of the Negro tended to emphasize the elements of his character which made him a valuable chattel: courtesy became humility, moral strength degenerated into submission, and the exquisite native appreciation of the beautiful became an infinite capacity for dumb suffering. The Negro, losing the joy of this world, eagerly seized upon the offered conceptions of the next; the avenging Spirit of the Lord enjoining patience in this world, under sorrow and tribulation until the Great Day when He should lead His dark children home,—this became his comforting dream. His preacher repeated the prophecy, and his bards sang,—

> "Children, we all shall be free
> When the Lord shall appear!"

This deep religious fatalism, painted so beautifully in "Uncle Tom," came soon to breed, as all fatalistic faiths will, the sensualist side by side with the martyr. Under the lax moral life of the plantation, where marriage was a farce, laziness a virtue, and property a theft, a religion of resignation and submission degenerated easily, in less strenuous minds, into a philosophy of indulgence and crime. Many of the worst characteristics of the Negro masses of to-day had their seed in this period of the slave's ethical growth. Here it was that the Home was ruined under the very shadow of the Church, white and black; here habits of shiftlessness took root, and sullen hopelessness replaced hopeful strife.

With the beginning of the abolition movement and the gradual growth of a class of free Negroes came a change. We often neglect the influence of the freed-

man before the war, because of the paucity of his
numbers and the small weight he had in the history
of the nation. But we must not forget that his chief
influence was internal,—was exerted on the black
world; and that there he was the ethical and social
leader. Huddled as he was in a few centres like Philadelphia, New York, and New Orleans, the masses of
the freedmen sank into poverty and listlessness; but
not all of them. The free Negro leader early arose and
his chief characteristic was intense earnestness and
deep feeling on the slavery question. Freedom became to him a real thing and not a dream. His religion became darker and more intense, and into his
ethics crept a note of revenge, into his songs a day of
reckoning close at hand. The "Coming of the Lord"
swept this side of Death, and came to be a thing to
be hoped for in this day. Through fugitive slaves and
irrepressible discussion this desire for freedom seized
the black millions still in bondage, and became their
one ideal of life. The black bards caught new notes,
and sometimes even dared to sing,—

> "O Freedom, O Freedom, O Freedom over me!
> Before I'll be a slave
> I'll be buried in my grave,
> And go home to my Lord
> And be free."

For fifty years Negro religion thus transformed itself and identified itself with the dream of Abolition,
until that which was a radical fad in the white North
and an anarchistic plot in the white South had become
a religion to the black world. Thus, when Emancipation finally came, it seemed to the freedman a literal
Coming of the Lord. His fervid imagination was
stirred as never before, by the tramp of armies, the
blood and dust of battle, and the wail and whirl of
social upheaval. He stood dumb and motionless before the whirlwind: what had he to do with it? Was it

not the Lord's doing, and marvellous in his eyes?
Joyed and bewildered with what came, he stood awaiting new wonders till the inevitable Age of Reaction
swept over the nation and brought the crisis of to-
day.

It is difficult to explain clearly the present critical
stage of Negro religion. First, we must remember that
living as the blacks do in close contact with a great
modern nation, and sharing, although imperfectly, the
soul-life of that nation, they must necessarily be
affected more or less directly by all the religious and
ethical forces that are to-day moving the United
States. These questions and movements are, however,
overshadowed and dwarfed by the (to them) all-im-
portant question of their civil, political, and economic
status. They must perpetually discuss the "Negro
Problem,"—must live, move, and have their being in
it, and interpret all else in its light or darkness. With
this come, too, peculiar problems of their inner life,—
of the status of women, the maintenance of Home,
the training of children, the accumulation of wealth,
and the prevention of crime. All this must mean a
time of intense ethical ferment, of religious heart-
searching and intellectual unrest. From the double
life every American Negro must live, as a Negro and
as an American, as swept on by the current of the nineteenth while yet struggling in the eddies of the fifteenth century,—from this must arise a painful self-
consciousness, an almost morbid sense of personality
and a moral hesitancy which is fatal to self-confi-
dence. The worlds within and without the Veil of
Color are changing, and changing rapidly, but not at
the same rate, not in the same way; and this must
produce a peculiar wrenching of the soul, a peculiar
sense of doubt and bewilderment. Such a double life,
with double thoughts, double duties, and double so-

cial classes, must give rise to double words and double ideals, and tempt the mind to pretence or revolt,
to hypocrisy or radicalism.

In some such doubtful words and phrases can one
perhaps most clearly picture the peculiar ethical paradox that faces the Negro of to-day and is tingeing and
changing his religious life. Feeling that his rights and
his dearest ideals are being trampled upon, that the
public conscience is ever more deaf to his righteous
appeal, and that all the reactionary forces of prejudice, greed, and revenge are daily gaining new
strength and fresh allies, the Negro faces no enviable
dilemma. Conscious of his impotence, and pessimistic,
he often becomes bitter and vindictive; and his religion, instead of a worship, is a complaint and a curse,
a wail rather than a hope, a sneer rather than a faith.
On the other hand, another type of mind, shrewder
and keener and more tortuous too, sees in the very
strength of the anti-Negro movement its patent weaknesses, and with Jesuitic casuistry is deterred by no
ethical considerations in the endeavor to turn this
weakness to the black man's strength. Thus we have
two great and hardly reconcilable streams of thought
and ethical strivings; the danger of the one lies in an-
archy, that of the other in hypocrisy. The one type of
Negro stands almost ready to curse God and die, and
the other is too often found a traitor to right and a
coward before force; the one is wedded to ideals re-
mote, whimsical, perhaps impossible of realization;
the other forgets that life is more than meat and the
body more than raiment. But, after all, is not this simply the writhing of the age translated into black,—the
triumph of the Lie which today, with its false culture,
faces the hideousness of the anarchist assassin?

To-day the two groups of Negroes, the one in the
North, the other in the South, represent these diver-

gent ethical tendencies, the first tending toward radicalism, the other toward hypocritical compromise. It
is no idle regret with which the white South mourns
the loss of the old-time Negro,—the frank, honest, simple old servant who stood for the earlier religious age
of submission and humility. With all his laziness and
lack of many elements of true manhood, he was at
least open-hearted, faithful, and sincere. To-day he is
gone, but who is to blame for his going? Is it not
those very persons who mourn for him? Is it not the
tendency, born of Reconstruction and Reaction, to
found a society on lawlessness and deception, to tam-
per with the moral fibre of a naturally honest and
straightforward people until the whites threaten to
become ungovernable tyrants and the blacks criminals and hypocrites? Deception is the natural defence of the weak against the strong, and the South
used it for many years against its conquerors; to-day
it must be prepared to see its black proletariat turn
that same two-edged weapon against itself. And how
natural this is! The death of Denmark Vesey and Nat
Turner proved long since to the Negro the present
hopelessness of physical defence. Political defence is
becoming less and less available, and economic defence is still only partially effective. But there is a patent defence at hand,—the defence of deception and
flattery, of cajoling and lying. It is the same defence
which peasants of the Middle Age used and which
left its stamp on their character for centuries. To-day
the young Negro of the South who would succeed
cannot be frank and outspoken, honest and self-asser-
tive, but rather he is daily tempted to be silent and
wary, politic and sly; he must flatter and be pleasant,
endure petty insults with a smile, shut his eyes to
wrong; in too many cases he sees positive personal
advantage in deception and lying. His real thoughts,

his real aspirations, must be guarded in whispers; he must not criticise, he must not complain. Patience, humility, and adroitness must, in these growing black youth, replace impulse, manliness, and courage. With this sacrifice there is an economic opening, and perhaps peace and some prosperity. Without this there is riot, migration, or crime. Nor is this situation peculiar to the Southern United States, is it not rather the only method by which undeveloped races have gained the right to share modern culture? The price of culture is a Lie.

On the other hand, in the North the tendency is to emphasize the radicalism of the Negro. Driven from his birthright in the South by a situation at which every fibre of his more outspoken and assertive nature revolts, he finds himself in a land where he can scarcely earn a decent living amid the harsh competition and the color discrimination. At the same time, through schools and periodicals, discussions and lectures, he is intellectually quickened and awakened. The soul, long pent up and dwarfed, suddenly expands in new-found freedom. What wonder that every tendency is to excess,—radical complaint, radical remedies, bitter denunciation or angry silence. Some sink, some rise. The criminal and the sensualist leave the church for the gambling-hell and the brothel, and fill the slums of Chicago and Baltimore; the better classes segregate themselves from the group-life of both white and black, and form an aristocracy, cultured but pessimistic, whose bitter criticism stings while it points out no way of escape. They despise the submission and subserviency of the Southern Negroes, but offer no other means by which a poor and oppressed minority can exist side by side with its masters. Feeling deeply and keenly the tendencies and opportunities of the age in which they live, their souls are bitter at the fate which drops the Veil between; and the very fact that this bitterness is natural and justifiable only serves to intensify it and make it more maddening.

Between the two extreme types of ethical attitude which I have thus sought to make clear wavers the mass of the millions of Negroes, North and South; and their religious life and activity partake of this social conflict within their ranks. Their churches are differentiating,—now into groups of cold, fashionable devotees, in no way distinguishable from similar white groups save in color of skin; now into large social and business institutions catering to the desire for information and amusement of their members, warily avoiding unpleasant questions both within and without the black world, and preaching in effect if not in word: *Dum vivimus, vivamus.*

But back of this still broods silently the deep religious feeling of the real Negro heart, the stirring, unguided might of powerful human souls who have lost the guiding star of the past and seek in the great night a new religious ideal. Some day the Awakening will come, when the pent-up vigor of ten million souls shall sweep irresistibly toward the Goal, out of the Valley of the Shadow of Death, where all that makes life worth living—Liberty, Justice, and Right—is marked "For White People Only."

XI

Of the Passing of the First-Born

O sister, sister, thy first-begotten,
The hands that cling and the feet that follow,
The voice of the child's blood crying yet,
Who hath remembered me? who hath forgotten?
Thou hast forgotten, O summer swallow,
But the world shall end when I forget.

SWINBURNE.

"UNTO you a child is born," sang the bit of yellow paper that fluttered into my room one brown October morning. Then the fear of fatherhood mingled wildly with the joy of creation; I wondered how it looked and how it felt—what were its eyes, and how its hair curled and crumpled itself. And I thought in awe of her,—she who had slept with Death to tear a man-child from underneath her heart, while I was unconsciously wandering. I fled to my wife and child, repeating the while to myself half wonderingly, "Wife and child? Wife and child?"—fled fast and faster than boat and steam-car, and yet must ever impatiently

226

await them; away from the hard-voiced city, away from the flickering sea into my own Berkshire Hills that sit all sadly guarding the gates of Massachusetts.

Up the stairs I ran to the wan mother and whimpering babe, to the sanctuary on whose altar a life at my bidding had offered itself to win a life, and won. What is this tiny formless thing, this newborn wail from an unknown world,—all head and voice? I handle it curiously, and watch perplexed its winking, breathing, and sneezing. I did not love it then; it seemed a ludicrous thing to love; but her I loved, my girl-mother, she whom now I saw unfolding like the glory of the morning—the transfigured woman. Through her I came to love the wee thing, as it grew strong; as its little soul unfolded itself in twitter and cry and half-formed word, and as its eyes caught the gleam and flash of life. How beautiful he was, with his olive-tinted flesh and dark gold ringlets, his eyes of mingled blue and brown, his perfect little limbs, and the soft voluptuous roll which the blood of Africa had moulded into his features! I held him in my arms, after wo had sped far away from our Southern home, —held him, and glanced at the hot red soil of Georgia and the breathless city of a hundred hills, and felt a vague unrest. Why was his hair tinted with gold? An evil omen was golden hair in my life. Why had not the brown of his eyes crushed out and killed the blue?—for brown were his father's eyes, and his father's father's. And thus in the Land of the Color-line I saw, as it fell across my baby, the shadow of the Veil.

Within the Veil was he born, said I; and there within shall he live,—a Negro and a Negro's son. Holding in that little head—ah, bitterly!—the unbowed pride of a hunted race, clinging with that tiny dimpled hand—ah, wearily!—to a hope not hopeless but

unhopeful, and seeing with those bright wondering
eyes that peer into my soul a land whose freedom is
to us a mockery and whose liberty a lie. I saw the
shadow of the Veil as it passed over my baby, I saw
the cold city towering above the blood-red land. I
held my face beside his little cheek, showed him the
star-children and the twinkling lights as they began to
flash, and stilled with an even-song the unvoiced terror of my life.

So sturdy and masterful he grew, so filled with
bubbling life, so tremulous with the unspoken wisdom of a life but eighteen months distant from the
All-life,—we were not far from worshipping this revelation of the divine, my wife and I. Her own life
builded and moulded itself upon the child; he tinged
her every dream and idealized her every effort. No
hands but hers must touch and garnish those little
limbs; no dress or frill must touch them that had not
wearied her fingers; no voice but hers could coax him
off to Dreamland, and she and he together spoke
some soft and unknown tongue and in it held communion. I too mused above his little white bed; saw the
strength of my own arm stretched onward through
the ages through the newer strength of his; saw the
dream of my black fathers stagger a step onward in
the wild phantasm of the world; heard in his baby
voice the voice of the Prophet that was to rise within
the Veil.

And so we dreamed and loved and planned by fall
and winter, and the full flush of the long Southern
spring, till the hot winds rolled from the fetid Gulf,
till the roses shivered and the still stern sun quivered
its awful light over the hills of Atlanta. And then one
night the little feet pattered wearily to the wee white
bed, and the tiny hands trembled; and a warm
flushed face tossed on the pillow, and we knew baby

was sick. Ten days he lay there,—a swift week and three endless days, wasting, wasting away. Cheerily the mother nursed him the first days, and laughed into the little eyes that smiled again. Tenderly then she hovered round him, till the smile fled away and Fear crouched beside the little bed.

Then the day ended not, and night was a dreamless terror, and joy and sleep slipped away. I hear now that Voice at midnight calling me from dull and dreamless trance,—crying, "The Shadow of Death! The Shadow of Death!" Out into the starlight I crept, to rouse the gray physician,—the Shadow of Death, the Shadow of Death. The hours trembled on; the night listened; the ghastly dawn glided like a tired thing across the lamplight. Then we two alone looked upon the child as he turned toward us with great eyes, and stretched his stringlike hands,—the Shadow of Death! And we spoke no word, and turned away.

He died at eventide, when the sun lay like a brooding sorrow above the western hills, veiling its face; when the winds spoke not, and the trees, the great green trees he loved, stood motionless. I saw his breath beat quicker and quicker, pause, and then his little soul leapt like a star that travels in the night and left a world of darkness in its train. The day changed not; the same tall trees peeped in at the windows, the same green grass glinted in the setting sun. Only in the chamber of death writhed the world's most piteous thing—a childless mother.

I shirk not. I long for work. I pant for a life full of striving. I am no coward, to shrink before the rugged rush of the storm, nor even quail before the awful shadow of the Veil. But hearken, O Death! Is not this my life hard enough,—is not that dull land that stretches its sneering web about me cold enough,—is not all the world beyond these four little walls pitiless enough, but that thou must needs enter here,—thou, O Death? About my head the thundering storm beat like a heartless voice, and the crazy forest pulsed with the curses of the weak; but what cared I, within my home beside my wife and baby boy? Wast thou so jealous of one little coign of happiness that thou must needs enter there,—thou, O Death?

A perfect life was his, all joy and love, with tears to make it brighter,—sweet as a summer's day beside the Housatonic. The world loved him; the women kissed his curls, the men looked gravely into his wonderful eyes, and the children hovered and fluttered about him. I can see him now, changing like the sky from sparkling laughter to darkening frowns, and then to wondering thoughtfulness as he watched the world. He knew no color-line, poor dear—and the Veil, though it shadowed him, had not yet darkened half his sun. He loved the white matron, he loved his black nurse; and in his little world walked souls alone, uncolored and unclothed. I—yea, all men—are larger and purer by the infinite breadth of that one little life. She who in simple clearness of vision sees beyond the stars said when he had flown, "He will be happy There; he ever loved beautiful things." And I, far more ignorant, and blind by the web of mine own weaving, sit alone winding words and muttering, "If still he be, and he be There, and there be a There, let him be happy, O Fate!"

Blithe was the morning of his burial, with bird and song and sweet-smelling flowers. The trees whispered to the grass, but the children sat with hushed faces. And yet it seemed a ghostly unreal day,—the wraith of Life. We seemed to rumble down an unknown street behind a little white bundle of posies, with the shadow of a song in our ears. The busy city dinned about us; they did not say much, those pale-faced

hurrying men and women; they did not say much,—
they only glanced and said, "Niggers!"

We could not lay him in the ground there in Georgia, for the earth there is strangely red; so we bore
him away to the northward, with his flowers and his
little folded hands. In vain, in vain!—for where, O
God! beneath thy broad blue sky shall my dark baby
rest in peace,—where Reverence dwells, and Goodness, and a Freedom that is free?

All that day and all that night there sat an awful
gladness in my heart,—nay, blame me not if I see the
world thus darkly through the Veil,—and my soul
whispers ever to me saying, "Not dead, not dead, but
escaped; not bond, but free." No bitter meanness now
shall sicken his baby heart till it die a living death, no
taunt shall madden his happy boyhood. Fool that I
was to think or wish that this little soul should grow
choked and deformed within the Veil! I might have
known that yonder deep unworldly look that ever and
anon floated past his eyes was peering far beyond this
narrow Now. In the poise of his little curl-crowned
head did there not sit all that wild pride of being
which his father had hardly crushed in his own heart?
For what, forsooth, shall a Negro want with pride
amid the studied humiliations of fifty million fellows?
Well sped, my boy, before the world had dubbed
your ambition insolence, had held your ideals unat-
tainable, and taught you to cringe and bow. Better far
this nameless void that stops my life than a sea of sorrow for you.

Idle words; he might have borne his burden more
bravely than we,—aye, and found it lighter too, some
day; for surely, surely this is not the end. Surely there
shall yet dawn some mighty morning to lift the Veil
and set the prisoned free. Not for me,—I shall die in
my bonds,—but for fresh young souls who have not

known the night and waken to the morning; a morning when men ask of the workman, not "Is he white?" but "Can he work?" When men ask artists, not "Are they black?" but "Do they know?" Some morning this may be, long, long years to come. But now there wails, on that dark shore within the Veil, the same deep voice, *Thou shalt forego!* And all have I foregone at that command, and with small complaint,—all save that fair young form that lies so coldly wed with death in the nest I had builded.

If one must have gone, why not I? Why may I not rest me from this restlessness and sleep from this wide waking? Was not the world's alembic, Time, in his young hands, and is not my time waning? Are there so many workers in the vineyard that the fair promise of this little body could lightly be tossed away? The wretched of my race that line the alleys of the nation sit fatherless and unmothered; but Love sat beside his cradle, and in his ear Wisdom waited to speak. Perhaps now he knows the All-love, and needs not to be wise. Sleep, then, child,—sleep till I sleep and waken to a baby voice and the ceaseless patter of little feet —above the Veil.

XII

Of Alexander Crummell

Then from the Dawn it seemed there came, but faint
As from beyond the limit of the world,
Like the last echo born of a great cry,
Sounds, as if some fair city were one voice
Around a king returning from his wars.

TENNYSON.

THIS is the story of a human heart,—the tale of a black boy who many long years ago began to struggle with life that he might know the world and know himself. Three temptations he met on those dark dunes that lay gray and dismal before the wonder-eyes of the child: the temptation of Hate, that stood out against the red dawn; the temptation of Despair, that darkened noonday; and the temptation of Doubt, that ever steals along with twilight. Above all, you must hear of the vales he crossed,—the Valley of Humiliation and the Valley of the Shadow of Death.

233

I saw Alexander Crummell first at a Wilberforce commencement season, amid its bustle and crush. Tall, frail, and black he stood, with simple dignity and an unmistakable air of good breeding. I talked with him apart, where the storming of the lusty young orators could not harm us. I spoke to him politely, then curiously, then eagerly, as I began to feel the fineness of his character,—his calm courtesy, the sweetness of his strength, and his fair blending of the hope and truth of life. Instinctively I bowed before this man, as one bows before the prophets of the world. Some seer he seemed, that came not from the crimson Past or the gray To-come, but from the pulsing Now,—that mocking world which seemed to me at once so light and dark, so splendid and sordid. Fourscore years had he wandered in this same world of mine, within the Veil.

He was born with the Missouri Compromise and lay a-dying amid the echoes of Manila and El Caney: stirring times for living, times dark to look back upon, darker to look forward to. The black-faced lad that paused over his mud and marbles seventy years ago saw puzzling vistas as he looked down the world. The slave-ship still groaned across the Atlantic, faint cries burdened the Southern breeze, and the great black father whispered mad tales of cruelty into those young ears. From the low doorway the mother silently watched her boy at play, and at nightfall sought him eagerly lest the shadows bear him away to the land of slaves.

So his young mind worked and winced and shaped curiously a vision of Life; and in the midst of that vision ever stood one dark figure alone,—ever with the hard, thick countenance of that bitter father, and a form that fell in vast and shapeless folds. Thus the temptation of Hate grew and shadowed the growing child,—gliding stealthily into his laughter, fading into his play, and seizing his dreams by day and night with rough, rude turbulence. So the black boy asked of sky and sun and flower the never-answered Why? and loved, as he grew, neither the world nor the world's rough ways.

Strange temptation for a child, you may think; and yet in this wide land to-day a thousand thousand dark children brood before this same temptation, and feel its cold and shuddering arms. For them, perhaps, some one will some day lift the Veil,—will come tenderly and cheerily into those sad little lives and brush the brooding hate away, just as Beriah Green strode in upon the life of Alexander Crummell. And before the bluff, kind-hearted man the shadow seemed less dark. Beriah Green had a school in Oneida County, New York, with a score of mischievous boys. "I'm going to bring a black boy here to educate," said Beriah Green, as only a crank and an abolitionist would have dared to say. "Oho!" laughed the boys. "Ye-es," said his wife; and Alexander came. Once before, the black boy had sought a school, had travelled, cold and hungry, four hundred miles up into free New Hampshire, to Canaan. But the godly farmers hitched ninety yoke of oxen to the abolition schoolhouse and dragged it into the middle of the swamp. The black boy trudged away.

The nineteenth was the first century of human sympathy,—the age when half wonderingly we began to descry in others that transfigured spark of divinity which we call Myself; when clodhoppers and peasants, and tramps and thieves, and millionaires and—sometimes—Negroes, became throbbing souls whose warm pulsing life touched us so nearly that we half gasped with surprise, crying, "Thou too! Hast Thou seen Sorrow and the dull waters of Hopelessness?

Hast Thou known Life?" And then all helplessly we peered into those Other-worlds, and wailed, "O World of Worlds, how shall man make you one?"

So in that little Oneida school there came to those schoolboys a revelation of thought and longing beneath one black skin, of which they had not dreamed before. And to the lonely boy came a new dawn of sympathy and inspiration. The shadowy, formless thing—the temptation of Hate, that hovered between him and the world—grew fainter and less sinister. It did not wholly fade away, but diffused itself and lingered thick at the edges. Through it the child now first saw the blue and gold of life,—the sun-swept road that ran 'twixt heaven and earth until in one far-off wan wavering line they met and kissed. A vision of life came to the growing boy,—mystic, wonderful. He raised his head, stretched himself, breathed deep of the fresh new air. Yonder, behind the forests, he heard strange sounds; then glinting through the trees he saw, far, far away, the bronzed hosts of a nation calling,—calling faintly, calling loudly. He heard the hateful clank of their chains; he felt them cringe and grovel, and there rose within him a protest and a prophecy. And he girded himself to walk down the world.

A voice and vision called him to be a priest,—a seer to lead the uncalled out of the house of bondage. He saw the headless host turn toward him like the whirling of mad waters,—he stretched forth his hands eagerly, and then, even as he stretched them, suddenly there swept across the vision the temptation of Despair.

They were not wicked men,—the problem of life is not the problem of the wicked,—they were calm, good men, Bishops of the Apostolic Church of God, and strove toward righteousness. They said slowly, "It is all very natural—it is even commendable; but the General Theological Seminary of the Episcopal Church cannot admit a Negro." And when that thin, half-grotesque figure still haunted their doors, they put their hands kindly, half sorrowfully, on his shoulders, and said, "Now,—of course, we—we know how *you* feel about it; but you see it is impossible,—that is —well—it is premature. Sometime, we trust—sincerely trust—all such distinctions will fade away; but now the world is as it is."

This was the temptation of Despair; and the young man fought it doggedly. Like some grave shadow he flitted by those halls, pleading, arguing, half angrily demanding admittance, until there came the final *No:* until men hustled the disturber away, marked him as foolish, unreasonable, and injudicious, a vain rebel against God's law. And then from that Vision Splendid all the glory faded slowly away, and left an earth gray and stern rolling on beneath a dark despair. Even the kind hands that stretched themselves toward him from out the depths of that dull morning seemed but parts of the purple shadows. He saw them coldly, and asked, "Why should I strive by special grace when the way of the world is closed to me?" All gently yet, the hands urged him on,—the hands of young John Jay, that daring father's daring son; the hands of the good folk of Boston, that free city. And yet, with a way to the priesthood of the Church open at last before him, the cloud lingered there; and even when in old St. Paul's the venerable Bishop raised his white arms above the Negro deacon —even then the burden had not lifted from that heart, for there had passed a glory from the earth.

And yet the fire through which Alexander Crum-

mell went did not burn in vain. Slowly and more soberly he took up again his plan of life. More critically
he studied the situation. Deep down below the slavery and servitude of the Negro people he saw their
fatal weaknesses, which long years of mistreatment
had emphasized. The dearth of strong moral character, of unbending righteousness, he felt, was their
great shortcoming, and here he would begin. He
would gather the best of his people into some little
Episcopal chapel and there lead, teach, and inspire
them, till the leaven spread, till the children grew, till
the world hearkened, till—till—and then across his
dream gleamed some faint after-glow of that first fair
vision of youth—only an after-glow, for there had
passed a glory from the earth.

One day—it was in 1842, and the springtide was
struggling merrily with the May winds of New England—he stood at last in his own chapel in Provi-
dence, a priest of the Church. The days sped by, and
the dark young clergyman labored; he wrote his ser-
mons carefully; he intoned his prayers with a soft,
earnest voice; he haunted the streets and accosted the
wayfarers; he visited the sick, and knelt beside the
dying. He worked and toiled, week by week, day by
day, month by month. And yet month by month the
congregation dwindled, week by week the hollow
walls echoed more sharply, day by day the calls came
fewer and fewer, and day by day the third temptation
sat clearer and still more clearly within the Veil; a
temptation, as it were, bland and smiling, with just a
shade of mockery in its smooth tones. First it came
casually, in the cadence of a voice: "Oh, colored
folks? Yes." Or perhaps more definitely: "What do
you *expect?*" In voice and gesture lay the doubt—the
temptation of Doubt. How he hated it, and stormed

at it furiously! "Of course they are capable," he cried; "of course they can learn and strive and achieve—" and "Of course," added the temptation softly, "they do nothing of the sort." Of all the three temptations, this one struck the deepest. Hate? He had outgrown so childish a thing. Despair? He had steeled his right arm against it, and fought it with the vigor of determination. But to doubt the worth of his life-work,—to doubt the destiny and capability of the race his soul loved because it was his; to find listless squalor instead of eager endeavor; to hear his own lips whispering, "They do not care; they cannot know; they are dumb driven cattle,—why cast your pearls before swine?"—this, this seemed more than man could bear; and he closed the door, and sank upon the steps of the chancel, and cast his robe upon the floor and writhed.

The evening sunbeams had set the dust to dancing in the gloomy chapel when he arose. He folded his vestments, put away the hymn-books, and closed the great Bible. He stepped out into the twilight, looked back upon the narrow little pulpit with a weary smile, and locked the door. Then he walked briskly to the Bishop, and told the Bishop what the Bishop already knew. "I have failed," he said simply. And gaining courage by the confession, he added: "What I need is a larger constituency. There are comparatively few Negroes here, and perhaps they are not of the best. I must go where the field is wider, and try again." So the Bishop sent him to Philadelphia, with a letter to Bishop Onderdonk.

Bishop Onderdonk lived at the head of six white steps,—corpulent, red-faced, and the author of several thrilling tracts on Apostolic Succession. It was after dinner, and the Bishop had settled himself for a pleasant season of contemplation, when the bell must needs ring, and there must burst in upon the Bishop a letter and a thin, ungainly Negro. Bishop Onderdonk read the letter hastily and frowned. Fortunately, his mind was already clear on this point; and he cleared his brow and looked at Crummell. Then he said, slowly and impressively: "I will receive you into this diocese on one condition: no Negro priest can sit in my church convention, and no Negro church must ask for representation there."

I sometimes fancy I can see that tableau: the frail black figure, nervously twitching his hat before the massive abdomen of Bishop Onderdonk; his threadbare coat thrown against the dark woodwork of the bookcases, where Fox's "Lives of the Martyrs" nestled happily beside "The Whole Duty of Man." I seem to see the wide eyes of the Negro wander past the Bishop's broadcloth to where the swinging glass doors of the cabinet glow in the sunlight. A little blue fly is trying to cross the yawning keyhole. He marches briskly up to it, peers into the chasm in a surprised sort of way, and rubs his feelers reflectively; then he essays its depths, and, finding it bottomless, draws back again. The dark-faced priest finds himself wondering if the fly too has faced its Valley of Humiliation, and if it will plunge into it,—when lo! it spreads its tiny wings and buzzes merrily across, leaving the watcher wingless and alone.

Then the full weight of his burden fell upon him. The rich walls wheeled away, and before him lay the cold rough moor winding on through life, cut in twain by one thick granite ridge,—here, the Valley of Humiliation; yonder, the Valley of the Shadow of Death. And I know not which be darker,—no, not I. But this I know: in yonder Vale of the Humble stand to-day a million swarthy men, who willingly would

"... bear the whips and scorns of time,
The oppressor's wrong, the proud man's contumely,
The pangs of despised love, the law's delay,
The insolence of office, and the spurns
That patient merit of the unworthy takes,"—

all this and more would they bear did they but know
that this were sacrifice and not a meaner thing. So
surged the thought within that lone black breast. The
Bishop cleared his throat suggestively; then, recollect-
ing that there was really nothing to say, considerately
said nothing, only sat tapping his foot impatiently.
But Alexander Crummell said, slowly and heavily: "I
will never enter your diocese on such terms." And
saying this, he turned and passed into the Valley of
the Shadow of Death. You might have noted only the
physical dying, the shattered frame and hacking
cough; but in that soul lay deeper death than that. He
found a chapel in New York,—the church of his father; he labored for it in poverty and starvation,
scorned by his fellow priests. Half in despair, he wandered across the sea, a beggar with outstretched
hands. Englishmen clasped them,—Wilberforce and
Stanley, Thirwell and Ingles, and even Froude and
Macaulay; Sir Benjamin Brodie bade him rest awhile
at Queen's College in Cambridge, and there he lingered, struggling for health of body and mind, until
he took his degree in '53. Restless still, and unsatis-
fied, he turned toward Africa, and for long years,
amid the spawn of the slave-smugglers, sought a new
heaven and a new earth.

So the man groped for light; all this was not Life,—
it was the world-wandering of a soul in search of itself, the striving of one who vainly sought his place in
the world, ever haunted by the shadow of a death that
is more than death,—the passing of a soul that has
missed its duty. Twenty years he wandered,—twenty

years and more; and yet the hard rasping question kept gnawing within him, "What, in God's name, am I on earth for?" In the narrow New York parish his soul seemed cramped and smothered. In the fine old air of the English University he heard the millions wailing over the sea. In the wild fever-cursed swamps of West Africa he stood helpless and alone.

You will not wonder at his weird pilgrimage,—you who in the swift whirl of living, amid its cold paradox and marvellous vision, have fronted life and asked its riddle face to face. And if you find that riddle hard to read, remember that yonder black boy finds it just a little harder; if it is difficult for you to find and face your duty, it is a shade more difficult for him; if your heart sickens in the blood and dust of battle, remember that to him the dust is thicker and the battle fiercer. No wonder the wanderers fall! No wonder we point to thief and murderer, and haunting prostitute, and the never-ending throng of unhearsed dead! The Valley of the Shadow of Death gives few of its pilgrims back to the world.

But Alexander Crummell it gave back. Out of the temptation of Hate, and burned by the fire of Despair, triumphant over Doubt, and steeled by Sacrifice against Humiliation, he turned at last home across the waters, humble and strong, gentle and determined. He bent to all the gibes and prejudices, to all hatred and discrimination, with that rare courtesy which is the armor of pure souls. He fought among his own, the low, the grasping, and the wicked, with that unbending righteousness which is the sword of the just. He never faltered, he seldom complained; he simply worked, inspiring the young, rebuking the old, helping the weak, guiding the strong.

So he grew, and brought within his wide influence all that was best of those who walk within the Veil.

They who live without knew not nor dreamed of that full power within, that mighty inspiration which the dull gauze of caste decreed that most men should not know. And now that he is gone, I sweep the Veil away and cry, Lo! the soul to whose dear memory I bring this little tribute. I can see his face still, dark and heavy-lined beneath his snowy hair; lighting and shading, now with inspiration for the future, now in innocent pain at some human wickedness, now with sorrow at some hard memory from the past. The more I met Alexander Crummell, the more I felt how much that world was losing which knew so little of him. In another age he might have sat among the elders of the land in purple-bordered toga; in another country mothers might have sung him to the cradles.

He did his work,—he did it nobly and well; and yet I sorrow that here he worked alone, with so little human sympathy. His name to-day, in this broad land, means little, and comes to fifty million ears laden with no incense of memory or emulation. And herein lies the tragedy of the age: not that men are poor,—all men know something of poverty; not that men are wicked,—who is good? not that men are ignorant,—what is Truth? Nay, but that men know so little of men.

He sat one morning gazing toward the sea. He smiled and said, "The gate is rusty on the hinges." That night at star-rise a wind came moaning out of the west to blow the gate ajar, and then the soul I loved fled like a flame across the Seas, and in its seat sat Death.

I wonder where he is to-day? I wonder if in that dim world beyond, as he came gliding in, there rose on some wan throne a King,—a dark and pierced Jew, who knows the writhings of the earthly damned, saying, as he laid those heart-wrung talents down, "Well done!" while round about the morning stars sat singing.

XIII

Of the Coming of John

> What bring they 'neath the midnight,
>   Beside the River-sea?
> They bring the human heart wherein
>   No nightly calm can be;
> That droppeth never with the wind,
>   Nor drieth with the dew;
> O calm it, God; thy calm is broad
>   To cover spirits too.
>   The river floweth on.
>
> MRS. BROWNING.

CARLISLE STREET runs westward from the centre of Johnstown, across a great black bridge, down a hill and up again, by little shops and meat-markets, past single-storied homes, until suddenly it stops against a wide green lawn. It is a broad, restful place, with two large buildings outlined against the west. When at

evening the winds come swelling from the east, and
the great pall of the city's smoke hangs wearily above
the valley, then the red west glows like a dreamland
down Carlisle Street, and, at the tolling of the sup-
per-bell, throws the passing forms of students in dark
silhouette against the sky. Tall and black, they move
slowly by, and seem in the sinister light to flit before
the city like dim warning ghosts. Perhaps they are;
for this is Wells Institute, and these black students
have few dealings with the white city below.

And if you will notice, night after night, there is
one dark form that ever hurries last and late toward
the twinkling lights of Swain Hall,—for Jones is never
on time. A long, straggling fellow he is, brown and
hard-haired, who seems to be growing straight out of
his clothes, and walks with a half-apologetic roll. He
used perpetually to set the quiet dining-room into
waves of merriment, as he stole to his place after the
bell had tapped for prayers; he seemed so perfectly
awkward. And yet one glance at his face made one
forgive him much,—that broad, good-natured smile in
which lay no bit of art or artifice, but seemed just
bubbling good-nature and genuine satisfaction with
the world.

He came to us from Altamaha, away down there
beneath the gnarled oaks of Southeastern Georgia,
where the sea croons to the sands and the sands listen
till they sink half drowned beneath the waters, rising
only here and there in long, low islands. The white
folk of Altamaha voted John a good boy,—fine
plough-hand, good in the rice-fields, handy every-
where, and always good-natured and respectful. But
they shook their heads when his mother wanted to
send him off to school. "It'll spoil him,—ruin him,"
they said; and they talked as though they knew. But
full half the black folk followed him proudly to the

station, and carried his queer little trunk and many
bundles. And there they shook and shook hands, and
the girls kissed him shyly and the boys clapped him
on the back. So the train came, and he pinched his
little sister lovingly, and put his great arms about his
mother's neck, and then was away with a puff and a
roar into the great yellow world that flamed and
flared about the doubtful pilgrim. Up the coast they
hurried, past the squares and palmettos of Savannah,
through the cotton-fields and through the weary
night, to Millville, and came with the morning to the
noise and bustle of Johnstown.

And they that stood behind, that morning in Altamaha, and watched the train as it noisily bore playmate and brother and son away to the world, had
thereafter one ever-recurring word,—"When John
comes." Then what parties were to be, and what
speakings in the churches; what new furniture in the
front room,—perhaps even a new front room; and
there would be a new schoolhouse, with John as
teacher; and then perhaps a big wedding; all this and
more—when John comes. But the white people shook
their heads.

At first he was coming at Christmas-time,—but the
vacation proved too short; and then, the next summer,
—but times were hard and schooling costly, and so,
instead, he worked in Johnstown. And so it drifted to
the next summer, and the next,—till playmates scattered, and mother grew gray, and sister went up to
the Judge's kitchen to work. And still the legend lingered,—"When John comes."

Up at the Judge's they rather liked this refrain; for
they too had a John—a fair-haired, smooth-faced boy,
who had played many a long summer's day to its
close with his darker namesake. "Yes, sir! John is at
Princeton, sir," said the broad-shouldered gray-haired

Judge every morning as he marched down to the
post-office. "Showing the Yankees what a Southern
gentleman can do," he added; and strode home again
with his letters and papers. Up at the great pillared
house they lingered long over the Princeton letter,—
the Judge and his frail wife, his sister and growing
daughters. "It'll make a man of him," said the Judge,
"college is the place." And then he asked the shy little
waitress, "Well, Jennie, how's your John?" and added
reflectively, "Too bad, too bad your mother sent him
off,—it will spoil him." And the waitress wondered.

Thus in the far-away Southern village the world lay
waiting, half consciously, the coming of two young
men, and dreamed in an inarticulate way of new
things that would be done and new thoughts that all
would think. And yet it was singular that few thought
of two Johns,—for the black folk thought of one John,
and he was black; and the white folk thought of another John, and he was white. And neither world
thought the other world's thought, save with a vague
unrest.

Up in Johnstown, at the Institute, we were long
puzzled at the case of John Jones. For a long time the
clay seemed unfit for any sort of moulding. He was
loud and boisterous, always laughing and singing, and
never able to work consecutively at anything. He did
not know how to study; he had no idea of thorough-
ness; and with his tardiness, carelessness, and appalling good-humor, we were sore perplexed. One night
we sat in faculty-meeting, worried and serious; for
Jones was in trouble again. This last escapade was too
much, and so we solemnly voted "that Jones, on account of repeated disorder and inattention to work,
be suspended for the rest of the term."

It seemed to us that the first time life ever struck
Jones as a really serious thing was when the Dean

told him he must leave school. He stared at the gray-haired man blankly, with great eyes. "Why,—why," he faltered, "but—I haven't graduated!" Then the Dean slowly and clearly explained, reminding him of the tardiness and the carelessness, of the poor lessons and neglected work, of the noise and disorder, until the fellow hung his head in confusion. Then he said quickly, "But you won't tell mammy and sister,—you won't write mammy, now will you? For if you won't I'll go out into the city and work, and come back next term and show you something." So the Dean promised faithfully, and John shouldered his little trunk, giving neither word nor look to the giggling boys, and walked down Carlisle Street to the great city, with sober eyes and a set and serious face.

Perhaps we imagined it, but someway it seemed to us that the serious look that crept over his boyish face that afternoon never left it again. When he came back to us he went to work with all his rugged strength. It was a hard struggle, for things did not come easily to him,—few crowding memories of early life and teaching came to help him on his new way; but all the world toward which he strove was of his own building, and he builded slow and hard. As the light dawned lingeringly on his new creations, he sat rapt and silent before the vision, or wandered alone over the green campus peering through and beyond the world of men into a world of thought. And the thoughts at times puzzled him sorely; he could not see just why the circle was not square, and carried it out fifty-six decimal places one midnight,—would have gone further, indeed, had not the matron rapped for lights out. He caught terrible colds lying on his back in the meadows of nights, trying to think out the solar system; he had grave doubts as to the ethics of the Fall of Rome, and strongly suspected the Ger-

mans of being thieves and rascals, despite his text-
books; he pondered long over every new Greek word,
and wondered why this meant that and why it
couldn't mean something else, and how it must have
felt to think all things in Greek. So he thought and
puzzled along for himself,—pausing perplexed where
others skipped merrily, and walking steadily through
the difficulties where the rest stopped and surrendered.

Thus he grew in body and soul, and with him his
clothes seemed to grow and arrange themselves; coat
sleeves got longer, cuffs appeared, and collars got less
soiled. Now and then his boots shone, and a new dignity crept into his walk. And we who saw daily a new
thoughtfulness growing in his eyes began to expect
something of this plodding boy. Thus he passed out
of the preparatory school into college, and we who
watched him felt four more years of change, which
almost transformed the tall, grave man who bowed to
us commencement morning. He had left his queer
thought-world and come back to a world of motion
and of men. He looked now for the first time sharply
about him, and wondered he had seen so little before.
He grew slowly to feel almost for the first time the
Veil that lay between him and the white world; he
first noticed now the oppression that had not seemed
oppression before, differences that erstwhile seemed
natural, restraints and slights that in his boyhood days
had gone unnoticed or been greeted with a laugh. He
felt angry now when men did not call him "Mister,"
he clenched his hands at the "Jim Crow" cars, and
chafed at the color-line that hemmed in him and his.
A tinge of sarcasm crept into his speech, and a vague
bitterness into his life; and he sat long hours wondering and planning a way around these crooked things.
Daily he found himself shrinking from the choked

and narrow life of his native town. And yet he always planned to go back to Altamaha,—always planned to work there. Still, more and more as the day approached he hesitated with a nameless dread; and even the day after graduation he seized with eagerness the offer of the Dean to send him North with the quartette during the summer vacation, to sing for the Institute. A breath of air before the plunge, he said to himself in half apology.

It was a bright September afternoon, and the streets of New York were brilliant with moving men. They reminded John of the sea, as he sat in the square and watched them, so changelessly changing, so bright and dark, so grave and gay. He scanned their rich and faultless clothes, the way they carried their hands, the shape of their hats; he peered into the hurrying carriages. Then, leaning back with a sigh, he said, "This is the World." The notion suddenly seized him to see where the world was going; since many of the richer and brighter seemed hurrying all one way. So when a tall, light-haired young man and a little talkative lady came by, he rose half hesitatingly and followed them. Up the street they went, past stores and gay shops, across a broad square, until with a hundred others they entered the high portal of a great building.

He was pushed toward the ticket-office with the others, and felt in his pocket for the new five-dollar bill he had hoarded. There seemed really no time for hesitation, so he drew it bravely out, passed it to the busy clerk, and received simply a ticket but no change. When at last he realized that he had paid five dollars to enter he knew not what, he stood stockstill amazed. "Be careful," said a low voice behind him; "you must not lynch the colored gentleman simply because he's in your way," and a girl looked up ro-

guishly into the eyes of her fair-haired escort. A shade
of annoyance passed over the escort's face. "You *will*
not understand us at the South," he said half impatiently, as if continuing an argument. "With all your
professions, one never sees in the North so cordial
and intimate relations between white and black as are
everyday occurrences with us. Why, I remember my
closest playfellow in boyhood was a little Negro
named after me, and surely no two,—*well!*" The man
stopped short and flushed to the roots of his hair, for
there directly beside his reserved orchestra chairs sat
the Negro he had stumbled over in the hallway. He
hesitated and grew pale with anger, called the usher
and gave him his card, with a few peremptory words,
and slowly sat down. The lady deftly changed the
subject.

All this John did not see, for he sat in a half-daze
minding the scene about him; the delicate beauty of
the hall, the faint perfume, the moving myriad of
men, the rich clothing and low hum of talking seemed
all a part of a world so different from his, so strangely
more beautiful than anything he had known, that he
sat in dreamland, and started when, after a hush, rose
high and clear the music of Lohengrin's swan. The infinite beauty of the wail lingered and swept through
every muscle of his frame, and put it all a-tune. He
closed his eyes and grasped the elbows of the chair,
touching unwittingly the lady's arm. And the lady
drew away. A deep longing swelled in all his heart to
rise with that clear music out of the dirt and dust of
that low life that held him prisoned and befouled. If
he could only live up in the free air where birds sang
and setting suns had no touch of blood! Who had
called him to be the slave and butt of all? And if he
had called, what right had he to call when a world
like this lay open before men?

Then the movement changed, and fuller, mightier harmony swelled away. He looked thoughtfully across the hall, and wondered why the beautiful gray-haired woman looked so listless, and what the little man could be whispering about. He would not like to be listless and idle, he thought, for he felt with the music the movement of power within him. If he but had some master-work, some life-service, hard,—aye, bitter hard, but without the cringing and sickening servility, without the cruel hurt that hardened his heart and soul. When at last a soft sorrow crept across the violins, there came to him the vision of a far-off home, the great eyes of his sister, and the dark drawn face of his mother. And his heart sank below the waters, even as the sea-sand sinks by the shores of Altamaha, only to be lifted aloft again with that last ethereal wail of the swan that quivered and faded away into the sky.

It left John sitting so silent and rapt that he did not for some time notice the usher tapping him lightly on the shoulder and saying politely, "Will you step this way, please, sir?" A little surprised, he arose quickly at the last tap, and, turning to leave his seat, looked full into the face of the fair-haired young man. For the first time the young man recognized his dark boyhood playmate, and John knew that it was the Judge's son. The White John started, lifted his hand, and then froze into his chair; the black John smiled lightly, then grimly, and followed the usher down the aisle. The manager was sorry, very, very sorry,—but he explained that some mistake had been made in selling the gentleman a seat already disposed of; he would refund the money, of course,—and indeed felt the matter keenly, and so forth, and—before he had finished John was gone, walking hurriedly across the square and down the broad streets, and as he passed the park he buttoned his coat and said, "John Jones, you're a natural-born fool." Then he went to his lodgings and wrote a letter, and tore it up; he wrote another, and threw it in the fire. Then he seized a scrap of paper and wrote: "Dear Mother and Sister—I am coming—John."

"Perhaps," said John, as he settled himself on the train, "perhaps I am to blame myself in struggling against my manifest destiny simply because it looks hard and unpleasant. Here is my duty to Altamaha plain before me; perhaps they'll let me help settle the Negro problems there,—perhaps they won't. 'I will go in to the King, which is not according to the law; and if I perish, I perish.'" And then he mused and dreamed, and planned a life-work; and the train flew south.

Down in Altamaha, after seven long years, all the world knew John was coming. The homes were scrubbed and scoured,—above all, one; the gardens and yards had an unwonted trimness, and Jennie bought a new gingham. With some finesse and negotiation, all the dark Methodist and Presbyterians were induced to join in a monster welcome at the Baptist Church; and as the day drew near, warm discussions arose on every corner as to the exact extent and nature of John's accomplishments. It was noontide on a gray and cloudy day when he came. The black town flocked to the depot, with a little of the white at the edges,—a happy throng, with "Good-mawnings" and "Howdys" and laughing and joking and jostling. Mother sat yonder in the window watching; but sister Jennie stood on the platform, nervously fingering her dress, tall and lithe, with soft brown skin and loving eyes peering from out a tangled wilderness of hair. John rose gloomily as the train stopped, for he was thinking of the "Jim Crow'" car; he stepped to the platform, and paused: a little dingy station, a black crowd gaudy and dirty, a half-mile of dilapidated shanties along a straggling ditch of mud. An overwhelming sense of the sordidness and narrowness of it all seized him; he looked in vain for his mother, kissed coldly the tall, strange girl who called him brother, spoke a short, dry word here and there; then, lingering neither for hand-shaking nor gossip, started silently up the street, raising his hat merely to the last eager old aunty, to her open-mouthed astonishment. The people were distinctly bewildered. This silent, cold man,—was this John? Where was his smile and hearty hand-grasp? " 'Peared kind o' down in the mouf," said the Methodist preacher thoughtfully. "Seemed monstus stuck up," complained a Baptist sister. But the white postmaster from the edge of the crowd expressed the opinion of his folks plainly. "That damn Nigger," said he, as he shouldered the mail and arranged his tobacco, "has gone North and got plum full o' fool notions; but they won't work in Altamaha." And the crowd melted away.

The meeting of welcome at the Baptist Church was a failure. Rain spoiled the barbecue, and thunder turned the milk in the ice-cream. When the speaking came at night, the house was crowded to overflowing. The three preachers had especially prepared themselves, but somehow John's manner seemed to throw a blanket over everything,—he seemed so cold and preoccupied, and had so strange an air of restraint that the Methodist brother could not warm up to his theme and elicited not a single "Amen"; the Presbyterian prayer was but feebly responded to, and even the Baptist preacher, though he wakened faint enthusiasm, got so mixed up in his favorite sentence that he had to close it by stopping fully fifteen minutes sooner than he meant. The people moved uneasily in

their seats as John rose to reply. He spoke slowly and
methodically. The age, he said, demanded new ideas;
we were far different from those men of the seven-
teenth and eighteenth centuries,—with broader ideas
of human brotherhood and destiny. Then he spoke
of the rise of charity and popular education, and particularly of the spread of wealth and work. The question was, then, he added reflectively, looking at the
low discolored ceiling, what part the Negroes of this
land would take in the striving of the new century.
He sketched in vague outline the new Industrial
School that might rise among these pines, he spoke in
detail of the charitable and philanthropic work that
might be organized, of money that might be saved for
banks and business. Finally he urged unity, and dep-
recated especially religious and denominational
bickering. "To-day," he said, with a smile, "the world
cares little whether a man be Baptist or Methodist, or
indeed a churchman at all, so long as he is good and
true. What difference does it make whether a man be
baptized in river or washbowl, or not at all? Let's
leave all that littleness, and look higher." Then, thinking of nothing else, he slowly sat down. A painful
hush seized that crowded mass. Little had they understood of what he said, for he spoke an unknown
tongue, save the last word about baptism; that they
knew, and they sat very still while the clock ticked.
Then at last a low suppressed snarl came from the
Amen corner, and an old bent man arose, walked over
the seats, and climbed straight up into the pulpit. He
was wrinkled and black, with scant gray and tufted
hair; his voice and hands shook as with palsy; but on
his face lay the intense rapt look of the religious fa-
natic. He seized the Bible with his rough, huge
hands; twice he raised it inarticulate, and then fairly
burst into words, with rude and awful eloquence. He

quivered, swayed, and bent; then rose aloft in perfect majesty, till the people moaned and wept, wailed and shouted, and a wild shrieking arose from the corners where all the pent-up feeling of the hour gathered itself and rushed into the air. John never knew clearly what the old man said; he only felt himself held up to scorn and scathing denunciation for trampling on the true Religion, and he realized with amazement that all unknowingly he had put rough, rude hands on something this little world held sacred. He arose silently, and passed out into the night. Down toward the sea he went, in the fitful starlight, half conscious of the girl who followed timidly after him. When at last he stood upon the bluff, he turned to his little sister and looked upon her sorrowfully, remembering with sudden pain how little thought he had given her. He put his arm about her and let her passion of tears spend itself on his shoulder.

Long they stood together, peering over the gray unresting water.

"John," she said, "does it make every one—unhappy when they study and learn lots of things?"

He paused and smiled. "I am afraid it does," he said.

"And, John, are you glad you studied?"

"Yes," came the answer, slowly but positively.

She watched the flickering lights upon the sea, and said thoughtfully, "I wish I was unhappy,—and—and," putting both arms about his neck, "I think I am, a little, John."

It was several days later that John walked up to the Judge's house to ask for the privilege of teaching the Negro school. The Judge himself met him at the front door, stared a little hard at him, and said brusquely, "Go 'round to the kitchen door, John, and wait." Sitting on the kitchen steps, John stared at the corn, thoroughly perplexed. What on earth had come over him? Every step he made offended some one. He had come to save his people, and before he left the depot he had hurt them. He sought to teach them at the church, and had outraged their deepest feelings. He had schooled himself to be respectful to the Judge, and then blundered into his front door. And all the time he had meant right,—and yet, and yet, somehow he found it so hard and strange to fit his old surroundings again, to find his place in the world about him. He could not remember that he used to have any difficulty in the past, when life was glad and gay. The world seemed smooth and easy then. Perhaps,—but his sister came to the kitchen door just then and said the Judge awaited him.

The Judge sat in the dining-room amid his morning's mail, and he did not ask John to sit down. He plunged squarely into the business. "You've come for the school, I suppose. Well, John, I want to speak to you plainly. You know I'm a friend to your people. I've helped you and your family, and would have done more if you hadn't got the notion of going off. Now I like the colored people, and sympathize with all their reasonable aspirations; but you and I both know, John, that in this country the Negro must remain subordinate, and can never expect to be the equal of white men. In their place, your people can be honest and respectful; and God knows, I'll do what I can to help them. But when they want to reverse nature, and rule white men, and marry white women, and sit in my parlor, then, by God! we'll hold them under if we have to lynch every Nigger in the land. Now, John, the question is, are you, with your education and Northern notions, going to accept the situation and teach the darkies to be faithful servants and laborers as your fathers were,—I knew your father, John, he belonged to my brother, and he was a good Nigger. Well—well, are you going to be like him, or are you going to try to put fool ideas of rising and equality into these folks' heads, and make them discontented and unhappy?"

"I am going to accept the situation, Judge Henderson," answered John, with a brevity that did not escape the keen old man. He hesitated a moment, and then said shortly, "Very well,—we'll try you awhile. Good-morning."

It was a full month after the opening of the Negro school that the other John came home, tall, gay, and headstrong. The mother wept, the sisters sang. The whole white town was glad. A proud man was the Judge, and it was a goodly sight to see the two swinging down Main Street together. And yet all did not go smoothly between them, for the younger man could not and did not veil his contempt for the little town, and plainly had his heart set on New York. Now the one cherished ambition of the Judge was to see his son mayor of Altamaha, representative to the legislature, and—w⁴ ꜱ could say?—governor of Georgia. So the argument often waxed hot between them. "Good heavens, father," the younger man would say after dinner, as he lighted a cigar and stood by the fireplace, "you surely don't expect a young fellow like me to settle down permanently in this—this God-forgotten town with nothing but mud and Negroes?" "I did," the Judge would answer laconically; and on this particular day it seemed from the gathering scowl that he was about to add something more emphatic, but neighbors had already begun to drop in to admire his son, and the conversation drifted.

"Heah that John is livenin' things up at the darky school," volunteered the postmaster, after a pause.

"What now?" asked the Judge, sharply.

"Oh, nothin' in particulah,—just his almighty air and uppish ways. B'lieve I did heah somethin' about his givin' talks on the French Revolution, equality, and such like. He's what I call a dangerous Nigger."

"Have you heard him say anything out of the way?"

"Why, no,—but Sally, our girl, told my wife a lot of rot. Then, too, I don't need to heah: a Nigger what won't say 'sir' to a white man, or—"

"Who is this John?" interrupted the son.

"Why, it's little black John, Peggy's son,—your old playfellow."

The young man's face flushed angrily, and then he laughed.

"Oh," said he, "it's the darky that tried to force himself into a seat beside the lady I was escorting—"

But Judge Henderson waited to hear no more. He had been nettled all day, and now at this he rose with a half-smothered oath, took his hat and cane, and walked straight to the schoolhouse.

For John, it had been a long, hard pull to get things started in the rickety old shanty that sheltered his school. The Negroes were rent into factions for and against him, the parents were careless, the children irregular and dirty, and books, pencils, and slates largely missing. Nevertheless, he struggled hopefully on, and seemed to see at last some glimmering of dawn. The attendance was larger and the children were a shade cleaner this week. Even the booby class in reading showed a little comforting progress. So John settled himself with renewed patience this afternoon.

"Now, Mandy," he said cheerfully, "that's better; but you mustn't chop your words up so: 'If—the—man —goes.' Why, your little brother even wouldn't tell a story that way, now would he?"

"Naw, suh, he cain't talk."

"All right; now let's try again: 'If the man—'"

"John!"

The whole school started in surprise, and the teacher half arose, as the red, angry face of the Judge appeared in the open doorway.

"John, this school is closed. You children can go home and get to work. The white people of Altamaha are not spending their money on black folks to have their heads crammed with impudence and lies. Clear out! I'll lock the door myself."

Up at the great pillared house the tall young son wandered aimlessly about after his father's abrupt departure. In the house there was little to interest him; the books were old and stale, the local newspaper flat, and the women had retired with heachaches and sewing. He tried a nap, but it was too warm. So he sauntered out into the fields, complaining disconsolately, "Good Lord! how long will this imprisonment last!" He was not a bad fellow,—just a little spoiled and self-indulgent, and as headstrong as his proud father. He seemed a young man pleasant to look upon, as he sat on the great black stump at the edge of the pines idly swinging his legs and smoking. "Why, there isn't even a girl worth getting up a respectable flirtation with," he growled. Just then his eye caught a tall, willowy figure hurrying toward him on the narrow path. He looked with interest at first, and then burst into a laugh as he said, "Well, I declare, if it isn't Jennie, the little brown kitchen-maid! Why, I never noticed before what a trim little body she is. Hello, Jennie! Why, you haven't kissed me since I came home," he said gaily. The young girl stared at him in surprise and confusion,—faltered something inarticulate, and attempted to pass. But a wilful mood had seized the young idler, and he caught at her arm. Frightened, she slipped by; and half mischievously he turned and ran after her through the tall pines.

Yonder, toward the sea, at the end of the path, came John slowly, with his head down. He had turned wearily homeward from the schoolhouse; then, thinking to shield his mother from the blow, started to meet his sister as she came from work and break the news of his dismissal to her. "I'll go away," he said slowly; "I'll go away and find work, and send for them. I cannot live here longer." And then the fierce, buried anger surged up into his throat. He waved his arms and hurried wildly up the path.

The great brown sea lay silent. The air scarce breathed. The dying day bathed the twisted oaks and mighty pines in black and gold. There came from the wind no warning, not a whisper from the cloudless sky. There was only a black man hurrying on with an ache in his heart, seeing neither sun nor sea, but starting as from a dream at the frightened cry that woke the pines, to see his dark sister struggling in the arms of a tall and fair-haired man.

He said not a word, but, seizing a fallen limb, struck him with all the pent-up hatred of his great black arm; and the body lay white and still beneath the pines, all bathed in sunshine and in blood. John looked at it dreamily, then walked back to the house briskly, and said in a soft voice, "Mammy, I'm going away—I'm going to be free."

She gazed at him dimly and faltered, "No'th, honey, is yo' gwine No'th agin?"

He looked out where the North Star glistened pale above the waters, and said. "Yes, mammy, I'm going—North."

Then, without another word, he went out into the narrow lane, up by the straight pines, to the same winding path, and seated himself on the great black

stump, looking at the blood where the body had lain.
Yonder in the gray past he had played with that dead
boy, romping together under the solemn trees. The
night deepened; he thought of the boys at Johnstown.
He wondered how Brown had turned out, and Carey?
And Jones,—Jones? Why, *he* was Jones, and he wondered what they would all say when they knew, when
they knew, in that great long dining-room with its
hundreds of merry eyes. Then as the sheen of the
starlight stole over him, he thought of the gilded ceiling of that vast concert hall, heard stealing toward him the faint sweet music of the swan. Hark!
was it music, or the hurry and shouting of men? Yes,
surely! Clear and high the faint sweet melody rose
and fluttered like a living thing, so that the very earth
trembled as with the tramp of horses and murmur of
angry men.

He leaned back and smiled toward the sea, whence
rose the strange melody, away from the dark shadows
where lay the noise of horses galloping, galloping on.
With an effort he roused himself, bent forward, and
looked steadily down the pathway, softly humming
the "Song of the Bride,"—

"Freudig geführt, ziehet dahin."

Amid the trees in the dim morning twilight he
watched their shadows dancing and heard their
horses thundering toward him, until at last they came
sweeping like a storm, and he saw in front that hag-
gard white-haired man, whose eyes flashed red with
fury. Oh, how he pitied him,—pitied him,—and wondered if he had the coiling twisted rope. Then, as the
storm burst round him, he rose slowly to his feet and
turned his closed eyes toward the Sea.

And the world whistled in his ears.

XIV

Of the Sorrow Songs

I walk through the churchyard
  To lay this body down;
I know moon-rise, I know star-rise;
I walk in the moonlight, I walk in the starlight;
I'll lie in the grave and stretch out my arms,
I'll go to judgment in the evening of the day,
And my soul and thy soul shall meet that day,
  When I lay this body down.

NEGRO SONG.

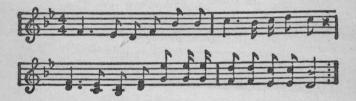

THEY that walked in darkness sang songs in the olden days—Sorrow Songs—for they were weary at heart. And so before each thought that I have written in this book I have set a phrase, a haunting echo of these weird old songs in which the soul of the black slave spoke to men. Ever since I was a child these songs have stirred me strangely. They came out of the South unknown to me, one by one, and yet at once I knew them as of me and of mine. Then in after years when I came to Nashville I saw the great temple builded of these songs towering over the pale city. To me Jubilee Hall seemed ever made of the songs themselves, and its bricks were red with the blood and dust of toil. Out of them rose for me morning, noon, and night, bursts of wonderful melody, full of the voices of my brothers and sisters, full of the voices of the past.

Little of beauty has America given the world save the rude grandeur God himself stamped on her bosom; the human spirit in this new world has expressed itself in vigor and ingenuity rather than in beauty. And so by fateful chance the Negro folk-song —the rhythmic cry of the slave—stands to-day not simply as the sole American music, but as the most beautiful expression of human experience born this side the seas. It has been neglected, it has been, and is, half despised, and above all it has been persistently mistaken and misunderstood; but notwithstanding, it still remains as the singular spiritual heritage of the nation and the greatest gift of the Negro people.

Away back in the thirties the melody of these slave songs stirred the nation, but the songs were soon half forgotten. Some, like "Near the lake where drooped the willow," passed into current airs and their source was forgotten; others were caricatured on the "minstrel" stage and their memory died away. Then in war-time came the singular Port Royal experiment after the capture of Hilton Head, and perhaps for the first time the North met the Southern slave face to face and heart to heart with no third witness. The Sea Islands of the Carolinas, where they met, were filled with a black folk of primitive type, touched and moulded less by the world about them than any others outside the Black Belt. Their appearance was uncouth, their language funny, but their hearts were

human and their singing stirred men with a mighty
power. Thomas Wentworth Higginson hastened to
tell of these songs, and Miss McKim and others urged
upon the world their rare beauty. But the world listened only half credulously until the Fisk Jubilee
Singers sang the slave songs so deeply into the
world's heart that it can never wholly forget them
again.

There was once a blacksmith's son born at Cadiz,
New York, who in the changes of time taught school
in Ohio and helped defend Cincinnati from Kirby
Smith. Then he fought at Chancellorsville and Gettysburg and finally served in the Freedman's Bureau at
Nashville. Here he formed a Sunday-school class of
black children in 1866, and sang with them and
taught them to sing. And then they taught him to
sing, and when once the glory of the Jubilee songs
passed into the soul of George L. White, he knew his
life-work was to let those Negroes sing to the world
as they had sung to him. So in 1871 the pilgrimage of
the Fisk Jubilee Singers began. North to Cincinnati
they rode,—four half-clothed black boys and five girl-
women,—led by a man with a cause and a purpose.
They stopped at Wilberforce, the oldest of Negro
schools, where a black bishop blessed them. Then
they went, fighting cold and starvation, shut out of
hotels, and cheerfully sneered at, ever northward; and
ever the magic of their song kept thrilling hearts,
until a burst of applause in the Congregational Council at Oberlin revealed them to the world. They came
to New York and Henry Ward Beecher dared to welcome them, even though the metropolitan dailies
sneered at his "Nigger Minstrels." So their songs conquered till they sang across the land and across the
sea, before Queen and Kaiser, in Scotland and Ire-

land, Holland and Switzerland. Seven years they sang, and brought back a hundred and fifty thousand dollars to found Fisk University.

Since their day they have been imitated—sometimes well, by the singers of Hampton and Atlanta, sometimes ill, by straggling quartettes. Caricature has sought again to spoil the quaint beauty of the music, and has filled the air with many debased melodies which vulgar ears scarce know from the real. But the true Negro folk-song still lives in the hearts of those who have heard them truly sung and in the hearts of the Negro people.

What are these songs, and what do they mean? I know little of music and can say nothing in technical phrase, but I know something of men, and knowing them, I know that these songs are the articulate message of the slave to the world. They tell us in these eager days that life was joyous to the black slave, careless and happy. I can easily believe this of some, of many. But not all the past South, though it rose from the dead, can gainsay the heart-touching witness of these songs. They are the music of an unhappy people, of the children of disappointment; they tell of death and suffering and unvoiced longing toward a truer world, of misty wanderings and hidden ways.

The songs are indeed the siftings of centuries; the music is far more ancient than the words, and in it we can trace here and there signs of development. My grandfather's grandmother was seized by an evil Dutch trader two centuries ago; and coming to the valleys of the Hudson and Housatonic, black, little, and lithe, she shivered and shrank in the harsh north winds, looked longingly at the hills, and often crooned a heathen melody to the child between her knees, thus:

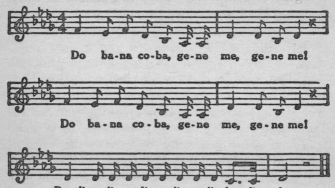

Do ba-na co-ba, ge-ne me, ge-ne me!

Do ba-na co-ba, ge-ne me, ge-ne me!

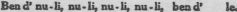

Ben d' nu-li, nu-li, nu-li, nu-li, ben d' le.

The child sang it to his children and they to their children's children, and so two hundred years it has travelled down to us and we sing it to our children, knowing as little as our fathers what its words may mean, but knowing well the meaning of its music.

This was primitive African music; it may be seen in larger form in the strange chant which heralds "The Coming of John":

> "You may bury me in the East,
> You may bury me in the West,
> But I'll hear the trumpet sound in that morning,"

—the voice of exile.

Ten master songs, more or less, one may pluck from this forest of melody—songs of undoubted Negro origin and wide popular currency, and songs peculiarly characteristic of the slave. One of these I have just mentioned. Another whose strains begin this book is "Nobody knows the trouble I've seen." When, struck with a sudden poverty, the United States refused to

fulfill its promises of land to the freedmen, a briga-
dier-general went down to the Sea Islands to carry
the news. An old woman on the outskirts of the throng
began singing this song; all the mass joined with her,
swaying. And the soldier wept.

The third song is the cradle-song of death which all
men know,—"Swing low, sweet chariot,"—whose bars
begin the life story of "Alexander Crummell." Then
there is the song of many waters, "Roll, Jordan, roll," a
mighty chorus with minor cadences. There were
many songs of the fugitive like that which opens "The
Wings of Atalanta," and the more familiar "Been
a-listening." The seventh is the song of the End and
the Beginning—"My Lord, what a mourning! when
the stars begin to fall"; a strain of this is placed before "The Dawn of Freedom." The song of groping—
"My way's cloudy"—begins "The Meaning of Progress"; the ninth is the song of this chapter—"Wres-
tlin' Jacob, the day is a-breaking,"—a pæan of hopeful
strife. The last master song is the song of songs—"Steal
away,"—sprung from "The Faith of the Fathers."

There are many others of the Negro folk-songs as
striking and characteristic as these, as, for instance,
the three strains in the third, eighth, and ninth chapters; and others I am sure could easily make a selection on more scientific principles. There are, too,
songs that seem to be a step removed from the more
primitive types: there is the maze-like medley,
"Bright sparkles," one phrase of which heads "The
Black Belt"; the Easter carol, "Dust, dust and ashes";
the dirge, "My mother's took her flight and gone
home"; and that burst of melody hovering over "The
Passing of the First-Born"— "I hope my mother will be
there in that beautiful world on high."

These represent a third step in the development of
the slave song, of which "You may bury me in the

East" is the first, and songs like "March on" (chapter six) and "Steal away" are the second. The first is African music, the second Afro-American, while the third is a blending of Negro music with the music heard in the foster land. The result is still distinctively Negro and the method of blending original, but the elements are both Negro and Caucasian. One might go further and find a fourth step in this development, where the songs of white America have been distinctively influenced by the slave songs or have incorporated whole phrases of Negro melody, as "Swanee River" and "Old Black Joe." Side by side, too, with the growth has gone the debasements and imitations—the Negro "minstrel" songs, many of the "gospel" hymns, and some of the contemporary "coon" songs,—a mass of music in which the novice may easily lose himself and never find the real Negro melodies.

In these songs, I have said, the slave spoke to the world. Such a message is naturally veiled and half articulate. Words and music have lost each other and new and cant phrases of a dimly understood theology have displaced the older sentiment. Once in a while we catch a strange word of an unknown tongue, as the "Mighty Myo," which figures as a river of death; more often slight words or mere doggerel are joined to music of singular sweetness. Purely secular songs are few in number, partly because many of them were turned into hymns by a change of words, partly because the frolics were seldom heard by the stranger, and the music less often caught. Of nearly all the songs, however, the music is distinctly sorrowful. The ten master songs I have mentioned tell in word and music of trouble and exile, of strife and hiding; they grope toward some unseen power and sigh for rest in the End.

The words that are left to us are not without interest, and, cleared of evident dross, they conceal much of real poetry and meaning beneath conventional theology and unmeaning rhapsody. Like all primitive folk, the slave stood near to Nature's heart. Life was a "rough and rolling sea" like the brown Atlantic of the Sea Islands; the "Wilderness" was the home of God, and the "lonesome valley" led to the way of life. "Winter'll soon be over," was the picture of life and death to a tropical imagination. The sudden wild thunder-storms of the South awed and impressed the Negroes,—at times the rumbling seemed to them "mournful," at times imperious:

> "My Lord calls me,
> He calls me by the thunder,
> The trumpet sounds it in my soul."

The monotonous toil and exposure is painted in many words. One sees the ploughmen in the hot, moist furrow, singing:

> "Dere's no rain to wet you,
> Dere's no sun to burn you,
> Oh, push along, believer,
> I want to go home."

The bowed and bent old man cries, with thrice-repeated wail:

> "O Lord, keep me from sinking down,"

and he rebukes the devil of doubt who can whisper:

> "Jesus is dead and God's gone away."

Yet the soul-hunger is there, the restlessness of the savage, the wail of the wanderer, and the plaint is put in one little phrase:

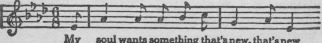

My soul wants something that's new, that's new

Over the inner thoughts of the slaves and their relations one with another the shadow of fear ever hung,
so that we get but glimpses here and there, and also
with them, eloquent omissions and silences. Mother
and child are sung, but seldom father; fugitive and
weary wanderer call for pity and affection, but there
is little of wooing and wedding; the rocks and the
mountains are well known, but home is unknown.
Strange blending of love and helplessness sighs
through the refrain:

> "Yonder's my ole mudder,
>   Been waggin' at de hill so long;
>   'Bout time she cross over,
>   Git home bime-by."

Elsewhere comes the cry of the "motherless" and the
"Farewell, farewell, my only child."

Love-songs are scarce and fall into two categories
—the frivolous and light, and the sad. Of deep successful love there is ominous silence, and in one of the
oldest of these songs there is a depth of history and
meaning:

Poor Ro - sy, poor gal; Poor Ro - sy,
poor gal; Ro - sy break my poor heart,
Heav'n shall - a - be my home.

A black woman said of the song, "It can't be sung without a full heart and a troubled sperrit." The same voice sings here that sings in the German folk-song:

"Jetz Geh i' an's brunele, trink' aber net."

Of death the Negro showed little fear, but talked of it familiarly and even fondly as simply a crossing of the waters, perhaps—who knows?—back to his ancient forests again. Later days transfigured his fatalism, and amid the dust and dirt the toiler sang:

"Dust, dust and ashes, fly over my grave,
But the Lord shall bear my spirit home."

The things evidently borrowed from the surrounding world undergo characteristic change when they enter the mouth of the slave. Especially is this true of Bible phrases. "Weep, O captive daughter of Zion," is quaintly turned into "Zion, weep-a-low," and the wheels of Ezekiel are turned every way in the mystic dreaming of the slave, till he says:

"There's a little wheel a-turnin' in-a-my heart."

As in olden time, the words of these hymns were improvised by some leading minstrel of the religious band. The circumstances of the gathering, however, the rhythm of the songs, and the limitations of allowable thought, confined the poetry for the most part to single or double lines, and they seldom were expanded to quatrains or longer tales, although there are some few examples of sustained efforts, chiefly paraphrases of the Bible. Three short series of verses have always attracted me,—the one that heads this chapter, of one line of which Thomas Wentworth Higginson has fittingly said, "Never, it seems to me,

since man first lived and suffered was his infinite
longing for peace uttered more plaintively." The second and thi'.? are descriptions of the Last Judgment,
—the one a late improvisation, with some traces of
outside influence:

> "Oh, the stars in the elements are falling,
> And the moon drips away into blood,
> And the ransomed of the Lord are returning unto God,
> Blessed be the name of the Lord."

And the other earlier and homelier picture from the
low coast lands:

> "Michael, haul the boat ashore,
> Then you'll hear the horn they blow,
> Then you'll hear the trumpet sound,
> Trumpet sound the world around,
> Trumpet sound for rich and poor,
> Trumpet sound the Jubilee,
> Trumpet sound for you and me."

Through all the sorrow of the Sorrow Songs there
breathes a hope—a faith in the ultimate justice of
things. The minor cadences of despair change often to
triumph and calm confidence. Sometimes it is faith in
life, sometimes a faith in death, sometimes assurance
of boundless justice in some fair world beyond. But
whichever it is, the meaning is always clear: that
sometime, somewhere, men will judge men by their
souls and not by their skins. Is such a hope justified?
Do the Sorrow Songs sing true?

The silently growing assumption of this age is that
the probation of races is past, and that the backward
races of to-day are of proven inefficiency and not
worth the saving. Such an assumption is the arro-
gance of peoples irreverent toward Time and ignorant
of the deeds of men. A thousand years ago such an
assumption, easily possible, would have made it diffi-

cult for the Teuton to prove his right to life. Two thousand years ago such dogmatism, readily welcome, would have scouted the idea of blond races ever leading civilization. So wofully unorganized is sociological knowledge that the meaning of progress, the meaning of "swift" and "slow" in human doing, and the limits of human perfectability, are veiled, unanswered sphinxes on the shores of science. Why should Æschylus have sung two thousand years before Shakespeare was born? Why has civilization flourished in Europe, and flickered, flamed, and died in Africa? So long as the world stands meekly dumb before such questions, shall this nation proclaim its ignorance and unhallowed prejudices by denying freedom of opportunity to those who brought the Sorrow Songs to the Seats of the Mighty?

Your country? How came it yours? Before the Pilgrims landed we were here. Here we have brought our three gifts and mingled them with yours: a gift of story and song—soft, stirring melody in an ill-harmonized and unmelodious land; the gift of sweat and brawn to beat back the wilderness, conquer the soil, and lay the foundations of this vast economic empire two hundred years earlier than your weak hands could have done it; the third, a gift of the Spirit. Around us the history of the land has centred for thrice a hundred years; out of the nation's heart we have called all that was best to throttle and subdue all that was worst; fire and blood, prayer and sacrifice, have billowed over this people, and they have found peace only in the altars of the God of Right. Nor has our gift of the Spirit been merely passive. Actively we have woven ourselves with the very warp and woof of this nation,—we fought their battles, shared their sorrow, mingled our blood with theirs, and generation after generation have pleaded with a headstrong, careless people to despise not Justice, Mercy, and Truth, lest the nation be smitten with a curse. Our song, our toil, our cheer, and warning have been given to this nation in blood-brotherhood. Are not these gifts worth the giving? Is not this work and striving? Would America have been America without her Negro people?

Even so is the hope that sang in the songs of my fathers well sung. If somewhere in this whirl and chaos of things there dwells Eternal Good, pitiful yet masterful, then anon in His good time America shall rend the Veil and the prisoned shall go free. Free, free as the sunshine trickling down the morning into these high windows of mine, free as yonder fresh young voices welling up to me from the caverns of brick and mortar below—swelling with song, instinct with life, tremulous treble and darkening bass. My children, my little children, are singing to the sunshine, and thus they sing:

Let us cheer the wea-ry trav-el-ler, . .

Cheer the wea-ry trav-el-ler, Let us

cheer the wea-ry trav-el-ler A-

-long the heav-en-ly way.

And the traveller girds himself, and sets his face toward the Morning, and goes his way.

THE AFTERTHOUGHT

Hear my cry, O God the Reader; vouchsafe that this my book fall not still-born into the world wilderness. Let there spring, Gentle One, from out its leaves vigor of thought and thoughtful deed to reap the harvest wonderful. Let the ears of a guilty people tingle with truth, and seventy millions sigh for the righteousness which exalteth nations, in this drear day when human brotherhood is mockery and a snare. Thus in Thy good time may infinite reason turn the tangle straight, and these crooked marks on a fragile leaf be not indeed

THE END

SELECTED BIBLIOGRAPHY

Works by William Edward Burghardt Du Bois

The Suppression of the African Slave Trade to the U.S.A., 1638-1870, 1896   Study

Atlanta University Studies on the American Negro, 1897-1915   Studies

The Philadelphia Negro, 1899   Study

The Souls of Black Folk, 1903   Essays and Sketches   (Signet Classic 0451-521757)

John Brown, 1909   Biography

The Quest of the Silver Fleece, 1911   Novel

The Negro, 1915   Study

Darkwater: Voices from within the Veil, 1920   Essays and Sketches

The Gift of Black Folk: The Negroes in the Making of America, 1924   Study

Dark Princess: A Romance, 1928   Novel

Black Reconstruction in America, 1860-1880, 1935   Study

Black Folk: Then and Now, 1939   Study

Dusk of Dawn: An Essay Toward an Autobiography of a Race Concept, 1940   Autobiographical Essay

Color and Democracy: Colonies and Peace, 1945   Study

The World and Africa, 1946   Study

In Battle for Peace: The Story of My 83rd Birthday, 1952   Autobiographical Essay

The Black Flame: A Trilogy
  The Ordeal of Mansart, 1957   Novel
  Mansart Builds a School, 1959   Novel
  Worlds of Color, 1961   Novel

An ABC of Color, 1964   Selected Writings

The Autobiography of W. E. B. Du Bois, 1963   Autobiography

Biography and Criticism

Broderick, Francis L. *W. E. B. Du Bois: Negro Leader in a Time of Crisis.* Stanford: Stanford Univ. Press, 1959.

Selected Biography and Criticism

Broderick, F. L.   *W. E. B. Du Bois: A Negro Leader in a Time of Crisis.* Stanford: Stanford University Press, 1959.

Rudwick, E. M.   *W. E. B. Du Bois: A Study in Minority Group Leadership.* Philadelphia: University of Pennsylvania Press, 1961.